TALKING OF THE ROYAL FAMILY

D0321174

The British public has an insatiable appetite for information about the Royal Family. Every day the media carry news and pictures about the most famous family in the world. Yet social scientists have virtually ignored this strange mass obsession.

Now Michael Billig, a social psychologist, examines the significance of this interest in royalty. He argues that the Royal Family is a symbol of continuity in national consciousness. He supports this claim with analyses of sixty-three English families discussing the Royal Family. As the families talk about royalty, they are talking about much more: about gender, nationality, family life, the media, inequality, sex. Above all, they are talking about themselves. The book shows how this talk can be simultaneously serious and funny. There are jokes, criticism, praise and, above all, acceptance. Billig does much more than simply portray 'attitudes' towards royalty: he shows how our commonsense attitudes and ordinary desires are constructed, and his book has important and entertaining new insights about ideology and popular memory.

Acutely observed and vividly reported, the picture of modern culture which emerges is striking and surprising. *Talking of the Royal Family* will be of interest to students of modern culture and to anyone perplexed by one of the oddest phenomena of today – the persistence of the monarchy in the modern age.

Michael Billig is Professor of Social Sciences, Loughborough University.

TALKING OF THE ROYAL FAMILY

Michael Billig

London and New York

First published in 1992
by Routledge
11 New Fetter Lane, London EC4P 4EE

Simultaneously published in the USA and Canada
by Routledge
a division of Routledge, Chapman and Hall, Inc.
29 West 35th Street, New York, NY 10001

© 1992 Michael Billig

Typeset by LaserScript, Mitcham, Surrey
Printed and bound in Great Britain by
Biddles Ltd, Guildford and King's Lynn

British Library Cataloguing in Publication Data
Billig, Michael
Talking of the royal family.
1. Royal families. 2. Great Britain
I. Title
305.52220941

Library of Congress Cataloging in Publication Data
Billig, Michael
Talking of the royal family/Michael Billig.
p. cm.
Includes bibliographical references and index.
1. Elizabeth II, Queen of Great Britain, 1926 – Family --
Public opinion. 2. Great Britain – Kings and rulers –
Public opinion. 3. Monarchy – Great Britain – Public opinion.
4. Public opinion – Great Britain. I. Title.
DA590.B55   1991
941.085′0922 – dc20   91-12628   CIP

ISBN 0–415–06745–6
0–415–06746–4 (pbk)

CONTENTS

PREFACE

Why listen to ordinary families talking about the British Royal Family? There must be more sensible ways for social scientists to spend their time. If you've got to listen to people talking, then surely to goodness there are other topics more worthy of investigation. So might a serious social scientist object to the project on which this book is based.

However, the objection would be misplaced. The British Royal Family is a phenomenon of curious sociological and psychological proportions. This family, almost certainly the best known in the world, is an object of mass public interest. Its televised ceremonies are observed by audiences of millions. The newspapers headline the most trivial details of royal life. The sovereign is a symbol of British nationhood, quite apart from being the constitutional head of other Commonwealth nations. Yet, little sociological or psychological research has been conducted into the survival of monarchy today.

There are several reasons for listening to ordinary families discussing the Royal Family. The first, and most obvious, is to search for clues to the fascination which royalty exerts. As people talk about royalty, so they voice desires and denials, admiration and discontent, seriousness and mockery. They are to be heard to strip away the mystery from royalty, and to demand that the mystery continues. Thus, the discussions provide material for a social psychology of contemporary monarchy.

But, there is more than this. Ordinary British people can talk readily about royalty, and, as they do so, their talk is not confined to individual royals. To talk about royalty is to talk of many other things: privilege, equality, nationality, morality, family and so on.

Important themes and issues flow through the seemingly trivial chatter about royalty. In addition, as families sit in their living-rooms, discussing the extraordinary life of royalty, so they give glimpses of ordinary ways of living. Thus, to study talk of royalty is to investigate the tones and patterns of contemporary consciousness.

In addition, there is a theoretical reason for analysing family discussions. The project emerges from the development of a 'rhetorical approach' to social psychology. This approach, which is critical of much experimental and survey research, emphasises the importance of argumentation. In effect, it says that if one wishes to understand how people think about issues – what their 'attitudes' are – one should listen to them discussing. This book represents one of the first full-length studies to emerge from this rhetorical perspective. As such, it reveals some of the characteristics which a rhetorical psychology might take.

Readers familiar with more orthodox social psychology will note differences, not merely in methodology and theoretical background, but also in style of presentation. The heavy, forbidding language, which typifies much social scientific writing, has been avoided, as far as possible. The commitment to an accessible style stems from the theoretical wish to recapture the voices of the speakers themselves. For the most part, these speakers expressed themselves clearly and pointedly, often with humour. The style of the analyst should not obfuscate where there was clarity. Nor should it avoid the sort of irony which is fit for the topic of contemporary royalty. In consequence, it is hoped that the book can be read, even enjoyed, by non-specialists, who might be indifferent to the internal debates of social scientists, but who are genuinely perplexed by monarchy's conspicuous survival in a democratic age.

ACKNOWLEDGEMENTS

This book is based upon a research project supported by the Economic and Social Research Council (ESRC): 'Socio-psychological analysis of family discourse' (Grant Number: R000231228). The support of the ESRC is gratefully acknowledged, especially given the nature of the project and the constraints under which the Council is forced to operate these days.

The effort and help of those who have worked on the project has been much appreciated. Marie Kennedy arranged and skilfully conducted the interviews. I am grateful for her sensitivity, in knowing when to nudge a conversation with a gentle question and when to remain silent, letting the participants talk amongst themselves. Belinda Cripps, Delia Perkins and Myra Hunt performed the difficult, painstaking task of transcribing the tapes. They showed incredible persistence, as they listened, re-listened and then listened again to passages hard to decipher. Their skills and their patience have been invaluable. And, of course, special thanks must be given to all those participants, who so generously gave of their time and, indeed, hospitality, to take part in the project. Without them, there would have been silence.

I would also like to thank my colleagues in the Department of Social Sciences at Loughborough University who have provided an atmosphere congenial for studying this topic. In particular, I am grateful to colleagues in the Discourse and Rhetoric Group, who have read and commented upon drafts of the manuscript: Derek Edwards, Mike Gane, Dave Middleton, Jonathan Potter, Anna Dempsey, Nigel Edley and Ros Gill. Also I am grateful for the general encouragement of John Shotter and Herb Simons.

Lastly, there is a final ritual to perform. The Royal Family is not the only family with rituals which perform latent functions. It has become customary for me to finish the acknowledgements page with thanks to my family. In reality the thanks are apologies. But how can one really apologise for ignoring the noises of one's own family, in order to spend so much time listening to other families talking about 'that' family? So, thanks and love to Sheila, Daniel, Rebecca, Rachel and Benjamin.

1

INTRODUCTION:
THE PROBLEM OF MONARCHY

The survival of monarchy in late twentieth century Britain is a socio-psychological phenomenon of strange proportions. In a country supposedly imbued with the values of democracy – indeed, in the country which proclaims itself to be the home of democracy – this ancient institution of inherited status still persists. It does not survive as an embarrassing relic, shuffling along like an elderly relative, conscious of being in the way of the younger generation. Quite the contrary, it survives by being noticed, over and over again. Sixty years ago, George V's second son apparently hurried on to a train at Grantham and started to pull down blinds. His wife, aware of the crowds on the platform, is said to have snapped 'Bertie, you must wave' (Thornton, 1986, p.70). In July 1986, another Duke of York, also the second son of the ruling sovereign, stood on the balcony of Buckingham Palace, having earlier that day been married. He needed no whispered reminder to wave to the crowd of thousands and to the television audience of millions. *The Times* reported the event: 'The Duke broadly cupped his ear to the chanting of: "Give her a kiss, then." So he gave her a kiss: not a moth's kiss, but a smacking naval kiss, like a tyre explosion, or as if he were trying to clear the drains' (23 August 1986).

This report in *The Times* reveals the sociological and psychological strangeness of the phenomenon. There was no hushed reverence, as the crowd gazed upwards towards the royal balcony. Instead, there was cheeky familiarity, and the prince was obliging the crowd. *The Times*, the self-proclaimed voice of establishment Britain, was also enjoying itself: reader and writer could smile at the drain-clearing kiss and at the *lèse-majesté* of the event's retelling. The twentieth century has seen monarchies disappear in Portugal,

1

Russia, Germany, Austria, Italy and Turkey. In other European countries, monarchies might survive by discreet use of regal carriages and by ostentatious use of public transport. But in Britain, you must wave, you must kiss. Or so it appears.

In a literal sense, monarchy is neither a sociological nor a psychological phenomenon, for the experts in sociology and psychology have not pronounced it such. Nowhere is the disparity between social scientific writing and popular writing more evident. The royal books, which are published by the pile, can be considered for a moment. Go to any high-street sale of unsold new books. There on display will be the hardback volumes of last year. The topics will reflect the interests of middle-brow publishing. There will be illustrated books about military transport, cookery and gardens. Perhaps there will also be some volumes about zodiacal signs. Shoppers looking for books about royalty are unlikely to be disappointed. Big, glossy volumes, with plenty of colour photographs, will record the lives of royals. Some publishers, combining various marketable interests, will offer insights into royal cookery, royal gardens or royal zodiacal signs. Wilson (1989) estimates that there are 'approximately 240 books about the Monarchy in print of generally uncritical, inane and sycophantic sorts, and just one critical work' (p.1). In 1989, one book club was advertising nationally a book entitled *Royal Knits:* 'Clothes and accessories for home and family all with a "royal" theme – from corgi slippers to an "ermine" trimmed loo'.

Repeat the search for royal volumes at an academic bookshop, or better still in a university library, and the results will be different. Walk along the shelves reserved for the sociology or psychology volumes. There will be titles about all manner of aspects of contemporary life, but, odds on, there will not be a single volume about the sociology or psychology of the British monarchy. Try leafing through recent editions of the *British Journal of Sociology* or of the *British Journal of Social Psychology*, and the quest will be as barren. There will be articles about race prejudice, sexual behaviour and misconduct at sporting occasions, but about interest in royalty, even about royalty itself, there will be nothing. Royalty is not an approved socio-psychological phenomenon. This adds to the strangeness of the matter.

The present book is about the interest in royalty, or, to be more precise, about what ordinary English families have to say about the Royal Family. The topic is not the Royal Family itself. The distinction can be illustrated by the example of the Duchess of York at

Grantham station all those years ago. As far as the present investigation is concerned, the interest would not be in the Duchess's actions, nor in her relationship with her husband. It would be in the crowd and what its members might say, not while waiting for the blinds to be raised, but later when discussing royal matters in general. An analogy might be made with sociologists or psychologists studying religious beliefs. They can put aside theological questions about the existence of gods, while studying what people believe. So the student of royal beliefs can avoid making judgements about the 'true' characteristics of various royal persona. However, the investigator of royal mythology has less room for doubt than does the examiner of religious mythology. Neither the existence of royal figures, nor the general conditions of their life are to be doubted. It must be remembered that the object of the popular interest is a family, which possesses immense wealth and which numbers amongst its members the constitutional head of the United Kingdom.

AN INTERESTING IDEA

Over a hundred years ago, Walter Bagehot wrote in *The English Constitution* that 'a family on the throne is an interesting idea' (1867/1965, p.85). The extent to which the Royal Family has become interesting today must have exceeded all the imaginings of the Victorian commentator. Bagehot had foreseen that monarchy, once it had lost its political power, needed to be transformed, if it were to survive usefully. Responsibility for the 'efficient' aspects of the state – for raising taxes and for passing legislation – had passed to the politicians. Royalty, argued Bagehot, should concentrate on the 'dignified' ceremonial aspects, because no common politician could command the sort of loyalty which the masses would show to a king or queen. This split between the 'efficient' and the 'ceremonial' aspects of state provided an opportunity to expand the cast of royal actors. Once the sovereign had relinquished the political power, which made him or her such a compelling figure, public interest could be directed on to the whole family. The public would be interested, deeply interested, if royalty were to display themselves as the first family of the nation. Bagehot's argument was barbed. He was slyly criticising the semi-retirement to which Queen Victoria had retreated since the death of Prince Albert. And he was *memorando* hinting that the Prince of Wales would be best advised to cease frequenting gaming tables, race tracks and married women.

Today, the faces of the British Royal Family are to be seen in newspaper and television pictures around the globe, making it the best known family of the world. No other family can claim such celebrity. In a MORI survey of January 1990, British respondents were shown pictures of members of the Royal Family and were asked to identify them. An extraordinary hundred percent identified the Queen Mother correctly. The figures dropped to ninety-nine percent for Prince Charles and Princess Diana, with ninety-eight percent identifying the Queen. The fame of the family cuts across distinctions of class, gender and age.

There is massive popular interest in the great royal occasions. With the advent of television, a royal wave can be seen by millions (Dayan and Katz, 1985; see also Chaney, 1983). David Cannadine (1983) has shown how coronations, royal weddings and funerals have been transformed into public spectacles in the last two hundred years. Previously, such ceremonies were witnessed by the privileged few. Without a mass audience, these occasions had lacked the slickness of the modern televised presentation. Queen Victoria wrote in her journal that her Coronation was the 'proudest' day of her life, but her jottings captured the chaos of the great moment: 'The Archbishop came in and *ought* to have delivered the Orb to me, but I had already got it, and he (as usual) was *so* confused and puzzled and knew nothing, and – went away' (*The Letters of Queen Victoria*, Volume 1, p.123, emphasis in original; see also Lant, 1979). Such confusion is not permitted to mar today's professionally organised royal rituals, which, nevertheless, are presented as if they were exact repetitions of ancient ones (Cannadine, 1983).

A disproportionate number of the few academic studies investigating contemporary monarchy have focussed upon the great ceremonial events. Blumler *et al.* (1971) examined the effect of Prince Charles's Investiture on public attitudes. Bocock (1974) discusses more generally the place of royal ritual in industrialised society (see also Lukes, 1977). Reactions to royal ceremonies have been documented by Mass Observation. For over fifty years, this project has been compiling a record of life in modern Britain, by recruiting ordinary individuals to record day-to-day observations. The directors of Mass Observation have appreciated the importance of common feelings towards royalty: diaries of the great royal days have been specifically collected. Jennings and Madge's book

May 12 1937 is a fascinating collage of material relating to the Coronation of George VI. Ziegler (1977) used the Mass Observation archive to compare popular reactions to various royal events. One enduring factor has been the public's keen interest. There might be initial indifference, but, as the great day approaches, this typically gives way to mounting excitement.

The Mass Observation programme has always been on the periphery of academic social science. This is not true of Shils and Young (1953) who provided one of the few mainstream sociological studies of a royal event. They analysed the 1953 Coronation, depicting a nation enthralled by the antiquity of the proceedings and collectively reaffirming its sacred values. This essentially uncritical image of the nation at one with itself was not without its opponents (Birnbaum, 1955; Lukes, 1977). Recently, it has taken a severe assault from Tom Nairn's superb analysis of British monarchy, *The Enchanted Glass* (1988), a book which is unlikely to be recognised as properly sociological by the disciplinary experts. *Don't go on.*

The studies of the great events will be somewhat misleading if they give the impression that public interest in royalty is tidal, with its water-line receding between the gaps in the irregular calender of ceremonial occasions. On the contrary, the interest is sustained daily. Practically every edition of the popular press brings information about the life of the royals (Edley, 1991). These items are not tucked away on the inside pages, but insignificant episodes will be blazoned across front pages. To give a single example: on 23 May 1987, the front-page headline of the *Daily Mirror*, occupying more space than the words of the story itself, was 'Bottoms Up Ma'am'. Princess Anne had fallen from a horse in the view of the paper's photographer. She had been completely unharmed. The angle of the camera and the words of the headline drew attention to the curve of the tumbling princess's buttocks. 'Furious Anne Comes A Cropper', declared the sub-heading. Bagehot may have predicted an interest in the royal personages, but he foresaw a dignified interest. Royal bottoms would be seated upon the throne, not tilted upwards for public entertainment.

The tabloid papers can publish such items regularly, because they retain staff specialising in royal matters. Papers, which think it unnecessary to have foreign correspondents stationed in major capital cities, employ permanent staff to chronicle the movements of royalty. Martin Walker, a *Guardian* reporter, followed these specialists during a royal visit to the United States. He commented that if this team of journalists were assigned to cover politics, 'the cabinet would hardly have a secret left by tea-time' (*Guardian*, 13 February 1989). A tenuous connection with royalty can transform journalistic dross into headline gold. The *Sun* specialises in such alchemy. 'Queen's Guards Eat Pub Pet Fish' screamed its front-page headline on 22 May 1990, pushing foreign and political news on to inside pages. Drunken soldiers eating tropical fish in a Home Counties public house are hardly newsworthy: but add the information that they are the Queen's soldiers, then the other news of the day is dimmed.

The television does not lag far behind the popular newspapers. Hugh Stephenson and a team of researchers from City University analysed the contents of BBC and ITV news for a week. The rationale for the survey had nothing to do with royalty, for it was reacting to complaints from senior Conservative politicians, particularly Norman Tebbit, that the BBC news had a 'left-wing bias'. The results, reported at length in the *Guardian* (16 March 1987), showed the frequency and prominence of royal news. On three of the five days, the BBC news presented royal stories in its headlines. One of these stories was that Prince Charles had visited a public house whilst foxhunting. The *Guardian* itself demonstrated the allure of the royal dimension. The report was accompanied by a photograph, not of Norman Tebbit, but of Prince Charles. 'In The News Out Foxhunting' was the caption. Once again, the Prince was in the news: this time, he was in the news for being in the news.

A royal dimension multiplies public interest exponentially. The viewing figures for the modest television game show, 'It's A Knockout', soared when younger royals participated in a special edition. That week the show became the single most watched programme on British television (*Daily Telegraph*, 30 June 1987). The story did not end when the credits rolled. The following morning, there were headlines about Prince Edward's comments at a press conference. Several books were planned to record the great event (*Observer*, 7 July 1987).

During the past twenty-five years the volume of press coverage has substantially increased. *The Sun Book of Royalty* reproduced the 'Royal Front Pages' during the first fourteen years of the paper's tabloid existence. For the first three years (1970–2) there were only nine royal front pages. The years 1981–3 produced nineteen. The upward graph has continued through the eighties. Edley (1991) conducted a survey of royal press coverage during a three-month period in 1988. He found that twelve percent of *Sun* issues had a royal story as the main front-page story. Thirty-five percent of issues had something about the royals on the front page, not necessarily the headline story.

If the amount of media coverage has increased in the past twenty-five years, then Buckingham Palace has not exactly been passive itself. It has deliberately sought to join the modern world of image-marketing. John Pearson, in *The Ultimate Family* (1986), documents the steps taken by royalty to employ professional press secretaries and publicity agents. Information-releases and photo-opportunities are regularly provided. The princes and princesses will even grant the occasional interview to chosen, trusted, reporters. The Palace and its professional publicists do their bit to ensure the continuing high profile of the product.

In short, royalty and the professionals working in the media act as if the public has an insatiable hunger for royal information. Psychological words spring easily to mind. Professor Stephenson, describing the results of his television survey, commented that 'both the BBC and ITN seem to share the obsession of the tabloid press with Royal stories and non-stories' (*Guardian*, 16 March 1987). However, this is an 'obsession' with a difference. It has not troubled psychologists. None has bothered to design a therapeutic treatment for the suffering nation.

ALL PROBLEMS – NO PROBLEM

The nature of the so-called obsession is related to its neglect by academic sociologists and psychologists. Social scientists have a tendency to study issues which are publicly declared to be 'problems', especially by government departments. They will be encouraged by funding agencies to conduct research on such identified 'problems' and they will hope that their findings will help in the search for 'solutions'. However, there seems to be no corresponding 'Monarchy Problem'. There is no popular movement for republicanism. In answer to pollsters' questions, around ninety percent of the British population agree that the country should have a sovereign (for summaries of the poll data, see Harris, 1966; Rose, 1965; Rose and Kavanagh, 1976; Ziegler, 1977). MORI, January 1990, reports that only six percent of the population responded that Britain would be better off if monarchy were abolished. The support for monarchy comes from all sections of the population: young and old, male and female, rich and poor. The British Social Attitudes Survey, which was designed to assess public opinion annually, initially included a general question about monarchy. The results were clear: 'Attitudes to the monarchy are strongly in the direction of uncritical support among all social groups' (Young, 1984, p.30). No identifiable section of the population defines monarchy as a problem. That being so, it was recommended that 'this question clearly need not be repeated annually' (p.30). If there is no 'Monarchy Problem' to be solved, then there is no need for expert advice and specialist research findings.

Certainly, no major political party in Britain puts republicanism on its policy agenda. That is left for the fringe Marxist groups. Even republicans in Northern Ireland do not campaign on the general principle of republicanism, but they advocate a re-drawing of the boundary between the Irish republic and the British monarchy. By the same token, nationalists in Scotland and Wales tend to advocate national boundaries between two adjacent monarchies sharing the same monarch. The case of the Labour Party is instructive. This is an avowedly socialist party, whose written constitution asserts the principle of equality. However, the party does not care to tackle the symbol of inherited privilege at the centre of the nation's unwritten constitution. In 1923, the Party Conference overwhelmingly rejected republicanism, and, as Schwartz (1986) comments, 'this appeared to close the issue once and for all' (p.177). Willie Hamilton, who for years was a lonely advocate of republicanism on the Labour parliamentary benches, criticised his party's timidity. 'Openly denouncing the monarchy could be political suicide', he wrote in his book *My Queen and I* (1975, p.117).

Diaries published by former Labour ministers show the weakness of the republican impulse in the governments of the socialist party. In the 1960s, Richard Crossman, cabinet minister and editor of Bagehot's *The English Constitution*, was confiding his republicanism quietly to his diary. Only feeble gestures were possible. In 1967, he declared that he would not attend the State Opening of Parliament. A discrete, even sympathetic, word from the Palace ('the Queen has as strong a feeling of dislike of public ceremonies as you do'), and the rebel dutifully attended (1979, pp.387–8).

Another diarist, and closet republican, during the first Wilson administration was Tony Benn. His republicanism was reduced to matters philatelic. As Postmaster General, he tried to broaden the range of stamp design. He records strenuous, time-consuming battles, as he struggled to get the Palace even to consider the possibility of stamps without the monarch's head. When, finally, he was permitted to present to the Queen designs, which omitted her profile, it was 'the best day since I took office' (Benn, 1988, p.232). Needless to say, all the headless designs were decisively rejected by the monarch. But she had seen them. It had been a victory of sorts.

During the Thatcher years, the room for republican manoeuvre within the Labour Party was further diminished. In newspapers, both serious and tabloid, there were rumours of rifts between monarch and prime minister, with the Queen allegedly objecting to Mrs Thatcher's regal style. The prime minister's grammar – 'We have become a grandmother' – hinted at pretensions beyond a common politician's station (see, for instance, Georgina Howell's 'The Queening of Mrs Thatcher' in the *Correspondent*, 22 April 1990). More seriously, there were stories that the Queen was anxious lest Mrs Thatcher's policies harmed the unity of nation and Commonwealth. In July 1986, *The Times* claimed authoritatively that the Queen was concerned about the British government's opposition to sanctions against South Africa and its effect upon the Commonwealth. The Queen's press secretary was later to resign, as a result of the story's publication. Judith Williamson (1987) noted that, with the political opposition to Mrs Thatcher so weakened in the mid-eighties, the Queen was being seen to represent the popular voice of liberalism (see also Brunt, 1988). On the one side was the harsh intolerance of Thatcherism, and on the other was the caring, internationally minded monarch. For left-wing Labour republicans, an awkward position was even more awkward than usual. After the appearance of *The Times* story about disagreements between the Queen and Mrs Thatcher, the *New Statesman*, left-wing and unvigorously republican, commented on the difficulty for socialists, now that the monarch was apparently in the vanguard of the fight against apartheid: 'The inferred collision between Queen and Prime Minister...is enough to make anyone of the Left try emigration (18 August 1986).

As regards conservatism, the Thatcher period was unusual in that there were critical murmurs against royalty within the Conservative Party. Remarks were made about individual royals, notably Prince Charles, whose social views have been deemed to be insufficiently right-wing. Free market enthusiasts have occasionally included monarchy when advocating the privatisation of all public bodies.

Andrew Morton, in the *Sunday Times* (21 January 1990), quoted a Conservative parliamentary hopeful saying that 'if there is no need for the state to mine coal, there is clearly no need for the state to keep palaces'. This is not republicanism as such. The monarchy is being told to pay its way like all business endeavours. If it fails to show a profit for its product, then market forces will dictate bankruptcy and abolition. This Conservative stance parallels the position of republicanism in the Labour Party. Both seem to be implied by the philosophy of their respective parties, but neither can be expressed too openly, and certainly not officially, for fear of offending the faithful. Even on the fascist far right, the same constraints apply. *Spearhead*, published by the British National Party, criticised royals for being inadequately racialist, but added that 'for practical reasons' it was not against monarchy (September 1988). The National Front's paper, *Flag*, in July 1988 published letters from members criticising the previous month's edition. Royalist members were disturbed by an editorial line which had asserted that, under a National Front government, royalty 'must do exactly as they are told'. Or else.

Without political parties pushing for abolition, and without dissent coming from an identifiable demographic group, there is no 'Monarchy Problem'. On the other hand, there is an infinity of royal problems. The topic would not be an interesting one were it not for the problems. Here Bagehot's conception of public interest was limited. Reverence towards majestic dignity can only sustain interest momentarily. And then it's back to normal life. Even photos of princesses falling from horses can pall after a while. It is necessary to have something controversial to discuss and argue about. This is what the daily press provides. Sometimes it is political controversy, such as the reported disagreement between the Queen and Mrs Thatcher; or there is the controversy between the Prince of Wales and the various experts whom he challenges; or there is constitutional controversy; but, over and over again, there is controversy about the personal behaviour of royals and about their character.

The possibilities are inexhaustible. The public is invited to hold attitudes on specific issues. The *Sun* and the *News of the World* frequently adopt the format of 'You The Jury'. The controversial issue is outlined, then readers are invited to communicate their views to the paper's office. The next issue of the paper will declare what 'You The Readers' think. 'Do you think a member of the Royal Family should go to Emperor Hirohito's funeral?', asked the *Sun* (9

January 1989), providing one phone number to ring for 'Yes' and another for 'No'. The *News of the World* (3 January 1988) headlined its story 'Fergie Sobs At Ugliest Woman Insults' and invited 'You The Jury' to telephone responses to the question: 'Do you think the critics are right to hammer Fergie as an ugly frump?'

The opinion polls, which report the public's general approval of monarchy, are usually commissioned by newspapers, because they provide easy copy. The headlines are not provided by evidence of continuing support for monarchy: even the experts of the British Social Attitudes Survey find such results tedious. The polls invariably contain items relating to controversies, which might provide headlinable differences of opinion. 'Should the Queen abdicate in favour of Prince Charles?' is a favourite item, which can be guaranteed to produce a split in public opinion and a story-line. Shifts in the popularity of individual figures will also be carefully recorded. For example, the *News of the World* commissioned the MORI January 1989 poll, which included questions on 'controversial' items: whether the Queen should pay poll tax, whether the royal children should seek the Queen's permission before marrying, and whether the Queen should be more active in controlling the behaviour of the younger royals. On all these questions, the public was divided. Also there were questions about individual royals. On this occasion, it was one of the latter items which provided the headline story. Under the banner 'Her Royal Idleness', the *News of the World* declared: 'Pleasure-seeking Fergie has earned herself a new shameful title'. It went on to record that 'a massive thirty-four percent of the population now believe Fergie is doing the most damage' (22 January 1989).

In this way, the problems of monarchy become defined. There is no general problem about the institution itself, but there are all manner of specific controversies about the conduct of its business and the character of its members. The very definition of these problems seems to exclude academic interest. In the first place, there is no need for academic social scientists to replicate the research which the professional surveys of MORI, Gallup and NOP conduct so efficiently and so regularly. There is a further point. Once the general issue of monarchy is defined as not a problem, then the specific problems seem to shrink into insignificance. Serious academics, not to mention the funding bodies who provide the financial wherewithal for research, are unlikely to be interested in the issues which the pollsters are commissioned to survey:

whether the Queen should discipline the younger royals, whether Prince Philip is a caring individual, whether the Duchess of York is frumpishly attired. The questions seem unworthy of academic interest, especially with so many proper problems awaiting grant applications. Thus, monarchy slips beneath scholarly consciousness.

IDEOLOGICAL PROBLEMS

On another level, this academic neglect is perplexing. The family, for whose welfare the British people show such concern, and whose activities feature so prominently in the press, is the richest family of the land. Just how rich is uncertain – and this is another sociological omission. The only recent investigation into the wealth of the Windsors is Andrew Morton's essentially uncritical book, glossily illustrated with crowns, diamonds and fabulous Fabergé eggs. Morton (1989) admits that the wealth of the royals escapes calculation. A public obsession with a family possessing incalculable wealth should in itself signify an interesting academic puzzle. Further, the Windsors possess another obvious significance. Theirs is the family which symbolises nationhood. How, one might ask, could an interest in such a family, an interest which seems to border on the obsessive, possibly be dismissed as unimportant?

At the minimum, the popular acceptance of monarchy must say something about the popular acceptance of inequality and national identity. What this 'something' is remains unclear; but to ignore such a visible element of popular consciousness, while studying the British 'social attitudes', is curious. As Tom Nairn (1988) stresses, it is time to take monarchy seriously, for, in an age of nationalism, it is the symbolic representation of English nationalism. Even if the socio-psychological effects of monarchy are unknown, one thing can be assumed: when people accept without reflection the appropriateness of being told as headlined news that a British prince went to a pub, or that a British princess has slipped from her horse, then echoes of inequality and nationhood are being registered. So too are they being registered when social scientists assume, without a second thought, that there is little worthy of professional attention in the royal news which they too witness daily.

In all this, it could be claimed that the operation of 'ideology' is discernible. The concept of 'ideology' is not a simple one in sociological writings. As McLellan (1986, p.1) claims, it is 'the most elusive concept' in all the social sciences. Two aspects of ideology can be mentioned. First, ideology refers to what passes for common-sense within a particular society. Often, ideology refers to those assumptions which are so taken-for-granted that they are not even considered to be worthy of attention. Second, ideology is seen to have a particular social function. It refers to beliefs which confirm the powerful in their position of power and which settle down the powerless into their respective positions of powerlessness. Thus, ideology denotes ways of talking and thinking which render ordinary people unrebellious and accepting of their lot in life. As Thompson (1987) writes, 'to study ideology is to study the ways in which meaning serves to sustain relations of domination' (p.518).

Patterns of belief about monarchs would clearly be ideological in this sense, if they lead ordinary people to be deferential to an all-powerful sovereign. For example, the sovereign's subjects might defer to the monarch as some sort of superior being, whose superiority was generally accepted as common-sense. Mediaeval monarchs were believed to be divinely anointed and to possess powers beyond the common mortal (Bloch, 1973; Nelson, 1987). Roman emperors were felt to be, if not actual gods, then gods in the making (Price, 1987). The point about such beliefs is that they not only represent the ruler as a superior being, but they also confirm the ordinary believer as an inferior being – a mere subject, who should defer to the majesty of the monarch.

However, modern beliefs about monarchy do not appear to fit this ideological pattern. First, the modern monarch is not a figure of political power, notwithstanding control over stamp design, and notwithstanding Bagehot's prediction that the masses would continue to believe in the power of the king. The second reason why modern monarchy does not fit the pattern of a deferential ideology is much simpler. Contemporary beliefs do not seem to be cast in reverence. Bagehot may have been correct in supposing that there would be mass interest in the family on the throne, but he was wrong in assuming that the interest would co-exist with unchanging deference. The more the public is interested in the private lives of royalty, the less divinely remote the royal personages will appear. Few could seriously believe that princes, who boldly kiss their brides on demand, have been touched by a divine mission. The popular press treats its readers to regular mockery of royals. A princess is to be seen toppling in a most undignified way. The headline ridicules the dignity of 'Ma'am', as she falls. The joke over,

13

the text returns to the more normal 'Anne' ('furious Anne'), as if she were a familiar friend to readers.

It is a theme of the present book that the mockery and the lack of deference do not indicate a lack of ideology. Quite the contrary, they represent contemporary ideological forms, by which the un-privileged accept their position of ordinariness in relation to extra-ordinary wealth. The common-sense talk about monarchy is much more complex than ascriptions of divine anointment; and it is more vocal than open-mouthed awe. In fact, complexity should be expected. The very existence of monarchy, as a visible and popular symbol of inherited privilege in outwardly egalitarian times, suggests a complicated consciousness, composed of cross-cutting themes. The tabloid press hints that 'You The Jury' should decide the official visit of the Queen's husband to Japan and the wardrobe of her younger daughter-in-law. It is as if the ordinary subject occupies the superior position, and royalty awaits the jury's decision. Symbols of inequity are being reversed.

In order to understand the ideological nature of thinking about monarchy, it is necessary to look beyond the specific controversies. It is not a question of detailing what percentage of the population believes that a particular princess is overweight. The underlying common-sense about monarchy and 'royalness' needs to be deciphered. At this point, one assumption can be made, for which the following chapters seek to provide substantiation. Apparently trivial talk about the Royal Family is not trivial, but flowing through it are themes of ideological importance. That being so, talk about the Royal Family will be more than talk about the specific family.

In the media's messages about royalty, cultural analysts can find a treasure-store of ideological meanings: a princess's posterior, a horse and a headline are gifts, more intellectually precious than Fabergé eggs, to the decoder of semiotic symbols. Roland Barthes (1972) set the semiotic tone with some ironical reflections on the extraordinarily ordinary figures of contemporary royalty. More recently, several others have looked at the symbolic representations of royalty in the British press, particularly examining how royals are presented as being simultaneously ordinary and extraordinary (Billig, 1988b, 1990b; Coward, 1983; Edley, 1991; Williamson, 1987). Nairn (1988) casts an ironic glance at the strange tone of press coverage. Looking at the reportage of Prince Charles, he writes of 'the mystic significance of a small bald patch' (see pp.25–9).

14

The study of ideology cannot end with an examination of what journalists are writing or what television cameras are reproducing, important though critical analyses of the media are. Ideology also refers to the thinking of ordinary people. This thinking is not to be inferred from the contents of the mass media (Jensen, 1990; Morley, 1986; Morley and Silverstone, 1990). As will be seen in later chapters, people have much to say about newspapers and television, and their thoughts are hardly flattering. At the same time, these thoughts are crucial to what they have to say about royalty, and about themselves as subjects in a monarchy.

Also, the public opinion polls, which indicate percentage responses to the controversial issues, can only go so far. Their findings present a disembodied and dessicated picture of popular thinking. The summaries of percentage responses provide no sense of people actually thinking about issues, nor of the underlying meanings contained in such thought. For this, there can be no substitute for actually listening at length to people talking.

THE FAMILY STUDY ~~rethorical~~ ?

It is impossible to conduct an empirical study of the way that people think without making some psychological assumptions about the nature of thought. The present investigation is no exception. Its theoretical background comes from the theoretical perspective of a 'rhetorical psychology', which is critical of much conventional social psychology. This rhetorical psychology has been discussed elsewhere at length (Billig, 1987 and 1991; Billig *et al.*, 1988; Shotter, 1990). A couple of brief points can be summarised here. The rhetorical perspective sees thinking as being essentially formed within discourse (Potter and Wetherell, 1987). In addition, it assumes that common-sense thinking is fundamentally argumentative and is composed of contrary, or 'dilemmatic', themes (Billig *et al.*, 1988). The implication is that if one wishes to observe thinking actually taking place, then one should listen to people discussing matters argumentatively. In the cut-and-thrust of discussion, one can hear the processes of thinking directly, witnessing the actual business of people formulating and using thoughts. When people argue, they justify and criticise, frequently appealing to common-sense, or to the values of accepted common-places (Billig, 1987; Perelman and Olbrechts-Tyteca, 1971). By listening to arguments about specific

Is this really knew

15

No Burke on Rhetoric of Motives

royal controversies – about a princess's weight, the royal home life or whatever – one should be able to hear much wider themes of common-sense being used.

Therefore, the present investigation did not use the methods of the pollsters, who ask individual respondents a series of pre-set questions. Instead, groups of people talking loosely around the topic of monarchy were observed. The groups were not artificial groups of strangers, which are employed in much experimental research in social psychology (Fraser and Foster, 1984). The participants knew each other very well. They were family groups, talking, for the most part, in the familiar context of their own homes.

The choice of using family groups, rather than any other sort of discussion group, was not fortuitous. The family represents the third symbolic element of contemporary monarchy. Over and above being a symbol of privilege and nationhood, the Royal Family overtly represents the family. In Bagehot's phrase, it is the family on the throne. By encouraging families to talk about the interesting family on the throne, the chances of observing ideological parallels between royal and ordinary lives would be maximised. As families talk about the Royal Family, they will be talking about family; and as they talk about family, so they will be talking about themselves. Therefore, as families talk of royalty, discussing its controversies, they will be providing glimpses of ordinary family life.

The study is based on sixty-three recorded interviews with families, all living in the East Midlands of England. A total of one hundred and seventy-five people took part in these sessions. This is a comparatively large sample for a qualitative study: i.e. a study which seeks to analyse the meanings of what people say, as opposed to analysing statistically the results from standard questionnaires. In setting up the discussions, 'family' was construed loosely. There was no strict definition of what should constitute a family (see Appendix for details of the participants). Families and households possessed a variety of structures, so did the composition of the discussion groups. Sometimes not all the family members living in the household were present: there were several mother and daughter discussions, with the husband absent. In one case, there was a single woman, living alone. Sometimes the family discussion included members who did not live in the household: older children, who had left home, visited for the interview, and occasionally other relatives took part. Once or twice, a friend dropped by to be included in the discussion. Not all the groups cut across generations:

16

there were couples without children, or whose children were absent or too young to participate. Formal marriage was not a necessary criterion for inclusion. Several couples were known to be legally unmarried; and there might have been more, but it was not part of the research to find out. In one instance, it was an all-male couple. There was one discussion in which none of the participants belonged to the same family: an unmarried mother, with small children, invited two other mothers along. Not all the respondents were English-born. There was one West Indian family. In all the discussions, the same interviewer, a graduate in her forties, was present.

The families were recruited in a number of ways. Some were suggested by friends or by people who had already participated. Some were recruited by knocking on doors. If a preliminary approach by the interviewer suggested that the family was willing to participate, then she made further contact, usually by telephone, in order to arrange the discussion session. It was left to the family members themselves to decide who would attend on the day of the interview. On three occasions, only a single member of the family was present for interview, because other members of the family had decided at the last moment not to participate. In each case, the sole participating member was a woman.

All the sessions, except for one, took place in family homes of respondents, mostly in evenings. The exception occurred because mother and daughter worked as secretaries in the same office; for reasons of convenience, the interview was held there, in a quiet room, during an extended lunch-break (interview 23). All potential participants were told by the interviewer that she was interested in hearing families talk about their views on the Royal Family. They were also told in advance that the discussions would be tape-recorded and that anonymity would be respected. The interviews were conducted in late 1988 and throughout 1989.

The interviewer did not have a fixed schedule of questions by which to shape the discussions. Instead, she sought to spark off discussion amongst the participants, and then, if possible, for herself to fade into the background. Sometimes this was achieved success-fully, with participants taking over the discussion, and the tran-scripts reveal that the interviewer said little. Sometimes, when the discussion started to flag, prompts were needed. Then, the inter-viewer might raise a topic or royal angle for the participants to consider. Sometimes, too, gentle nudges were given to stop the

17

conversation drifting too far from royal topics. Occasionally, the discussions were rather halting, and then the interviewer had to work to keep the talk going.

Towards the end of the discussions, the interviewer asked some formal questions. Participants were asked their age, occupation, educational background, voting preference and which newspapers they read. They were also asked two questions which were taken from a MORI opinion survey (October 1987, commissioned by the *Sunday Times*). The first question was: whether respondents thought that on balance Britain would be better off, worse off, or no different, if monarchy were abolished. The second question asked respondents how interested they themselves were in news about the Royal Family.

Because the discussions were open-ended, some were longer than others. By and large, most lasted between one and two hours. Later, the interviewer contacted the respondents to thank them for their participation. Several contacted her to say how much they had enjoyed the experience. Afterwards, the discussions were transcribed, yielding in all over two thousand, eight hundred pages of typed transcript. The longest transcript for a single interview ran to one hundred and fifty pages. The result was a corpus of material, rich in conversational detail.

One advantage of conducting qualitative research in an area already covered by the professional pollsters is that the general picture is already known. Therefore, there was no attempt to recruit respondents who would reproduce in exact proportions the demography of the general population of England. However, demographic questions about age, occupation, voting etc. were included as a general check, in order to ensure that identifiable demographic groups were being included in the sample. Respondents included middle and working classes (although, demographically speaking, the middle class was over-represented in the sample); town, city and rural dwellers; supporters of all the main political parties, as well as non-voters; there were young and old, with the ages of participants ranging from eleven to eight-seven.

The inclusion of the pollsters' questions about monarchy permitted a check lest a disproportionate number of 'republicans' had been included. In practice, checking the qualitative material against the questionnaire responses is not easily done, for the former can throw the meaning of the latter into question. Only five percent of those answering the question thought that Britain would be worse off if monarchy were abolished: a figure not too out of line with the national surveys. However, it would be wrong to label those, and only those, answering in this way as 'republican'. The discussions show that what people have to say is not easily summarised by an answer to a questionnaire item (see Billig, 1989a, for an analysis of a 'republican', whose republicanism is by no means straightforward in the context of a family argument). When one listens closely to conversational talk, one goes beyond the broad, and rather coarsely depicted, patterns of attitude surveys, in order to feel the textured intricacies of common-sensical thinking.

ANALYTICAL NOTES

Several general remarks can be made about the strategy for analysing the family discussions.

Common themes of common-sense

As was said earlier, the aim was to reconstruct patterns of common-sense thinking, by searching for underlying themes. This involves looking for the common patterns of thinking, rather than searching for the divisions between respondents. There is a fundamental difference in this strategy from that which guides most attitude research studies. Typically, socio-psychological research, as well as the opinion poll surveys, look for differences between social groups; for example, differences in attitudes between middle- and working-class respondents, or between the young and old, or male and female. For such research, the interesting findings are those which reveal statistically significant differences between population groups. As the example of the British Social Attitudes Survey testifies, a 'failure' to find such differences renders an issue uninteresting. And that is the end of the matter. By contrast, such 'failures' are the start of things here. Ideology is to be discovered in those patterns of common-sense thinking which cut across class, age and gender distinctions. This means looking for commonalities in what is said. And just as importantly, it means looking for the common patterns in what is not said. The silences, or the unspoken gaps between the words, can be just as ideologically revealing as spoken words.

The search for commonalities affects the presentation of the material. The analysis is not organised in terms of demographic

19

groupings. For instance, there is not a separate section to show the 'working-class view' and another to show the 'youth view' and so on. Commonalities are often indicated by providing similar examples of thinking from respondents who belong to different demographic groupings. For this reason, when giving examples, individual respondents are frequently described by age, occupation and family position. The descriptions then enable commonalities to be observed.

For similar reasons, the material is not organised in terms of particular controversies. There are not special sections detailing views on the 'abdication issue', the 'Thatcher issue', the 'frump issue' and so on. Nor generally is there an attempt to discover who takes which position on such issues – that can be left to the opinion surveys. The aim here is to go beyond the particular controversy, in order to uncover the more general common-sensical themes which permit the controversies to appear so controversial.

Glimpses of family life

In uncovering the common-sense themes, the investigation also aimed to catch glimpses of ordinary family living. Family discussions proved to be a fitting method for gaining the sorts of insights into family life which are not usually produced from survey research. A brief example can be given. A mother and father were condemning scurrilous tabloids, and in so doing were making claims for their own respectability (interview 22). Their older son then interrupted. But, he said, 'we always get the *Sun* when we go on holiday'. Hasty denials came from mother and father. No, we don't, it's only when we go on holiday with your uncle, says the mother. The son persists: No, it isn't uncle who buys the paper. A glimpse of a family's life, the relations between its members and the place of tabloid newspapers, has been revealed. This glimpse would not have emerged in a formal questionnaire, administered individually to either husband or wife. 'Do you read the *Sun*?' – 'Never'. Next question.

Presentation of material

The analysis involves presenting a considerable number of extracts from the discussions. There are a number of ways in which conversational examples can be presented. Two principal ways are used here. There are extracts which are reproduced directly from the transcripts. These presentations use some of the conventions of Conversation Analysis, in order to indicate hesitations, interruptions and two speakers talking at once (see the Appendix of Potter and Wetherell, 1987, for details of these conventions; see also Atkinson and Heritage, 1984[1]). This detailed way of reproducing speech is only used occasionally. Often, the minutiae of interaction are less important than the general content of what is being said. Then, there is a more relaxed form of reconstructing conversations. Minor hesitations may be omitted, but, apart from occasionally resolving grammatical ambiguities, remarks cited within quotation marks are taken verbatim, except with one proviso: when participants refer to each other by name, these names have been altered in order to respect anonymity, which the participants were promised.

A very brief example of such a reconstruction has already been given, with the example of the family's holiday-reading. The reconstructions use literary devices for representing dialogue: 'He said..., then she said..., then he said', and so forth. These devices are more usually found in fiction or journalism than in social scientific writing. There is a theoretical reason for using this style. Every family has its own uniqueness, and each individual is unique within the family. The conversations represent unique moments in their lives. The heavy theoretical categories, so commonly encountered in social psychological and sociological texts, can easily obscure this sense of individuality. It is necessary to use a style which conveys that the remarks made in the course of unfolding were moments occurring in the course of lives being led. Moreover, the participants often had very funny things to say. Social scientists should not plod along with their serious concepts, spoiling all the fun. Especially when the joke is on royalty.

Royal nomenclature

There is a dilemma when referring to royals: formal titles or informal first names can be used and both are in common use. The respondents tended to use familiar address, when talking about most members of the Royal Family: Di and Fergie, Andy and Charles, and so on. There were consistent exceptions: virtually never were the Queen or Queen Mother referred to by their first names. This itself is an issue, which would bear further examination, but it is not something which is directly discussed here. The strategy of formality is adopted here, except when reconstructing the dialogue of speakers who specifically used the informal terms. Generally, it is the Prince of Wales and the Duchess of York, not Charles and Sarah, let alone Charlie and Fergie.

The reason for the formality is simple. The popular informality, unsuspected by Bagehot and represented by that explosive kiss on the balcony after the royal marriage, is part of the phenomenon of contemporary monarchy. Part of the strangeness would be blurred by using, and thereby taking-for-granted, its own vocabulary. The critical analyst can achieve a distance by being somewhat formal. Under other rhetorical circumstances this formality might signify deferential loyalty, but here it is a reminder of the position of royalty. After all, if 'Andy' were not Prince Andrew, the crowds would not have gathered below the balcony; nor would the families have talked so animatedly about his family.

A POPULATED SOCIAL PSYCHOLOGY

Given the volume and richness of material, it would be impossible to recapture all that was said in the family discussions. A triumvirate of ideological themes guided the inevitable selection: nationality, inequality and family. The themes were not neatly organised in the discussions, but as participants discussed royal controversies, a shifting kaleidoscope of themes could be heard. In analysing these themes, it is hoped to present 'a populated social psychology' – that is, a psychological account which is filled with people.

Chapter 2 deals with the theme of nationalism. Respondents showed the importance of monarchy in their conception of British nationhood, and, thus, in their conceptions of themselves as members of the nation. The theme of family is involved in Chapter 3, as respondents are heard to discuss the extraordinary ordinariness of the family on the throne. The royals are only human after all, say the respondents, disclaiming themselves to be old-fashionedly deferential. These themes reappear in Chapter 4, as respondents talk about how the Royal Family should set examples of family life. This talk has a complexity which makes it inadequate simply to say that ordinary families 'identify' with the national family on the throne. Chapter 5 continues these themes by considering why respondents deny being envious of royalty's life. It is not deference which keeps envy in check. These issues are further examined in the following chapter, as respondents sympathise with royalty for being 'persecuted' by the press. The persecutors can include those very newspapers which the respondents themselves purchase. A complexity of desires and denials is to be heard in this talk. Chapter 7 confronts the issues of gender and family directly, by following the common-sense claim that interest in the Royal Family is essentially a woman's business. The final chapter deals with the reconstruction of time – past, present and future – in the common-sense depictions of royal matters. This returns the analysis back to nationhood, a topic which was never really left behind. It is suggested that monarchy does not merely represent the heritage of the nation's past, but also, comfortingly, the heritage of the future.

The chapters might appear to deal with separate topics, but throughout the themes are interconnected. There is the force of nationalism, and the ways which the familiar figures of royalty permit the nation to be imagined as a community. Then, there are the various ways in which the common-sense talk about royalty settles ordinary people down into their place within the imagined national community. The notion of 'double-declaiming' will be used: as people make claims about the Royal Family, justifying its position of privilege, so they will be heard making claims about the desirability of their own unprivileged lives. This double-declaiming is not confined to a particular topic, but is to be heard time and again.

The so-called obsession with the ancient institution is phrased in a cynicism, which is not simple. The modern subject 'knows' that royals are basically ordinary: they can fall from horses in ungainly ways. Yet, as images are demystified, so people will claim that the images should continue: the bald patch must maintain its mystic significance. In order to articulate these themes, people will draw upon common-sense notions beyond the topic of royalty. Thus, their talking reveals a wider pattern of thinking – a cynical consciousness, whose patterns match what is often called 'postmodernism'. In this sense, the modern monarchy is not a modern phenomenon; nor is it a survival from pre-modern modes of thought. Instead, as will be argued in the final chapter, the thinking of its supporters reproduces the tones of post-modernism.

In outlining these themes, and in reconstructing the patterns of thinking, there is an attempt to keep technical concepts to a minimum. This does not indicate a lack of concern with theory. Quite the contrary, the style of writing is itself part of a theoretical argument, which opposes the social science of statistical averages and abstracted theorising (Billig, 1989b). Much writing in the social sciences today is curiously depopulated – pages of theory and data

23

without a human being in sight. This is true of orthodox social psychology, with its search for the statistically significant result. In most social psychological texts, people seem to have been buried beneath a landslip of graphs, histograms and data tables. There is also a genre of critical analysis, which addresses itself to the study of ideology. This writing likewise is frequently depopulated – deserted landscapes of complex concepts, eerily silent of the chatter of humans. This depopulation seems out of keeping with the claim by Marx and Engels, who declared in *The German Ideology* that the analysis of ideology should start with the activity of 'real men' (1970, p.42).

The subsequent chapters are filled with real women and men, who are to be heard talking, joking and arguing. If the analysis aims to reconstruct the patterns of common-sense thinking, which are revealed in this talk, nevertheless, one assumption is not to be forgotten: thinking cannot occur without there being thinkers. Thus, it is hoped that the reconstructions give a sense of individual people, living their lives, voicing their desires and their discontents. In short, this aims to be a populated social psychology.

NOTES

1 The main signs used in the transcriptions are as follows:
   = to be found at the end of one speaker's utterance and at the beginning of another's: no audible gap between the two speakers. This would be expected if the second speaker were interrupting the first, who then gives way.
   [two or more speakers making utterances at the same time.
   (.) short pause. If the pause is of sufficient duration to be measurable, then the time is indicated in seconds: i.e. (2) indicates a pause of two seconds.
   ... omitted or inaudible material.
   { } clarificatory addition, often referring to tone or gesture i.e. {*laughing*}.
   underlining of words in the text indicates emphasis through raised voice; capitalisation indicates particular emphasis or volume.

An awful lot of *gff* – as Ito' he'd
inverted l-stemy
No Tony Parker / Gostwy /

2

THE ENVY OF THE WORLD

Kenneth Burke

The topic of nationhood provides an obvious starting-point for examining monarchy's appeal. In the modern world, to be king or queen is to be a king or queen of a nation – a King of Denmark, a Queen of the Netherlands, a King of Belgium and so on. To be a king in the abstract, without claiming to be a king of somewhere, is not to be a king. Monarchs can simultaneously be the sovereign head of several places. The Queen of the United Kingdom is a case in point; she is queen of a whole series of Commonwealth nations. There might be nations without monarchs, but there cannot be monarchs without nations. This is true of monarchs who have been rejected by the nation over which they claim their sovereignty. The King of Romania might not be welcomed in Romania, but still he claims to be the king of that nation. Various claimants dream of ascending to the throne of France (Dupuis, 1990). They aspire to something more than being French and being royal: they dream of being sovereign head of the national state.

Monarchy's connection with nationhood ensures that the topic is essentially serious, for nationalism cannot be contemplated with frivolity. Millions have fought and died in its various causes. As the twentieth century enters its last decade, nationalism is being asserted in those lands which had aspired in theory to establish the unities of socialism above the divisions of nationality. Now, most militantly, rival expressions of nationalisms confront each other. In this context, the King of Romania makes his claim. Nor is nationalism confined to those dramatic situations in which nations are in the process of being created or refashioned. Established nations are sustained by beliefs and myths of nationhood. To use Benedict Anderson's (1983) evocative term, they are 'imagined communities'.

Anderson emphasises that nations, as imagined communities, are essentially modern creations. The same point is made forcefully by Ernest Gellner (1983 and 1987). In a number of European countries, including Great Britain, the re-creation of monarchy in its popular, constitutional form was directly related to the formation of the national state. The Netherlands provides the most dramatic indication that the modern monarchy was not a pre-modern remnant which chance permitted to survive in modern conditions. The Dutch monarchy was established in 1813, in order to provide unity for the national state being created after a period of French domination. A national kingdom, fit for modern times, was replacing an old-fashioned, pre-national republic (Wilterdink, 1990).

Nationalism as an ideology is paradoxical: it is a product of the modern age but it creates myths about the antiquity and pre-modernity of nation states. The symbolism of nationhood hides its own recency (Hobsbawm, 1983). As Tom Nairn (1988) stresses, monarchy has made a unique contribution to the imagining of the British nation's past. Monarchy has a lineage of great antiquity, and, if placed at the centre of the modern state, it confers an imagined antiquity on that state. For this purpose, as David Cannadine (1983) has shown, royal traditions have been invented in the past two hundred years, and old rituals have been transformed by being put to new uses. The process of invention still continues. New rituals, such as the Investiture of the Prince of Wales in 1969, have been devised to represent the continuation of antiquity. The Investiture was like a new piece of furniture, made in the 'traditional style' with the latest technology applying genuine-look, antique finish. Lord Snowdon designed the proceedings so that, at the most dramatic moment, the Prince would utter archaic mumbo-jumbo about becoming 'liege man of life'. The words might have been incomprehensible to the television audience, but this incomprehensibility carried an important, readily understood message: the words cried 'We are ancient, we are your past'.

It could be argued that contemporary monarchy is a post-modernist, rather than modernist, phenomenon. This is a point to be considered later, when the thoughts of the ordinary families have been heard in detail. There is much more to be said about the post-modernist aspects of contemporary monarchy, which include both pastiche and self-parody. This is especially so, if one takes seriously Peter Sloterdijk's (1987) notion that contemporary consciousness is essentially cynical. Rationalist ways of thinking demystify mysteries, with rationalism turning against itself to mock its own pretensions of enlightenment. The result is, according to Sloterdijk, that cynicism permeates today's thinking. The argument of later chapters can be anticipated. People demystify the mystique of monarchy; yet, the demystification produces its own form of mystification and cynical justifications.

It would be too simple to start from the assumption that contemporary common-sense echoes to the single tone of cynicism. There are also the deep stains of nationalism, which are beyond pastiche and parody. In particular, there are two assumptions which are rarely questioned and which are accepted as expressing entirely 'natural' facts. The first is that the world is 'naturally' divided into separate nations. There might be disputes about where national boundaries should be drawn, but there is little dispute about the 'naturalness' of drawing boundaries. The second assumption is that each person is presumed 'naturally' to belong to a nation, so that part of what it means to be a person today is to have a national identity (Smith, 1979 and 1986). These assumptions convey the 'naturalness' of a world in which nations reinforce their separateness, by imagining their own unique, historic destinies (Schwartz, 1990; Schwartz *et al.*, 1986). These assumptions are not to be found in pre-modern times (Anderson, 1983).

Sometimes it is claimed that the English have no nationalism. Certainly, the English often show confusion about the name of their nation. As will be heard in the family interviews, English people seem unclear what to call their nation, using 'England' and 'Britain' interchangeably. Nairn (1988) argues persuasively that such confusion does not indicate a lack of national consciousness. It is a feature of an English nationalism, asserting its hegemonic position over the rival celtic nationalisms of the United Kingdom, whilst not appearing to do so.

In listening to participants discussing 'their' nation and 'their' monarchy, the limits of cynical consciousness are quickly reached. However, it might be inaccurate to refer to the 'limits of cynicism' as if there existed a whole area of thinking, untouched by rationalism; or, by contrast, as if there was a field of cynicism untouched by nationalism. Instead, rationalist and nationalist ways of talking are intertwined, and monarchy, as a topic, reproduces the dialectic between the two.

IMAGINING THE UNIMAGINABLE

First, the possibility that monarchy expresses some relic of a pre-modern 'taboo' can be considered. Public polls have suggested the reluctance of the British public to imagine the nation without a monarchy. The NOP survey of 1986 showed that eighty-one percent of the population could not foresee Britain in their life-times without a monarchy. Harris (1966), complementing surveys with longer interviews, noted that queries about imagining Britain as a republic were greeted almost by silence. It would be easy to slip into the language of 'taboo', in order to describe this reluctance.

Certainly, opponents of monarchy often use 'taboo' as part of their critical rhetoric. Edgar Wilson has a high 'taboo' count in the early pages of his book *The Myth of British Monarchy* (1989). He complains of 'the *taboo* protecting Monarchy from healthy scrutiny', claiming that 'the first step towards solving the problem of the Monarchy is to break the *taboo*' (p.5, emphases in original). In early 1990, the *Observer* newspaper published a series of articles 'challenging established opinions'. Christopher Hitchens wrote against monarchy, using an extended anthropological metaphor. An anthropologist who looked at 'our tribe' would recognise two things: a 'fetish' with royalty and 'a taboo on the discussion of it' (7 January 1990).

'Taboo' does not seem to be quite the right word. In the context of the critic's argument against monarchy, 'taboo' carries a particular rhetoric. It suggests that monarchy is a hang-over from 'primitive' times, unfit for modern society. Hence, Hitchens imagines an anthropologist looking at Britain, as if looking at some exotic 'tribe'. The implication is clear: if Britain wishes to be a modern nation, rather than a primitive tribe, it must do away with ancient taboos, which have no place in the modern world of rationality. There is a rhetorical consequence, following from these references to 'taboos', 'anthropologists' and 'tribes'. The modernity of many monarchical forms and their historical ties with the creation of the modern nation state are obscured. Whether intentionally or not, today's irrationalities are blamed on the past. In consequence, there is a hinted suggestion that the world would be a rational place, were it not for the strange survival of outdated taboos.

There is a further reason for being wary of the notion of 'taboo'. The use of the word begs the question about the nature of the British public's reluctance to contemplate republicanism. Certainly, public horror does not greet the infringement of the so-called 'taboo'. Hitchens's article did not provoke post-bags of outrage. Wilson's book was politely reviewed in the national press. Taboos of the sort which an anthropologist would recognise are not so painlessly broken. On the other hand, there is evidence that the British public is reluctant to imagine the end of monarchy, and this resistance, and its socio-psychological significance, deserve detailed examination. In particular, attention can be paid to two aspects: the ways that the resistance is maintained in 'polite' conversation, and the consequences which occur when the resistance is broken. As will be suggested, this resistance might not constitute a taboo in the anthropological sense, but it is bound deeply to feelings of national identity in contemporary Britain.

Certainly, in the family discussions there was a resistance to consider republicanism. This reluctance was managed by a number of conversational strategies. Frequently, the interviewer asked respondents whether they could imagine Britain without a Royal Family. Responses were typically negative, delivered with a brevity which indicated 'closure' of the conversation flow. Such closure would be employed by people who chatted quite freely, even intimately, at other moments. But an invitation to republicanism was to be firmly resisted.

A mother and father, who owned a small wool shop, were talking with their seventeen year old son (interview 3). The father tended to give his views of the world lengthily, with his wife and son then taking issue. On one matter, the loquacity and argument were curtailed. The interviewer asked whether they could imagine Britain without a Royal Family. 'Oh, I can't, no, no', replied the mother quickly. 'No, no', added her husband. Then, the question was specifically addressed to the son. 'No, I can't, no', he replied. The interviewer rephrased the question: 'You wouldn't like it?'. Back came the same reply: 'No, not at all' said the mother. For once, the whole family was in agreement. All had uttered brief replies, whose negatives close off discussion.

The interviewer persisted, asking the father to specify how things would be different without the Royal Family. He talked of other nations, like Italy and South American countries, always 'overthrowing the government and the queues'. The family returned to its argumentative mode: the son said that France was a republic and it didn't have queues. The father countered: France had seventeen presidents between 1940 and 1955 – 'You didn't know that'. His son conceded 'No, no'. Father was back in charge.

Initially, all the members had used unadorned negatives, as if erecting a fence with a sign, informing the interviewer that conversational trespassers were not welcome. Theirs was not an isolated case. A wife, who had been a market gardener before she had children, laughed slightly before answering: 'No, I wouldn't like to see it without one' (interview 7). She paused. The interviewer was still waiting. Her husband remained silent. She continued 'I don't think, no, I wouldn't be able to'. A sixty-four year old retired engineer admitted that, as a young man, he had been very anti-royalist. Shortly after this admission, the interviewer asked whether he could imagine Britain without royalty: 'No, not really, I don't think, no, no, I can't imagine what it would be like at all' (interview 4). Again the negatives fall thickly. The youthful imagination is now declared closed.

When, on another occasion, the interviewer asked what it would be like 'if we had a president that we elect?', the mother was emphatic: 'Oh, my goodness, NO' (interview 24). Again a fence was being erected. The interviewer persisted: 'What would it be like without them (the Royal Family)?'. The daughter, a sixteen year old school girl, hesitated at first, 'I don't think, err'. Then she found her answer: 'I think it's something that makes this country special really, because there's not many royal, that many royal families, is there really, in countries'. Her father agreed.

Once over the fence, the theme of nationality is revealed. Monarchy adds a unique dimension to the country (England or Britain). Remove monarchy and you remove the very thing which distinguishes this country from other countries: England/Britain would cease to be like England/Britain. Such a future should be avoided, even in the imagination: to imagine the imagined community without its special element would be to de-imagine it.

If this interpretation is correct, then a non-nationalist theme should be less effective than a nationalist one for justifying why a republican future is not to be imagined. A self-employed salesman of fifty-two, and his wife, a forty-three year old secretary, were talking (interview 26). He suggested that monarchy was 'part of the permanent structure of our society'. The interviewer then asked: 'Can you imagine Britain without them, without a monarchy?'. The husband split the two meanings in the question – the capacity to imagine and the wish to imagine: 'I can, but I don't like, I wouldn't like to think of it without one'. His wife cut in: 'No I wouldn't like to think of it at all'. 'How would it be?' asked the interviewer. 'Horrible', she replied.

Her words seemed to close off the discussion, which his claim to be able to imagine a royal-free future had opened. The interviewer pushed him for details and he answered:

> 'Well I mean, the thing that puts me off most is there would obviously be, err (.), supposedly democratic society, um, I mean the level of debate we see in Parliament sometimes I think is quite appalling, in, in, in terms of personal abuse, and, err, general blinkered, err, outlook. And I think if, if, that if the Royal Family weren't there, I could see that rising up a little further, which would be a very bad thing. I mean we're getting back to this, this thing we said earlier of stability and, err, having a certain sense of, of, err, something that is permanent and also a good example'.
>
> (interview 26)

It is not easy going imagining the royal-free future: ums, errs and pauses show this. He complains about parliamentary behaviour – 'quite appalling'. Without a Royal Family, this would rise up 'a little further'.

The interviewer continued her pursuit: 'What else might change?'. The husband was stumbling 'Um, I don't know, difficult one, isn't it, um'. He paused, then continued: 'Presumably business would go on pretty much the same, I mean it seems to do in the States'. The wife added that she couldn't 'imagine what it would be like really'. He agreed: 'No, I can't. I mean, that's, that's the quick answer to that; I find it impossible'.

Originally, he had confidently claimed that he could imagine a republican Britain. Now he withdraws the claim. In between, he has been able to imagine the republican future. But the imaginings were not so horrible. It seemed so ordinary, with business progressing much the same and parliamentary behaviour just a little worse. Suddenly, the matter must be closed. It's impossible to imagine, horrible.

He had been searching for horrors, but he has been looking in the wrong places. All the time, the clue was there, if not staring him in the face, then, at least, issuing from his lips. Its obviousness was like the purloined letter in Edgar Allen Poe's famous story. Lesser

31

Patronising

detectives than Auguste Dupin overlooked the ordinary letter, visible in the letter-rack. Business would be much the same, said the father, just like in the United States. He was searching for the vital clue in that ordinary business. Common-sense was urging him: just look up and see the air-mail letter with its American stamp.

Wife and husband, both civil servants, were talking of the constitutional benefits of monarchy (interview 18). The unimaginable was reached by another direction – via America. 'You've got to look what would replace it', said the husband. His wife interrupted: you'd get 'something like the American system'. It was his turn to interrupt: 'You'd get a presidency'. They were moving together towards a conclusion: 'I think it would be a dreadful state of affairs, really sad', she said. 'I can never see that happening', he said.

A further example shows how the unthinkability of republicanism is framed by an assumption of nationhood. An engineer and his wife, outlining their conventionally pro-royal views, were emphasising the virtues of respectable behaviour in front of their two teenage daughters (interview 27). The interviewer asked about imagining Britain without monarchy. The mother couldn't imagine it. Suddenly, the father switched from traditionalist to sceptic: 'Maybe you wouldn't notice it any different'. The mother reacted immediately: 'You would'. The sceptic persisted: 'How?', he asked. The mother could not specify: 'Well, I don't know, you just know they're there'. His sceptical mood was not appeased: 'We all think that the Royal Family hold the country together, but there's no real facts'. Perhaps it wouldn't matter and 'I wouldn't like to say that it'd change'.

There it was: the unthinkable out in the conversational open. The reaction was not one of shock, as if the lust and violence of the Freudian unconscious had spilled on to the antimacassars of a Victorian sitting-room. The conversation continued agreeably, around the old-style fire in the modernised cottage. No gods were demanding retribution for a broken taboo. Why the father lapsed from his conventional monarchism is not clear. Perhaps, it was an intended display of masculinity – the man of the house displaying worldly scepticism in front of his womenfolk. Maybe, it was a chance occurrence; two minutes earlier, or two minutes later, the thought might not have popped into his mind. What matters is that the sceptical argument was easily made. His talk about 'real facts' would, in other contexts, be quite conventional.

Whatever the reasons for the sceptical turn, its fate showed the persuasive force of nationalist themes. He proceeded to claim that a change to proportional representation would 'have a bigger influence' than the abolition of monarchy. The interviewer then asked whether he would like a presidential system. The reaction was immediate, brief and collective. 'No', they all answered in unison. The father went on: 'It's just Mickey Mouse, isn't it, when you see how America, I mean, untrained people, well I mean Ronald Reagan'.

The borders of scepticism had been reached, and they were national borders. The father gives reasons, and these point to America. But there was more. He had found the essential difference, whose existence he had just been doubting. The sceptic returns to the paths of common-sense. One glance across the Atlantic and the British Dupin has triumphantly recovered the lost justification.

✳ EQUATING NATION WITH MONARCHY

The reasoning behind the recovery of the lost justification was over-determined, in the sense that it contained several argument-ative themes. The father was offering a constitutional argument about the political neutrality of the Head of State (interview 27). In addition, there is the national theme of superiority and inferiority. The American presidency is mere Mickey Mouse, as compared with royalty, who are properly trained for the job.

The mixture of national and rational argumentative themes was quite common. A forty-four year old supermarket cashier said she would rather have a Royal Family than a dictator (as if there was a choice). The interviewer then asked what it would be like without the Royal Family. 'I wouldn't like to see them go', she said, 'I wouldn't feel as safe...if we had just a president' (interview 55). Her husband, a fitter, expanded the point: 'In everyday life there would be no difference but culturally...there would be a great void'. He went on to make the national equation: 'You know, the Queen and that...it's what Britain is, the Queen the Royal Family'.

In the equation of monarchy and nation, there is claim to a deeper level – everyday life might continue, but, at another level, England/Britain would no longer be itself. A housewife, married to a self-employed butcher, used a metaphor: The Royal Family was 'like the root of a tree, they're the root and we're all the little branches...and once that root's gone, the tree dies, doesn't it' (inter-view 21). There is nothing to stop an argumentative juxtaposition between pragmatic, rational justifications and nationalist ones. A

33

sixty-eight year old mother had been taking a critical position, and now her son was giving rational justifications for monarchy (interview 60). He was talking tourism, trade and business. Economic rationality slipped into a deeper nationality: 'I think it's nice, it's, it's, it's England, it's England', he concluded.

The equation of monarchy with nation implies that an attack upon monarchy is an attack upon the fundamental uniqueness of the nation. If 'our' selves are equated with the nation, then the attack is also a threat to the unique identity of 'our' national selves. To imagine the imagined community without monarchy is to do more than de-imagine the nation: it is to de-imagine 'our' selves. To use the metaphor of the butcher's wife, 'we', the branches, die when the national root is destroyed.

This sort of theme is not easily expressed: it would be silly for speakers to say that they would not be themselves if the Windsors vacated the throne. The metaphor of root and branch achieves this obliquely. The theme of identity can surface more directly. Interview 39 was a lively occasion. The daughter-in-law, a young mother who worked in a factory, was provocatively citing economic criticisms of royalty. Her mother-in-law, who annually travelled to London to see the Trooping of the Colour, resisted strongly. The father-in-law conceded some of the economic arguments, but he drew the line firmly when his daughter-in-law stretched the point of provocation by envisaging the end of monarchy.

She was talking about royalty becoming more and more lax – 'there's not so many rules'. She then said that young people like herself had less interest in royalty, and 'we're the people of the future'. Monarchy would not continue: 'I don't think the Royal Family will last for a gener-'. She paused, as if stuck in the middle of the word 'generation'. She rephrased the end of the sentence: 'for long'. Her parents-in-law voiced quick dissent. She backed down immediately: 'I think they'll last for hundreds of years'. She then explained that she was talking about the 'twenty-fifth century'. It was at this point that her father-in-law equated nation and monarchy: 'Oh I think that they'll last as long as the country lasts'. The daughter-in-law disassociated herself from her imagined republican scenario: 'I mean I'd be dead in five hundred, six hundred years' time, but I don't think there'll be a Royal Family then'. The father-in-law repeated his equation: 'If you've not got the Royal Family there, then you'll not have the British Isles as we know it, we'll perhaps be another state of America or something like that'.

Very irritating annotations . *Prescribe a cure in*
Tony Parker

The daughter-in-law, in imagining the end of monarchy, switched her pronouns. 'We' are no longer the people of the future. 'They', the people of the twenty-fifth century, would commit the fateful deed: 'One day they'll say "Right, we'll become a republic"'. The republican future would belong to others – 'them', not 'us', who will be long dead. In this way, she and her generation are dissociated from the imagined sedition. Her father-in-law's grammar indicates a 'we', which continues into the twenty-fifth century, long after 'our' deaths. This continuing 'we' is threatened by the distant republicanism. Without the Royal Family, 'we' will be another state of America; Britain would be like other nations; 'we' would be foreign to ourselves.

These reasonings hint at the void within 'us', which would be opened up by an absence of monarchy. Even the critic shrinks from the void, stopping herself in mid-sentence. She projects the imagined republicanism into a distantly safe future: others will be the republicans. This projection is not safe enough for her parents-in-law. If England/Britain ceases to be England/Britain, then 'we', the English/British, cease to be ourselves. And how can 'we' imagine ourselves as being not ourselves? As Americans? Italians? South Americans? No, no, it is unimaginable. Horrible.

PRIDE AND PREJUDICE

Nationalism involves more than depicting one's own nation; it involves depicting the nation's place amidst the world of nations. Here, a sense of the superiority can be invoked. As speakers talked about the uniqueness of England/Britain and its monarchy, so aspersions were cast upon other nations – their revolutions, queues and Micky Mouse presidents. Ideas of national superiority are not to be easily made, for they conflict with the assumptions of liberal tolerance. The universal aspirations of liberalism are as much a part of modern common-sense as is the particularity of nationalism. If it is common-sense that the world is 'naturally' divided into separate nations, it is just as common-sensical that 'we' are all members of the human race. As Stuart Hall remarks with irony, in England liberalism has 'become almost as "settled" and inescapable as the English weather' (1986, p.36).

One aspect of the liberal common-sense is a norm against appearing 'prejudiced'. This can be seen in the way that racism is commonly expressed. Modern racists feel the need to proclaim their own reasonableness with disclaimers of prejudice (Hewitt and Stokes, 1975; Lauerbach, 1989). 'I'm not prejudiced but...', they commonly assert before voicing their complaints about foreigners, immigrants and/or homosexuals (Barker, 1981; Billig *et al.*, 1988; van Dijk, 1987; Wetherell and Potter, 1988). These complaints are phrased as 'matters-of-fact', not 'matters-of-prejudice'. In speaking thus, modern racists are, in effect, denying that they possess that state of mind which psychologists have called 'ethnocentric'. The thinking of the ethnocentrist is seen to be irredeemably narrow, characterised by an unambiguous contempt for other groups, and an unthinking pride for one's own group. It is a mentality which is rigidly contained within its own nationalist assumptions (Adorno *et al.*, 1950; Forbes, 1986).

Some psychologists have contrasted the ethnocentric way of thinking with decentred thinking. The former is seen as nationalist thinking, whilst the latter represents the liberal cast of mind. Whereas ethnocentrists view the world from the narrow perspective of their own group, decentred individuals are said to exercise a crucial act of imagination: they can view themselves, and their own national groups, as outsiders might see them (Aboud, 1988; Helkama, 1987 and 1988). By such imagination, they can free themselves from the limited prejudices of ethnocentric thinking.

These psychological theories emphasise the difference between ethnocentric and decentred thinking, and, thereby, between the nationalist and the liberal mentality. However, the formula 'I'm not prejudiced but...' shows that the distinction might be an over-simplification: denials of racism, citing liberal values, can be used to articulate racism. This has a direct implication for the ways that nationalist themes are to be expressed. Denials of national pride and claims to be tolerantly decentred (i.e. to see 'our' nation as foreigners see 'us') can be employed, not to criticise notions of national superiority, but to articulate them.

First, there is the matter of pride in the nation. In the family discussions, there were few outright expressions of national pride. Interestingly, these tended to be made by critics of monarchy. One father, a motor mechanic, was known to his family as a vociferous opponent of royalty (interview 2). That afternoon he had torn up the Sunday paper, because of an article which had outraged him (see Billig, 1989a, for a detailed analysis of his views). The family discussion was argumentative from start to finish, with the father's

36

views as the focus. This was not the family's first disagreement on the topic. Nor was it likely to be the last. The son was talking about the devoted royalism of the older generation. The father said that this was because that generation 'had gone through the war'. He added: 'Because I don't like royalty, do *not* like royalty whatsoever, I'm still very patriotic'. He declared that he would be prepared to die for his country, but not, of course, for his queen.

This declaration must be understood in its rhetorical context: the common-sense equation of monarchy with nation leaves the anti-royalist vulnerable to the charge of national disloyalty. A widowed mother was taking an anti-monarchist line, much to the annoyance of her teenage son (interview 58). Her son, the royalist, had muttered rudely about the national flag. She countered, putting him in his place: 'I'm proud of England, England's still great to me...I'm quite proud of the fact that I am English'.

Royalists did not tend to speak in such terms, but they had little rhetorical need to do so. No-one was going to accuse them of being unpatriotic, unless they muttered about the flag. Their royalism was doing the patriotic business for them. Instead, they have a different rhetorical problem: the need to disclaim the prejudices of pride. This interpretation would explain the general absence of royalist 'pride'. However, the absences on their own do not confirm the explanation. It is necessary to consider what conversation analysts call the 'deviant cases', in which the unusual occurs (Heritage, 1988). The reactions of participants to the deviant case are all-important, for they can indicate whether the unusual is unusual, because it risks infringing social norms.

When a middle-class mother and father were talking with their two unmarried sons, there occurred an instance of a royalist citing national pride (interview 41). The father was an electronics engineer, the mother had a small health foods business and the twenty-seven year old son was doing well as a financial assistant. Those three were solidly Conservative and traditionally royalist. The older son, a photographer, was left-of-centre and critical of royalty. He did not hesitate to express his criticisms, nor the others to criticise his criticisms.

They were talking about watching royal events on the television. The mother was questioning her critical son, trying to elicit an admission that he had watched the royal weddings – and that he had felt proud.

(Interview 41)

Mother. ...did you watch the royal weddings, Rob?...

Older son: Yeah, I did, yeah

Mother. Were you proud? (2) [did you feel

Older son: [I can't remember my feelings at the time, but I remember [I remember watching it on TV but

Mother.   [No but you felt that you wanted to watch it

There she has him. The radical confesses to watching the weddings. She wants further confessions: Were you proud? He can't remember his feelings, or so he claims. She continues probing. The father breaks in. He tells his spouse – his argumentative ally – that 'pride' was inappropriate.

> *Father.* I think no, I think the (.) I don't know whether pride comes into it, Kate, I think that you realise at the time, even watching it on telly, that all that pomp and pageantry, probably you couldn't see, find, anywhere else in the world
>
> *Mother.* for definite, for absolute definite you couldn't
>
> *Father.* because people, this is what I was saying a while ago, that come from all over the world just to see little brief snatches of it

After this, the mother said that people come 'just to see' the Changing of the Guard and Buckingham Palace. Then, she returned to the ceremonies. If Charles were to be crowned king, she said turning to her radical son, wouldn't you feel it was a memorable event, something to tell your grandchildren about? Hang on a minute, he replied, what have you told me about the Coronation of '53? 'We've never had reason to', she answered, 'I mean you've never said "Mum tell us about 1953"'.

For the deviant case, it is the notion of 'pride' which matters. The mother did not say that she personally felt pride, when she saw the royal weddings. Nor did anyone else. Her husband intervenes specifically to deny the appropriateness of pride: 'I don't know whether pride comes into it, Kate'. She does not disagree with his disagreement: they are arguing on the same side. All the while he is expounding, the mother is expressing hearty agreement: 'For definite', she repeats. She has readily yielded the idea of 'pride'.

In place of 'pride', the father offers another way of talking about nation and foreigners: you 'realise' that the pomp and pageantry are unique. The emotion of 'pride' has been replaced by a term of rationalism – 'realise'. The person who claims to 'realise' something is claiming to notice the 'realities' of the situation. The facts have been 'realised', or made real, in the mind. Thus, the father, in denying the relevance of 'pride', makes a claim about 'reality'. People come from all over the world, just to catch a glimpse of something, which *is* unique. Yes, people come to see the Changing of the Guard and to look at Buckingham Palace, agrees his wife. More facts.

In two ways, the focus has shifted from inner world to outer world. There is the shift from inner feeling to outer reality. It's not a matter of an emotion, such as pride, it's a matter of realising. At the same time, there is a shift from the national ingroup to the rest of the world. It is no longer 'us', the English/British audience, proudly watching the national pageant. 'We' are watching the outer world of foreigners, watching 'us'. Neither pride, nor any other irrational emotion, are said to come into it. As the controversial psychoanalyst Jacques Lacan (1977) claimed, we project our ideal selves on to the gaze of others. An admirably unique national self is described as being realised within gaze of other nations. They see 'us' as unique; 'we' realise this. In so realising, 'we' lay claim to 'our' lack of prejudiced pride: 'we' are only seeing 'ourselves' as others see 'us'. Thus, the critic of royalty is confronted with something more argumentatively powerful than pride and prejudice. He is shown the 'realities' of 'our' unique national destiny. All the world realises 'us' to be unique. He should realise this too.

THE TOURIST DEFENCE OF THE REALM

The mother and father (interview 41), in talking of the Royal Family attracting tourists, were citing a common-place, whose commonality is confirmed by the opinion surveys. Blumler *et al.* (1971) presented respondents with a series of statements about monarchy; for instance, that the Queen was a lovely person or that the Royal Family sets standards for family life. The statement which received the highest degree of assent was that the Royal Family was good for the tourist trade. MORI, January 1990, asked about the consequences if monarchy was abolished. Eighty-seven percent agreed that the nation would be less attractive to tourists – a greater assent than for any of the other dire consequences listed by the pollsters. At first sight, this might appear remarkable. The venerable institution, equated with nationhood itself, is being treated as a tourist attraction. Cynicism seems to be reducing the palaces to dollar-earning heritage-parks.

However, the rhetorical over-functioning of utterances must be taken into account. When speakers say something, they are often doing several different things at once. The father, who disclaimed that pride came into it, is a case in point. He was doing a number of things simultaneously. He was arguing against his son; he was qualifying his wife's criticisms; he was claiming his own rationality. There was something else: he was also talking *about* the world. To be more precise, he was imagining the imagined national community in the imagination of the rest of the world.

The argumentative function of the tourist theme would appear to be simple: it provides a rationally economic counter to economic criticisms of monarchy. Should critics raise the issue of cost, then back can come the tourist argument. Sure, the palaces and the servants are expensive; and sure, the royals pay no tax; but look at the money they bring from tourism. The critical older son was using an economic argument to criticise the cost of monarchy. The father answered him: 'What you've got to remember Rob that...a lot of people forget is that, I don't know how many tourists go to London *every year*, but there's an awful lot of money'. Yes, joined in his mother, 'they go to the Palace' and her husband cut in with agreement and emphasis, they 'come into London *purely* because we've got a Royal Family'. The cynic has been answered in his own terms.

The critical mother and her royalist son, a school care-taker, have already been mentioned (interview 60). The mother was complaining about royal expense and extravagance. Her arguments elicited counter-economics from her son: 'I think it's good for the country and I think it brings a lot of trade in, it brings a lot of business in, it brings a lot of tourism'. It was then he made the remark, already quoted, equating monarchy with England ('it's England, it's England'). Later, he expanded the point: 'The government's not going to say "We're not giving you any money" because it's bringing in billions a year in tourism alone...I don't think they're going to stop it, it's bringing in billions and that's my reasoning, why I don't mind it really'. Again, monarchy was the major tourist attraction: 'It's our biggest tourist draw...without that we've got nothing...there's nothing to top it, nothing to compare with the monarchy'.

A retired fitter was considering, under prompting from the interviewer, the possibility of the country without a Royal Family (interview 52). The imagination was hesitant at first, but soon imagined tourists were flowing forth: 'Well (.), if, um, you know, if it stopped (.), if if you abolish royalty straight away and it stopped, say, your tourists coming in, and things like that (.), then we're bound to suffer until we've found something else to take its place by...attracting tourists'. The Americans, in particular, are drawn by the Royal Family: 'That's the only thing they come for'. He went on to say that royalty was 'the biggest drawing power of the lot'. 'Yes, I agree', said his wife.

The point was repeated in other discussions. After all, said the forty-four year old cleaner, it's not as if 'we' have the weather (interview 50). 'It brings the Americans over here and a lot of the tourists over here and if we didn't have the monarchy we wouldn't have anything' said a forty-two year old mother (interview 1). Her son and husband quickly agreed. A forty-seven year old father, a telephone engineer, noted: 'The Americans and the rest of the world come over here and they'll spend thousands of pounds just to look at Buckingham Palace and they'll spend thousands of pounds just to see the heritage of them' (interview 61).

A common-place belief is not merely one which is commonly held. It is also likely to be used as an argumentative justification, with speakers supporting their case by citing a piece of accepted common wisdom (Billig, 1987; Perelman and Olbrechts-Tyteca, 1971). Argumentative opponents can be thrown off balance for they too might accept the common-sense belief. When the son (interview 61) had used the tourist argument, citing the billions of pounds, his mother did not dispute his figures. All she did was to shift her defence. She complained that royalty when 'they go abroad they come back with expensive gifts'. The son could then continue with economic man-of-the-world cynicism: gifts are expected, there'd be trouble if one was refused. It was all so economically trivial compared to the reasonable reasoning about the billions.

The critical motor mechanic also revealed the power of the tourist argument (interview 2). This father continually used economic arguments against royalty: they were paid too much, their houses were too big, 'we' are supporting 'them' and so on. Back he kept coming to the economic point. But the mother played the tourist defence: 'They must bring a lot of money into the country because of tourism'. She mentioned people visiting Buckingham Palace. The father, far from challenging the point, added his agreement: 'The Tower, the Changing of the Guard, there's all that sort of thing, we know that'. Even the critic acknowledges 'we know that'. But it wasn't the point, he went on. They shouldn't have all the big houses and the estates. His daughter was agreeing with him on this point. Crucially, their argument had shifted to morality. The economics had been conceded.

The tourist theme is an effective argumentative defender of the realm. The argument of the critics, submitting the traditional institution to a harshly rational cost-benefit analysis, is returned in kind. The critics, substituting morality for economics, are in retreat. They drop their economic arguments, as they flee. The advancing royalists pick up the discarded weaponry, firing it back at the retreating rationalists. The Americans bring money – bang! They come to see the Queen – bang! Don't you want a wealthier Britain? – bang! bang! bang! The critics, dodging the bullets, can only complain about the unfairness of it all.

The defender of monarchy has not made a complete switch from nationalist arguments to rationalist economics. The two ideological forms – rationalism and nationalism – are entwined, for the economics, and their terms of reference, were always nationalist. The claims about the tourist income assume the naturalness of national economic interests. 'We' have the Royal Family. If the argument appears to be rational, then its rationality is very much that of nationality.

DEFLECTING DOUBT

There are further points to be made about the rhetorical functions of the tourist argument. McGuire (1964) produced experimental evidence to show that common beliefs, which are rarely criticised, have few ready-made argumentative defences. The institution of monarchy seems to be an exception to McGuire's rule. It is not subject to regular criticism – there are even complaints that it is protected by 'taboo'. Yet, there it stands, well defended against occasional skirmishers by the tourist argument. The armoury of the defence seems disproportionate to the threat of enemy attack. However, the weaponry would be needed if the critical position, despite the rarity of republicanism, was quite common-sensical. The enemy would be within the ranks of loyal subjects.

The same rationalist thinking, which provides the tourist argument, also provides those critical questions which the tourist argument counters. The criteria of costs and benefits are common-

This is straightforwardly written – it is

heavy-footed, leaden

sensical. There is no actual taboo to prevent them being applied to the topic of monarchy, to ask whether the royals are value for money. The father (interview 41) was facing the economic criticism, and his choice of words was significant. He played the tourist defence, but he added a preface: 'What you've got to remember Rob that...a lot of people forget'. He is not suggesting that his son's criticisms are beyond the bounds of common-sense. Far from it, he is assuming that the criticism is commonly made and needs to be countered by a little remembered piece of economics, which he is about to introduce decisively into the discussion.

If common-sense provides the wherewithal for questioning monarchy's expense, then the tourist argument can be useful for reassuring the doubting voice in the loyalist's own mind. This can be seen in discussions between sympathisers. A mother, father, son and daughter all voiced conventionally royal views, stressing the virtues of tradition and national heritage (interview 1). At one point, the father started questioning the economic cost: 'With this pomp and circumstance, there's a lot of waste'. But then, he added a qualification, 'I suppose really the waste is paying other people', and the making of paper flags was creating jobs. There again, the money 'could be better spent'. Around he went: 'But having said that...it's giving people work'. Argument and counter-argument were chasing each other through his thoughts (see Billig, 1990a, for an extended analysis). The discussion about the cost of ceremonies led to the general question whether royalty was value for money. 'Well, that's very difficult', commented the mother. The father conceded that the Queen 'gets a lot of money'. 'I don't begrudge them the money', said the mother. Nor did the son. The mother, then, voiced the tourist argument: 'I think it brings the Americans over here and a lot of the tourists over here, and if we didn't have the monarchy we wouldn't have anything'. Son and husband quickly agreed. The matter was settled; they had answered their own doubts.

Oh GOD

One might say that the tourist argument is a rationalisation for nationalist themes. There are two senses of 'rationalisation' and both are relevant to the economic justifications of monarchy (Billig, 1988a). First, there is the ideological sense of justifying the values of rationality, as opposed, for example, to those of religious faith. In this sense, the economic argument is a rationalisation, for it makes monarchy appear perfectly attuned to a world where profitable income is a criterion for rationality. Second, there is the psychological sense of rationalisation. Rationalising in this sense occurs when people give reasonable justifications for a belief, but the belief is held for other reasons, which are not being openly admitted. A speaker might concede the reasonableness of the rationalisation in an argument, but would not necessarily concede the position which is being justified by the rationalisation.

The tourist argument can be seen as a rationalisation in both senses of the term. Argumentatively, it is a powerful argument, sweeping common-sense doubts from its path. Its persuasive power is derived from common-sense and not from any technical calculation. Speakers could talk imprecisely about thousands of pounds, billions of pounds, or merely of an awful lot of money. No-one cited any relevant statistics to show that royal credits exceed debits. Critics did not quote that three times as many tourists visit the Tower of London than Windsor Castle (*Independent*, 18 August 1988); or that the London Tourist Board rates the Changing of the Guard lower as a tourist attraction than it does the Tower, Westminster Abbey and St Paul's Cathedral, with Buckingham Palace nowhere in sight (*Guardian*, 29 December 1989; see Wilson, 1989, pp.51–5 for a critical analysis of the tourist argument).

Even without such figures, it would not have been difficult for the rationalist critic to query whether the royal blue was in the credited black. Yet, this move was seldom made. Again the 'deviant cases' are instructive. On the rare occasions when the tourist argument was challenged, royalists would hastily withdraw their rational justifications, replacing them with the protected power of nationalism. The critical son (interview 41) twice challenged his mother's use of the tourist argument. The first time he tried to interject the economic doubt ('it's difficult to get the figures'), his voice was swamped by the combined effort of the rest of the family. He could hardly make his doubt heard in between the talk of Buckingham Palace, the Japanese, the Americans. The Royal Family, including 'the old Queen Mother', were ambassadors '*all* over the world', said the mother. She turned to dismiss the economic argument, reversing its value: 'That's *priceless* I think'.

The second time, the mother also shifted from price to priceless: 'You can't count it like that Rob; all you know is that wherever you go in the world, people look toward England, because we've got this tradition of pomp and pageantry and sort of Royal Family that goes back generations'. You can't count it like, she says, when she has just been counting it like that. The pounds are argumentatively

44

conceded. Accountancy is not the way to account for royalty: it is beyond money, it is priceless.

A nationalist image of the whole world gazing towards England has supplanted the cool tones of economics. It is back to the 'realisation' which denies its own pride. The speed with which the tourist argument was put aside suggests that it is was a rational-isation, in both senses of the term. However, nationality and rationality are not arranged into a neat ideological ordering, with the former residing at a deeper level than the latter. The tourist argu-ment is not *merely* a surface rationalisation for underlying nationalism, for the economics is already national, and nationality already seems rational. Rationality has been nationalised, even as nationality is being rationalised.

ENVY OF THE WORLD

The tourist argument has further content, for it depicts a relationship between England/Britain and the rest of the world. The relations between tourists and hosts can be ambivalent. The hosts can view the tourists cynically as punters, who are to be parted from their money and who might be resented for having the money in the first place (Furnham and Bochner, 1986). Alternatively, the tourists can be seen as pilgrims who have come to pay their respects. If tourists are imagined as pilgrims, rather than punters, then 'we' can imagine ourselves to be worthy of respect in their gaze. Those who come to pay their respects are to be respected for their respectful stance towards 'us'.

The mother, talking about tourists looking to 'us', was imagining something other than interest or respect in their gaze (interview 41). There was a look of jealousy. She was arguing economics with her older son: 'I think they're worth more...I've travelled abroad and people say "Aren't you lucky"; you know, they always envy the Brits their Royal Family'. Her husband agreed: no other country has 'got the hundreds and hundreds of years to look back on'. Here were further common-places: the rest of the world envies England/Britain its monarchy, its history and thereby its special place among the nations.

Across class, gender and generation, the same thoughts could be heard. The working-class family did not dispute the father when he declared that 'we're the envy of the world because we've got them' (interview 39). A forty year old mother, a domestic assistant, said that she would not like to see England 'without a monarch' (interview 57). Her husband, a lorry driver, voiced his approval by saying that 'they're all envious of it'. It was the heritage, 'the British heritage', said the mother. No-one was disagreeing. 'What's a monarch?', asked the sixteen year old daughter. 'Something England's got', answered her mother.

A young couple, civil servants living in a detached house, were giving the financial argument for monarchy (interview 18). The husband was talking 'revenue'. His wife then added: 'I mean it's so historic, people are envious of our Royal Family...it's just part of our culture and country'. Two sets of grandparents were talking of the value of monarchy (interview 38). One grandfather said that without it 'we would feel that we had lost something valuable'. The other grandfather agreed: 'the rest of the world' would feel that as well. A grandmother added: 'We've got something here everybody else admires'. 'They envy it', said the second grandmother.

The theme of international envy can be used to dispel the critical thought. The interviewer asked whether monarchy might be out of date. The wife, who worked with her husband in their wool shop, countered the very suggestion (interview 3). 'No, no, not at all', she said 'I think we're the envy of the world, a country with our queen; no, I think a lot of countries must envy us having a queen and a Royal Family'. Her husband agreed without hesitation: 'Definitely, I'm sure they do'. A salesman and his wife, living in the suburbs, had no doubt about the world's envy: 'I'm sure they do, yes', said the husband. 'Yes', said the wife (interview 26).

An electrical engineer felt able to describe the world's envy with precision (interview 36). Other countries envy England? 'I would say probably seventy-five percent of countries do'. Unprompted, he continued his calculations: 'Even some Arab countries do'. The countries which don't envy 'us' were those 'going through communist government periods'. But even then, one couldn't be too sure: 'Probably the communist government doesn't, but a lot of the day-to-day people would anyway'. His wife mentioned one place which he had neglected in his world survey: 'America, I should think places like that do'.

Again, unbidden, the transatlantic theme makes its appearance. A forty-three year old home-help and ex-barmaid specifically mentioned the Americans: 'They love us, don't they' (interview 10). Her husband agreed: there weren't many countries which have 'our history and I think we are envied'. In another interview, the interviewer had asked whether other countries envy Britain? The young wife and her mother both answered together: 'I think America does' (interview 53). 'They'd all love our Royal Family', said a forty-eight year old housewife, 'the Americans would love our Royal Family' (interview 21).

The theme of envy could be used to stop the critic. A mother was taking the critical line against her son and his wife (interview 60). Other countries haven't got a monarchy, she said to make the point that 'we' don't need one. Her son reacted quickly. No, that's the point, he said, it brings in the tourists: 'I mean the Americans love it...I'm sure if we said to the Yanks "Look we're dismissing the Royal Family, we've had enough of them"...they'd take 'em across in a crate...they would, they'd snap them up, pay millions for them'. The mother was silent.

A wife and husband, retired cleaner and fitter respectively, were talking about tourism (interview 52). Royalty was 'the biggest drawing power of the lot', he said. 'Yes, I agree', said his wife. She mentioned the 'beautiful uniforms and things like that, I mean you don't see that anywhere else in the world, do you'. She looked across the Atlantic: 'The Americans would give their eye-teeth for a Royal Family'. That's why they come to Britain, said her husband: 'Whatever we've got, they've got it ten times the size'. Yes, there's only one thing they haven't got and 'that's the only thing they come for', he added.

It could have been the disabled upholsterer and his wife talking (interview 15). Royalty was tradition, said the husband. His wife agreed: 'They come from all over the world to see it, don't they, the Americans go mad for it, don't they'. Theirs was a madness of desire. As her husband put it: 'I mean the Americans say "if you ever get the sack, come here and be our queen"'.

As always, the strength of a common-place is to be observed in argumentative exchange. The vociferously anti-royal father (interview 2) has already been mentioned. The interviewer asked whether other countries would want a monarchy like 'ours'. The daughter had no doubt: 'Yeah'. The mother was more cautious: 'Probably'. The father also replied, 'Probably'. Then, he gave reasons: 'France and all those' are probably envious, and 'I mean we may regret it if we got rid of them'. At the mention of France, the daughter jumped in to say how special England/Britain and its monarchy was: 'Look at France, I don't even know the names of their king and queen'. The father laughed: 'They did the right thing at the time and beheaded them'. He giggled.

The Robespierre in his modern semi-detached home has been unmasked. He does not escape the common-sense belief that the French envy 'our' monarchy. If they are envious, then there is a lesson for 'us': perhaps 'we' would have regrets, if 'we' were to get rid of 'our' monarchy. The doubts, so foreign to a Robespierre, are creeping in. He laughingly recalls the revolutionary end of monarchy in France. It is just a joke. But it's more than a joke. He can imagine that he is being observed: the republican world is looking at him and his country. He might not like it, but he too is caught in this collectively imagined gaze of envy.

THE KALEIDOSCOPE OF COMMON-SENSE

A number of themes have emerged so far. There are the common-sense beliefs in the uniqueness of England/Britain and its monarchy, the commercial returns of this uniqueness and the ascription of envy to the rest of the world. The themes are not neatly organised in consciousness, as if common-sense were an axiomatic theory, containing a small number of basic premises, several rules of deduction and a large number of derived propositions. Instead, common-sense is a kaleidoscope, whose brightly coloured elements are constantly changing their positions.

This kaleidoscope is to be seen in the patterns of shifting justification. It is not the case that some beliefs are always used as justifications (as *explanans*) which support axiomatically a set of beliefs to be justified (the *explanandum*). *Explanans* and *explanandum* swap places. One moment a belief acts as a justification, and the next moment it finds itself being justified by the very bit of common-sense which it has just been justifying. Around the beliefs can go in their kaleidoscopic whirl.

The tourist argument can be used to justify the belief that the world envies 'us'. One interview involved three unrelated mothers, who were close friends (interview 54). These left-of-centre women liked to consider themselves beyond the lure of royalty. The interviewer raised the notion of foreigners envying Britain. Lynn and Ann immediately drew attention to the common-sensicality of the belief, whilst sceptically distancing themselves. 'They say the

Americans do, don't they, whether it's true', said Lynn. To which Ann added: 'Perhaps we like to think that they envy us our Royal Family, whether they do or not'. She was interrupted by Sue, who offered a justification for the common-sense belief: 'They're certainly a great tourist attraction, aren't they'. Then, they started to tell stories of foreign interest: French, German and American stories were told. Envy might have been in doubt, but foreign interest was a 'reality'. These stories were being told as evidence.

The tourist theme was often used as a warrant, whose relevance was scarcely challenged. A father, a fitter in his early forties, was starting to justify his belief that foreigners envied Britain: 'I think they do, you know and I think more so America because they're...err' (interview 55). He hesitated – a suitable *explanans* did not seem to be at hand. His wife gave help: 'Well, when you go to London and you see the crowds of people from other countries, they do come to go to Buckingham Palace and Kensington Palace and what have you, I mean, they must, they do like the idea'. She went on to say that 'there's always a lot of foreign people there at the Changing of the Guards...I think they do like it, I think they do envy us, I think more Americans than anybody'.

The ascription of envy has been justified by the evidence of tourism. A thirty year old mother of two young children gave the same chain of reasoning (interview 34). As she spoke, her husband, a thirty-eight year old computing student, voiced background 'yesses'. Do other countries envy Britain? 'I think so because they're always coming to see them' began the wife. If ever there's a royal announcement 'you usually find that the people outside waiting, you know, who've come from miles, aren't the local people so much as people who come from America'.

By such means, the imagining of world envy is given 'factual' bases. The 'reality', which is 'realised', is justified by the evidence of tourists. The common-sense availability of such 'facts' permits ethnocentric prejudice to be denied. The father had denied that pride came into it (interview 41). He called on the rest of the world as his witness that Britain is the centre of the world's gaze. Another father, a forty-three year old dentist, also denied personal pride: 'It doesn't make me feel particularly proud to be told that other people envy the Royal Family' (interview 13). He continued: 'I don't feel superior to the Americans in that I have a Royal Family to head my country'. It's just that 'it is a better system'. No feelings of superiority are involved. Just facts – it *is* better.

49

This is the context in which decentred claims, disavowing pride and prejudice, can be heard. These claims are permitting the case for superiority to be expressed, even as it is denied. The mother and father, who owned the wool shop, were denying that monarchy was archaic. The mother raised the matter of world envy: 'I think we're the envy of the world...I think a lot of countries must envy us having a queen and a Royal Family' (interview 3). Britain was a bit special, she continued. At this point, her husband raised a decentred doubt: 'Oh I think so, but of course we're looking from the inside, aren't we, I mean we're not looking from the outside..., we're inside looking out'. He was not contradicting his wife, but he was arguing that those looking from the outside would come to the same conclusion as they both did. He continued, settling the doubt: 'You could go anywhere in the world and you could ask them what was the name of the Queen of England' and 'they would be able to tell you'. But they wouldn't be able to tell you who was the Queen of Spain. So it wasn't the prejudice of being inside, gazing outwards. The Queen of England really is special: the whole outside world will tell you that.

The course of justification can run in the opposite direction, with the world's interest turning from *explanans* to *explanandum*. Why should the tourists come here? It's because 'our' royalty is unique. This sort of justification could follow hard on the heels of a justification of envy in terms of tourism. Two different examples can be given, where the claim of world envy is justified in terms of interest. A forty-four year old supermarket cashier said about envy: 'Well, I think the Americans do because they've got no real history theirselves...I think they're a bit envious of it and they're envious of the history and I mean, when you go to London, it's steeped with history and all the likes of that isn't it, where America only goes back what just over two hundred years, isn't it' (interview 55). The same reasoning was offered by the wife of the mature computing student. Other countries 'haven't got anything like it themselves'; as for our Royal Family, 'it goes right back...it's got a long ancestry, but a lot of other people's royal families are...sort of like elected in...a lot of them haven't got such a long standing' (interview 34).

The reality of 'our' history, heritage and uniqueness has become the justification, rather than the fact in need of justification. 'Our' uniqueness is recognised by the rest of the world: that is why they come here. The dentist (interview 13) spoke of 'the sense of history' that the English have – 'an inherent feeling in almost every

Englishman that he's got a little bit more to him than the average foreigner'. The engineer (interview 41) said that he couldn't think of any other country with such a history. Even countries with monarchies were said not to be comparable. As for Holland, according to a thirty year old mother and part-time civil servant, 'it's just not so historical, is it' (interview 18). An eighteen year old son, following up his family's discussion of tourists coming to see the royal castles and palaces, said 'the other places haven't really got a past' (interview 14). A sixty-two year old manager asserted with finality 'we're unique and we ought to stay unique' (interview 59).

'Our' royalty is more authentic than any other, so it is claimed. 'Years ago you got some guy who set himself up as King of Spain and that's all that basically has followed on, whereas, I mean, ours can look right back to Ethelred the Unready', said a security guard (interview 39). A mother and her young married daughter were comparing 'our' royalty with foreign royalty (interview 23). They couldn't think of the name of the Spanish king and queen. The mother said with emphasis, 'I don't know much about them, I mean, our Royal Family is *the* Royal Family'. She added a decentred doubt: 'I just don't know, maybe it's because I'm English'. The doubt was there to be assuaged. Mother and daughter agreed that 'we' are envied by other countries 'very much'. 'Countries have said there's no royal families like ours', said the daughter. It's not just because 'we' are English that 'we' think 'we' are special: other countries say 'we' are. So 'we' must be special.

In talking thus, there is little hint of cynicism. The foreigners are pilgrims, paying respect to what is to be respected. The justifications can whirl around kaleidoscopically, protecting each other. Do they envy us? Yes, because they come here. Why do they come here? Because they envy us. Why do they envy us? Because we're special. Are we special? Obviously, because they come to see us. Around and around go the common-places. Queries, which can be common-sensically raised, have their own readily rational and steadily national answers.

Of the various common-place themes, none is too high to provide a humble supporting role to its fellow, should the context of discussion demand it. Premises and conclusions can exchange their enthymemic positions to do battle with the doubts which commonsense also provides (see also Edwards and Potter, in press; Potter and Edwards, 1990; Potter and Wetherell, 1987; for other examples). The resulting structure is not an inverted pyramid, with all views resting upon a single point of agreement. Instead, there is a continual kaleidoscope of common-sense.

The red-white-and-blue flakes of nationalism might rest upon the clear crystals of rationalism; turn the drum a fraction and the pieces fall into a new pattern. The crystals might now lean on the flakes. The kaleidoscope still contains the same limited number of glass pieces – the chips of foreign money, the old glass of heritage, the unique royal blue – but there are infinite possible patterns. Each discussion can reveal new argumentative turns of justification and criticism. This shifting mosaic has no law, decreeing that certain stones must always be placed at the centre.

NARCISSISM OF MINOR NATIONALISM

The respondents seem to be expressing their nationalism in a rather muted way. Coarse ethnocentrism is avoided; nevertheless there are echoes of harsher tones. Assertions of national uniqueness (without monarchy, 'we' would be like other nations) are accompanied by innuendoes of superiority. 'Our' history is longer, more authentic than that of other nations. They have Micky Mouse leaders, whilst 'our' monarchs have biological lines, stretching back in their purity to the dawn of history. Such is the value of this purity that the rest of the world is looking to 'us' to lead the world's parade.

Often, a transatlantic comparison was spontaneously made: 'we' are gazing at the Americans, who are imagined to be gazing enviously at 'us'. Three particular themes can be noted in such comments. First, there is the assertion of difference: 'we' differ from 'them', and 'our' possession of royalty maintains this difference. Second, there is the fear of incorporation: without monarchy, the difference would disappear and 'we' would become like 'them'. Third, there is the theme of superiority. The differences are not neutral, but what distinguishes 'us' from 'them' is something enviable. A housewife and former factory worker said that it 'puts us *above* America because they've got none' (interview 46). Yet there is a tension. As 'our' superiority is imagined, so simultaneously is it threatened: the Americans are imagined to want exactly that which keeps us different from them.

These themes might be said to express an ideology of national decline. Their outlines are not to be found in times of imperial confidence. Walter Bagehot may have written about the theatricality of monarchical pageantry, but the imagined audience was not the

perhaps agree that the idea is good

other nations of the world, coming to London to capture royal sights on their Fox Talbots. He conceived the audience to be the lower classes of the nation itself. It was their loyalty which he mistrusted. He did not even mention India. Just seven years after the publication of *The English Constitution*, the Prince of Wales was to be greeted in Bombay by cheering crowds and a carefully erected canopy bearing the legend 'Tell Mama We're Happy' (Roby, 1975). Bagehot certainly did not mention the value of an American audience.

World power may have been conceded to the Americans, but monarchy is a prized consolation. It is a reassuring thought. Increasingly, one eye is kept upon the royal pageant itself whilst the other looks towards the foreign audience, whose imagined gaze of jealousy is part of the occasion. Cannadine (1983) cites the reaction of the *Daily Mirror* to the Silver Jubilee of 1977: 'We can still show the world a clean pair of heels when it comes to a ceremonial' (p.160). Ziegler (1977), in his analysis of the Mass Observation data, notes the growing tendency for the public to make international comparisons. He quotes a middle-class man at the 1953 Coronation: 'I think the Americans are a bit jealous...as if they wished it was theirs'. According to Ziegler, 'the note of national self-approval, that in some ways we were scoring off other nations, was perceptibly more strident than at the last Coronation' (p.100). Nowadays the stridency is common-place.

Monarchy has become a topic in which the ambivalence of the relationship with America can be expressed. American envy is desired, as is suggested by the leaping generalisation, which takes handfuls of tourists as evidence of general American jealousy. There is ambivalence, murmurings of hostility. The Americans are richer and more powerful than 'us'. They can buy anything they want ten times over. But they cannot buy that which they are imagined to desire above all else. They cannot buy 'our' monarchy, 'our' history, 'our' nation. They cannot buy 'us'. In this argumentative turn, the tourist theme has transcended its own rationality. Money is no longer the rational justification, but tourism provides a justification beyond rationality. 'We' need the imagined admiration and 'we' need the threat of envy, for these confirm what is 'priceless' beyond the reach of dollars.

These beliefs resemble those by which a displaced aristocracy might comfort itself. Successful parvenus have money in abundance; they might even purchase their own country houses; but they only possess mere money, not the ineffable stamp of breeding. Envy is projected on to the bourgeois *arrivistes*. 'We' do not envy 'them' for their money – 'they' envy 'us'. 'We' have something more enviable than cash: 'we' have class, background and irreplaceable history. If the present, and perhaps the future, is conceded to the *arrivistes*, who only have money, then comfort is taken in the past. Splendid pageants can bring alive this history, and reassure 'us' that the *arrivistes* can never be heirs to 'our' history.

This pride in the past – a pride which is denied – is meaningful for a nation or class which has conceded the present and whose imagined future is filled with the fear of absorption. Robert Hewison (1987) links the growth of the British heritage industry to national decline. The monarchical symbols might also help to settle the nation into its declined position. The eyes of the world are still said to turn towards Britain. Not all has been lost: 'we' still lead the world in history.

There is a further function in the over-functioning of this rhetoric. If 'we' are the metaphorical aristocrats among nations, then this belief binds 'us' to the actual aristocrats within the nation. The talk about the tourists coming enviously to see the palaces is used to justify royalty's occupation of the same palaces. In justifying monarchy's wealth in terms of the world's gaze, the speakers are not only depicting nations and royalty. They are also depicting themselves, affirming their own position as subjects. The tourists, visiting palaces in a monarchical nation, are not imagined to be envying royals, but envying 'us'. The Americans are not said to want to be king and queen. They want to *have* a king and queen; they wish to *be* subjects, just like 'us'. That is the most enviable position of all.

Freud (1964a), in his 'Group psychology and the analysis of the ego', used the term the 'narcissism of minor differences' to describe the intense mutual hostility felt by neighbouring countries, which were greatly similar to each other. According to Freud, such hostility was a means of maintaining the separate identity of each group. His notion of the narcissism of minor differences would seem to be translatable to the context of decentred English/British nationalism. The Americans are the near neighbour – the powerful ally, which shares the same language and whose television programmes are nightly shown on British screens. There is fear of incorporation, and there is envy.

The nationalism, which Freud was calling the narcissism of minor differences, differs from that expressed by the respondents. The transatlantic aspersions do not resonate with hatred, but there is ambiguous respect for the respectful pilgrims. Nevertheless, the contemporary English/British nationalism is all the more self-regarding and self-serving. In the classic myth, Narcissus catches sight of his own reflected image in the fountain's pool, and he falls in love with this image. Nationalists are said to be in love with the image of their own nation, especially as they distinguish themselves from closely similar neighbours. Today, this narcissism has changed. Narcissus is still looking into the pool, but he is too knowing to be fooled by his own reflection, beauteous though it might be. Bent over the pool's edge, he sees something else. As he gazes down, Narcissus imagines the whole world looking up from the waters with envious admiration.

3
THE CONTINUING MYSTERY

Monarchy today broadcasts its heritage. Some of its traditions may have been invented in the past two hundred years, but they bear the appearance of great antiquity. This raises a problem for understanding the psychological force of royalty. The appearance of antiquity might be appealing to something genuinely old within the psyche of monarchy's subjects. Is there some pre-modern corner of the mind, perhaps a vestige of an ancient archetype, which resonates to the images of kings and queens? Or, on the other hand, is one dealing with an institution whose mass appeal is firmly rooted in the times of today? As will be argued in this chapter, the latter possibility is the more convincing: present times are producing states of mind which are drawn to the appearances of tradition. Monarchy, thus, fits today's modern, perhaps post-modern, times. This is indicated by its psychology, which carries the mark of contemporary cynicism, rather than pre-modern superstition.

SURVIVING FOSSILS

First, it is necessary to take seriously the idea that older, pre-modern sentiments have survived into the modern age and that these provide the basis of monarchy's appeal. The idea that the ordinary person's consciousness might bear the traces of previous ages can be found in the writings of Antonio Gramsci (1971), the Italian Marxist who has greatly influenced modern cultural analysis. In his *Prison Notebooks*, written between 1929 and 1935, Gramsci suggested that older, religious superstitions were being preserved within mass consciousness. The ordinary person was 'a walking anachronism, a fossil, and not living in the modern world, or at

56

least...he is strangely composite' (p.324). On this account, monarchy could be understood as an institution, which is tapping the fossilised parts of the mind of its anachronistic subjects.

Certainly, it is not difficult to draw parallels between today's reactions to monarchy and those found in pre-modern ages. In former times, monarchs, anointed in God's holy name, were believed to possess magical healing powers. A touch of the royal hand, and a ritual blessing, was believed to provide a cure for scrofula. People would travel immense distances and wait outside the palaces for hours in the hope of receiving the curative touch (Bloch, 1973). These customs did not withstand the demystifying force of the Enlightenment. As Voltaire ironically remarked of the royal power of healing, 'this sacred gift departed when people began to reason' (*Philosophical Dictionary*, p.442).

If modern common-sense is the essentially 'desacralised, post-magical common-sense', which Frederick Jameson (1988) claims it to be, then it would have little time for the magic of the royal touch. Yet, it would seem too simple to say that faith has been replaced by cynicism, mystery by rationality. Today, crowds will queue for hours to catch a glimpse of a royal figure. A queen's handshake or a prince's smile will produce dramatic effects. Philip Ziegler (1977), having studied the diaries in the Mass Observation archive, wrote that even 'the most tenuous brush with royalty...remains vivid in the mind' (p.77). Following a visit by the Princess of Wales to the National Hospital, a doctor reported without embarrassment: 'She seems to have extraordinary healing powers', adding that 'you could almost compare it with the laying on of hands' (*Today*, 28 November 1987). You could almost compare it, he says. But not quite, he implies.

It is easy to slip into the psychology of 'ancient mysteries', while considering the popularity of today's royal figures. For instance, Katherine Whitehorn, a normally hard-headed journalist, commented on 'people's apparently unhinged joy in their royalty', and proceeded to claim that 'nobody is rational at the levels where the old race memories twang, where ancient loyalties stir' (1986, p.12). Ernest Jones (1951), the illustrious British psycho-analyst and biographer of Freud, wrote a rather slight article about the psychological appeal of modern constitutional monarchy. He claimed that there was an 'element of magic belief', and 'just as princesses cannot be abolished from fairy-tales without starting a riot in the nursery, so it is impossible to abolish the idea of kingship in one form or another from the hearts of men' (pp.228–9; see also Sibony, 1990). Again, it is the fossils of superstition within the modern mind.

Shils and Young (1953) conducted their classic sociological study of Queen Elizabeth's Coronation in a similar spirit. They drew upon Durkheim's notions about the sociological functions of religious belief, in order to argue that British television audiences were affirming the sacral values of their society. Just as Durkheim in *The Elementary Forms of Religious Life* had claimed that religious rituals bound together 'primitive' societies, so Shils and Young saw Britain being united in a communal act of reverence. They were depicting a consciousness which is basically uncynical and deferentially obedient.

These evocations of past magic and deference accept the royal heritage on its own account. There is something slightly superior about observers using the language of modern psychology, whether technical or common-sensical, to talk about ancient magical stirrings. In so talking, observers are looking down at the irrationalities of others, for they assume that their own analyses are not magical superstitions. Furthermore, this talk seems to offer a very partial account of modern monarchy and contemporary consciousness. Democratic ways of reacting are omitted; or they are assumed to be psychologically superficial, swept away the moment when a queen steps forward to release the ancient forces of the soul.

For example, Ernest Jones, with his comments about princesses and magic, provided an analysis which is ill-prepared to deal with those other sides of monarchy: the subjects laughing at a princess falling from a horse; or demanding that the prince kisses his bride; or talking about the heritage as a money-making enterprise. These aspects must be taken seriously. It is necessary to listen carefully to what people have to say about monarchy and not to jump to conclusions that the fossilised elements of mystery are being perpetuated. After all, the doctor did not actually say that the Princess had the powers of healing. He almost made a comparison. And he knew he was almost making one. There was a knowingness in his remarks. This sort of knowingness is to be heard time and again.

THE VICTORIAN CYNIC

Walter Bagehot's classic work, *The English Constitution*, also evoked the image of a primitive psychology being stirred by the present monarchical parade. His book, originally published in 1867, has achieved the status of textbook in the twentieth century, being especially appreciated by practitioners of politics. A Labour cabinet minister edited the 1965 popular edition, and a former Conservative cabinet minister is the editor of a popular edition of his *Historical Essays* and of his *Collected Works*. *The English Constitution* has even become part of the royal curriculum. Nicolson (1952, pp.61f) identified the passages which the future George V was required to learn in the schoolrooms of Windsor Castle.

The English Constitution is worth considering in detail, because Bagehot's own brand of pragmatic cynicism seems highly contemporary today. Bagehot was countering the embryonic republican movement of his time. His argument for monarchy was not phrased in terms of traditional conservatism. There are no declarations of his own reverence towards God's anointed sovereigns. Instead, Bagehot argued in terms of usefulness, starting his famous chapter on monarchy with the word 'use': 'The use of the Queen, in a dignified capacity, is incalculable' (1867/1965, p.82). Once dignity has become a commodity to be used, and to be justified as useful, then inevitably that dignity is diminished.

Bagehot feared that the masses were fossils from a previous age, who would not accept that political power in Britain now rested with politicians. They would react fearfully if they discovered the truth about modern times. Therefore, concealment was necessary: monarchy 'acts as a *disguise*', because 'the masses of Englishmen are not fit for an elective government; if they knew how near they were to it, they would be surprised, and almost tremble' (p.97, emphasis in original). The sovereign was 'a visible symbol to those still so imperfectly educated as to need a symbol' (p.90).

Monarchy would usefully capitalise on the religious superstitions of its subjects: 'If you ask the immense majority of the Queen's subjects by what right she rules...they will say she rules by "God's grace"; they believe that they have a mystic obligation to obey her' (pp.89–90). Such mystic feelings of deference were to be harnessed in the cause of the state's stability: 'The English Monarchy strengthens our Government with the strength of religion' (p.86). Here, Bagehot was offering something akin to a classic Marxist account of ideology, assuming that superstitions concealed the realities of power. Unlike Marxists, Bagehot was not exposing the disguise, but was advocating its use. Religion would continue as the opium of the masses, with the royal coat-of-arms reproduced on each metaphorical jar of laudanum.

There are two accounts of the royalist mentality in *The English Constitution*. There is the royalism which Bagehot *depicts*, and there is the royalism which he *expresses*. In depicting the masses as superstitiously loyal, Bagehot was distancing himself from them. He presents himself as the rational author – the cool observer, who demystifies mystery. The masses would tremble with fright if they knew those shocking truths revealed in *The English Constitution*. When Bagehot uses the phrase, 'by God's grace', he places it in *oratio obliqua*: it belongs to the voice of the masses, not to his own. While God's grace is ironically mocked, its usefulness is recognised. Mysteries are demystified, but the cynical author argues that the mystery continues. The framework for this defence of mystification is a commitment to nationality. Bagehot associates himself with the 'English' and their national character: 'we' are unphilosophical and 'we' love the theatrical. As he cheers the royal parade, he imagines that he does so in a different manner from the masses.

Bagehot, in ascribing superstitions to the masses, was depicting a pre-modern mentality, which may itself have been a fiction. As Tom Nairn (1989) points out, the Dorsetshire peasant, who believed that the Queen made the laws, 'never existed outside Bagehot's pages' (p.75). Bagehot required this image of superstition in order to justify his own justification of monarchy. The Dorsetshire peasant may never have existed, but Bagehot's mentality, with its pragmatic cynicism, has a reality. His cynicism resembles that which Peter Sloterdijk (1988) has called 'enlightened false consciousness'. If, as Sloterdijk argues, modern consciousness is fundamentally cynical, and if, as will be heard, ordinary people today echo the tones of Bagehot's cynicism, nevertheless there is a difference between Bagehot's cynicism and that of today. The masses cannot easily depict a deceived mass, for they would be imagining their own deception. For this, a more complex cynicism – a more knowing cynicism – is required.

THE ABSENT VOICE

As a preliminary step, it is necessary to discount the possibility that echoes of 'God's grace' have persisted in the mass mind. Two generations ago, 'God's grace' might still have been just about audible. Harris (1966) in *Long to Reign Over Us?* noted that thirty percent of respondents agreed that 'the Queen is someone especially chosen by God'. This figure marked a decline from previous

surveys, and agreement was particularly concentrated among o
respondents. The surviving fossils were ageing rapidly and passi.
into history. Today, the pollsters no longer include the question
about God's choice in their surveys, for assent would be minimal.

The family discussions revealed barely a trace of religious senti-
ment when discussing monarchy. Even amongst the religiously
observant, 'God's grace' was notable by its absence. For example,
there was a family, which was deeply involved in its local church
(interview 59). The father, a quality assurance manager, had actually
helped to build the church, and, with his wife, he attended services
regularly. His justifications for monarchy contained no religious
element. The interviewer asked why 'England' still had a monarchy,
when other countries had discarded theirs. The father replied:
'Because we're unique and I feel we ought to stay unique'. Nationhood was present, but God was missing. A religious, thirty year old
childminder could countenance royal divorce, without mentioning
the vows of marriage (interview 34). She thought that the Queen
was preparing to abdicate in favour of Prince Charles ('she is stepping down very slowly'). Again, the absence was significant. It was
a matter of retirement and job-training: divine mission and anointment were missing.

The case of the forty-seven year old domestic cleaner and her
husband, a telephone engineer, provides an instructive exception
(interview 61). She was a deeply religious woman, although she no
longer attended the Evangelical church, to which she had previously belonged. This membership had created problems between
her and her unreligious husband. On her behalf, he started to tell
her story: she had been depressed after the birth of their son, and
she had started searching for something else. She interrupted
sharply to contest his account of her life: 'I wasn't depressed when
I went to church, I know for a fact I wasn't'. She continued: 'I was
reasonably attractive, I wasn't too young, I was thirty in fact;
basically it was about the most happiest time of my life'. But the
church had drawn her away from the family. The husband had
resented her involvement, and she had resented the resentment. She
no longer participated in the church, but she had retained her faith:
'I'm committed to the Bible totally', she said.

When it came to talking about royalty, this total commitment was
largely irrelevant. Like her son, a twenty-one year old plumber, she
criticised royalty for being too aloof: 'I like the idea that they're not
put on a pedestal any more'. Shortly afterwards, the son said: 'I'm

sure they still believe in the Divine Right of Kings'. This was said as criticism, and the mother agreed with the criticism. The implication was that the royals had no right to the Divine Right. This, far from being a theological matter, was down-to-earth: the royals should not consider themselves high and mighty. Divinity as such did not intrude upon the talk.

At one point, the mother cited the Bible. They had been talking about the morality of divorce (still no mention of the Deity). She had firm views: 'If there's any scandal, I think they should be out, yes, I think they should be sent into exile'. Again, no Bible. Then, the interviewer asked the mother if she was interested in royalty. This time she attempted to draw upon the Bible. But it was not easily done:

> 'It all depends what news it is, I mean, if they're here, they're here aren't they, I mean, I mean {*laughing slightly*}, I've got to say, I've, I've, um, I'm, I'm a believer in the Bible (.) you don't, do you, I mean, he's, he's, he's neither here nor there and the Bible talks, talks of, of, so I suppose a lot of some of my respect is, is because of that, because of the Bible'.
>
> (interview 61)

Her talk is marked by hesitations and repetitions. The meaning is unclear, except that the Bible is being claimed as the source of her morality. She comes close to incoherence, as she haltingly approaches the holy book: 'I've got to say, I've, I've, um, I'm, I'm a believer in the Bible' – pause. Perhaps she was embarrassed, speaking in front of a stranger, not to mention an unsympathetic husband and son. The embarrassment is not merely a matter of individual circumstance. It illustrates the lack of religious common-places, which can be used uncontroversially in conversation. There are no handy little phrases to use – no scriptural equivalent of liking 'the idea that they're not put on a pedestal any more'. Even this platitude has its moral message: it sets the conversation against a common-sense, which assumed the naturalness of Divine Right and deference. In short, the handy conversational gambits of today's common-sense reflect a secularity, which is disturbed by the spirit of religion.

There was one interview in which the tones of religious talk were central. This exception shows by contrast the general secularity of the usual common-sense to be heard in the other discussions. It was

Oh dear

a middle-aged West Indian couple, she a hospital orderly and he a waste disposal operator (interview 63). Religious posters were hung on the walls of their tidy council house: 'You Need Bodyfelt Salvation More Than Anything Else' declared the poster above the fireplace. Their commitment to the Bible was expressed in their conversation. When the wife talked about Princess Margaret's divorce, she cited the Bible: 'She broke her vow of divorcement'. If I took up the Bible now, she continued, it's all there: 'It's in there, you know, for her Majesty Queen of England'. It's based 'upon the law of righteousness and...it should be, because the head, the head, the throne should be all law, come out, they should stand clean'. Later, when she was talking about Mrs Thatcher, the husband interrupted to quote a passage in Isaiah, which supposedly had predicted dire things, should a woman ever become prime minister: 'Everything which has been written into the Bible is coming to pass, it's war upon war, rumours of war, earth crack in diverse places, famine, pestilence, it's coming to pass, nation against nation, it's coming to pass'. His wife denied that woman was to blame: 'When you're not talking about woman, *leave us alone*'. She laughed.

This couple's way of talking differed from that of all the other interviews. There is the matter of Jamaican dialect and syntax, but there was more than that. Their thinking was suffused with the language of the Bible: 'pestilence' and 'righteousness' are words which sat without embarrassment in their home. Their arguments were justified by scriptural references, with the Bible cited as the arbiter of disputes. Even the religious families of other interviews did not talk remotely like this. Their religious talking was confined to the Sunday morning ceremonies. Perhaps the West Indian couple were using a religious common-sense, which has been disappearing from England during the past century, but which has survived elsewhere. Was it a coincidence that this way of talking was confined to the sample's only Jamaicans, and middle-aged respondents at that? Or, perhaps, the source of their religious tones should be sought in the particular evangelical sect to which they belonged. Whatever the reasons, the bodyfelt salvationists' common-sense was not the common-sense to be commonly heard in the sitting-rooms of late twentieth century England. For this couple, Her Majesty really did rule by 'God's grace'. As for the rest, their thinking had descended from the heavens to earth.

THE OBLIQUE VOICE OF RELIGION

Talk about God and royalty was not completely absent, but it appeared as a fossil, clearly labelled as a specimen within a collector's cabinet. The young plumber had mentioned the belief in the Divine Right of Kings (interview 61). The belief is mentionable, but it is placed within *oratio obliqua*. The son indicated that it was neither his belief, nor one which he considered to be reasonable. He presents the belief in *oratio obliqua*, just as Bagehot presented 'God's grace'. Whereas Bagehot had attributed 'God's grace' to the lowest in the land, the plumber attributes it to the highest.

Two further examples can be given. In the first, a keenly royalist mother and married daughter were talking (interview 23). The second incident comes from the discussion of three mothers, who were more detached when it came to royal matters (interview 54). Both sets of speakers showed similar patterns of speaking about the divine aspect, and both resembled the notable Victorian journalist before them.

The mother and her married daughter worked as secretaries in the same office. Their discussion was recorded there during a lunch-break: the father, a chauffeur, was not present. They talked animatedly about the various members of the Royal Family. They were sympathising with Prince Charles: 'He seems to have had a lonely life', said the daughter. The mother agreed, using a word which expressed a common-sense sociology: 'Charles' seems to have no 'role in life'. 'He's just waiting, isn't he', said her daughter. Then, they discussed abdication, which they both firmly opposed. The daughter, finishing a sentence begun by her mother, said that 'Charles' shouldn't 'take it till she's gone'.

At this point, the mother interrupted, introducing the Deity into the conversation: 'No, no, you are anointed as Queen in God's name or whatever in this Abbey by the Archbishop of whatever, and that's what you are till you die, and nobody else should be one until you die; it should be the traditional role, I think'. The daughter agreed. Here seemed to be the religious voice, which Bagehot would have expected from members of the toiling classes: ancient ceremony and the name of God were being invoked.

Nevertheless, the conversation has not suddenly retrogressed into antiquity. As the mother talks of sacred themes, she distances herself from them. The Queen is not merely anointed in God's name, but in 'God's name or whatever': vagueness is suggested. This is not a chance mumble, for it is repeated: the 'Archbishop of whatever' does the anointing. The Abbey in which the ceremony takes place is unspecified: 'in this Abbey'. This mother regularly reads books about royalty. Throughout the discussion, she displayed her considerable knowledge, talking authoritatively about the marriage of Edward VII and Queen Alexandra. She recalled hearing the Coronation ceremony on the radio when she was thirteen. She travels annually to London for the Trooping of the Colour. It is difficult to imagine that she has forgotten, even momentarily, that the Coronation took place in Westminster Abbey and that it is conducted by the Archbishop of Canterbury.

Her daughter, generally so quick to express agreement by finishing her mother's sentences, did not respond as if information was being sought. She volunteered no facts to clarify her mother's imprecisions. The vagueness had another message and seems to have been recognised as such by the daughter. It enabled the mother to speak of a religious ceremony, and even of 'God's name', whilst distancing herself: it happened somewhere, conducted by someone and involved something or other (see Chapter 8 for another example of similar dissociation by this mother).

The mother signals distance by putting God's name into *oratio obliqua*, while she herself claims other words, sociological words: 'It should be the traditional role, I think'. This is a more comfortable language, with no sign of distancing. There is a mark of personal possession: 'I think'. The sociological thought is her thought, as she presents herself as an analyst of monarchy, using the demystifying tones of a Durkheim. God is construed as possessing a useful sociological function. She is examining the *conscience collective* of the anthropological exotica at Windsor or somewhere.

Another example of religious distancing occurred when three friends, all working mothers in their late thirties, were talking (interview 54). The topic of abdication had been raised, and the three were showing sympathy for Prince Charles: 'I feel sorry for Old Charlie, I think it's absolutely awful', said Lynn. 'Old Charlie' – here was no deferential obsequy. She laughed at the possible difficulty of the Queen Mother becoming the 'King Grandma'. Then, Sue raised a serious point about the Queen, hesitating as she did so. Her comment, and the reactions which it provoked, can be quoted in full:

At last

(Interview 54)

Sue: But surely, in in her own view she is there as the rightful heir to the throne, and, um, (.), doesn't she actually believe, er, I don't know about the Divine Right of Kings

Lynn: [um that's right

Sue: [but actually that it=

Lynn: = There is a God, yeah, God-given=

Sue: = Yes in her, in her role of Head of the Church that it's God's will that she's there

Lynn: Um

Sue: And therefore, if she believes that, she *can't* actually abdicate

Lynn: Um yes true=

Ann: = I think you'd find she probably does think like that

Sue: Yes I think she *does* and also I think she considers that she is one of the main figureheads of the country (.) and therefore to promote that *with* every other country she has to take herself very seriously and I don't think abdication goes along with that.

The passage is packed with distancing disclaimers; the speakers, like the young plumber, put the Divine Right of Kings safely behind the perimeter fence of reported speech. Sue signals reportage clearly: it is the Queen's 'view', which she is talking about. Even so, she hesitates, as if something difficult is about to be said. She distances herself from the Divine Right of Kings ('I don't know'). The others agree with her belief about the Queen's belief. Ann says: 'I think you'd find she probably does think like that'. Yet again, Sue emphasises the point: 'Yes, I think she *does*'. 'I think' they say, as they link themselves to the belief about the Queen's divine belief. The sacral voice is not theirs.

The speakers indicate that they are discussing a remarkable belief, which is outside the normal range of beliefs: yes, she *actually* does believe in it. People often treat the holding of unusual beliefs as something which needs to be explained (Gilbert and Mulkay, 1984; Potter and Wetherell, 1987). The belief in the divine rights of monarchs might appear so far removed from desacralised common-sense that an explanation is called for. The speakers do not offer psychological explanations: the Queen's always been a bit eccentric, so it's no wonder that she believes in Divine Right....Such psychology was unnecessary. In both instances, the speakers specifically talked sociologically, using the word 'role'. Sue says that it is part of the Queen's 'role' as Head of the Church to believe in God's will. The mystery of the mysterious belief is solved: it's a role requirement.

In this way, God's will serves the material sociology of the nation. If Bagehot projected irrational beliefs downwards on to the masses, the speakers project upwards to archbishops and queens. Like Bagehot, the speakers are giving justifications for monarchy. They are arguing that the Queen cannot lightly discard her responsibilities. A common-sensical sociology, with its demystifying language, protects the traditional mystery. The end result is not a clear victory for demystification over mystification, but irrationality is preserved by being rationalised.

THE ROYAL JOB

The concept of 'role', as a common-sense idea, bears a moment's thought. Sociological consciousness, of the sort pioneered by Durkheim, sought to demystify ancient taboos, by showing their pragmatic usefulness to the society of the believers. Common-sense versions of sociological thinking seem to demystify ordinary life. To say that someone is performing a role is to explain that person's behaviour, making it appear less mysterious and more pragmatic. The Queen is fulfilling her role by believing in that role. Accordingly, the notion of 'role' renders the mysterious belief in Divine Right less mysterious.

On the other hand, the notion of 'role' introduces the possibility of other mysteries, modern mysteries. The concept hints at a split between the public and the private individual. The role-player is the public person. The modern world is full of role-players – police, airline pilots, professional beauticians – who hang up their uniforms, returning home as private selves. The contrast between the private self and the public role-player invites mystery: there might always be the doubt that the role is *just* a piece of public display, at variance with the *real* person beneath the role.

What if the Queen didn't actually believe in the public role? I think she *actually* does believe in it, said Ann (interview 54). They were talking about a mysterious job: 'It's not just a job really, I suppose', said Lynn. 'No, it's her *life*,' Sue emphasised. 'Yeah that's right', agreed Lynn. Sue joked about 'Diana' getting maternity leave 'with full pay and a six-week option afterward to come back to work'. Ann added seriously: 'Yeah, it's not a job like that, though, is it; I mean it's not in that way a job'. But in some way it was.

As will be seen more clearly in the next chapter, it is common-sensical to talk of the royal position as a 'job'. The language of 'jobs' is demystificatory, for it strips away mystique, making monarchy appear ordinary. So common is this language that royalty is reported to use its vocabulary. Edward VII, it is said, frequently called king-ship his '*métier*'; on hearing about the assassination of the Serbian King, he declared that he could not be indifferent to the murder of 'a member of my profession' (Andrews, 1975, p.182). In 1929, Queen Mary deputised for her sick husband at Court; it was a duty, she claimed, which had to be done 'for the sake of "the trade"' (Lacey, 1977, p.56). The *Daily Mirror* claimed that 'they call themselves The Firm' and that 'the Queen is chairman and around her is the most famous Board of Directors in the world'. It is, the paper continued, 'Britain's oldest family business' (14 December 1987).

This modernly pragmatic way of talking about royalty can con-flict with the demand that monarchy represents something other than modern pragmatism. The job for which they are paid is to be mysterious. The language of 'jobs' demystifies a role which is justi-fied in terms of its mystery. The ambivalences were caught by a forty-four year old cleaner (interview 50). She and her daughters, both shop workers, were discussing the economics of monarchy, justifying costs in terms of benefits. The mother said: 'Princess Di...has done the British fashion industry a lot of good'. True, her clothes 'might cost a lot of money'; but, when you think what 'some of these places spend on advertising', you realise the boost she gives if she is photographed in a Zandra Rhodes dress and the picture 'goes all over the world'. She went on: 'The British fashion industry could never pay the money for that kind of advertising'. Here was economic cynicism: royal mystique was a commodity for marketing British industry.

Her daughters then asked about the other royals and whether they were worth the money. The mother countered by a question: 'Don't you think they'd lose some of their charisma if...you'd got someone like Princess Michael working in Woolies?'. If they weren't paid, they would do inappropriate jobs, like advertising. They would start 'endorsing products, you know, and advertising and saying "We use Fairy Soap" and "I'm Princess Beatrice of the what-have-you, but I get no money from the state, so I'm selling this soap"'. And if that happened, she said, 'the Royal Family is going to start losing credibility and charisma'.

Mystery and economics are mixed. Because royals have 'charisma', they are the national advertiser, promoting British products around the world. Their commodity of 'charisma' pays its way, and that is why 'we' gain from paying royalty. If 'we' stop paying the royals, they will be forced to become advertisers. Then, they will lose their charisma and be unable to fulfil the advertising job they do so well at present. 'Charisma' and 'credibility' are their trade, but turn them into a trade, and their successful business will be ruined.

A forty-one year old mother, a former teacher, also alluded to this link between mystification and payment (interview 30). She complained that too many members of the Royal Family were paid: 'Princess Diana, yes, but after that I think that there should be sort of demystification for the rest of the family...not being given a special allowance'. To demystify was to remove from the payroll. Mystification was a matter of receiving a monetary allowance to be professionally mysterious. The very thought was demystifying the mystery, whose financing it was justifying. Mystification and demystification seem to chase each other around.

The concept of a 'royal role' invites demystification for it implies that an ordinary human being stands behind the extraordinary role. Strip off the royal robes and the naked truth will be revealed: a royal body, as blotchy and pimply as anybody else's. Such claims, and the cynicism which they express, permit the pretensions of superiority to be mocked from below. Sloterdijk (1988) refers to such mockery of social superiors as the 'kynical impulse', using the Greek spelling in tribute to that great deflator of pretensions, Diogenes of Sinope.

Over and again, respondents uttered the common-place that royals were ordinary human beings. The common-place can be used to justify royal lapses, to claim similarity with royals and to bring royalty down to earth, should they start believing in their special destiny too ardently. A supermarket cashier commented that 'basically they're just ordinary people like everybody else' (interview 55). Her husband agreed: 'They come into the world same as anybody else, they go out of the world same as anybody else'. 'They're only human', said a security guard, using a phrase often repeated (interview 39). 'They're not superhuman, are they', declared a forty-seven year old housewife, 'they're only born the same way as us' (interview 56). 'They're ordinary people, but their lifestyle is completely different, isn't it, it's bound to be', said the fifty-five year old childminder (interview 48). According to one mother, a former factory worker, 'inside' they're just 'ordinary people'. Her daughter agreed: 'They know they're Royal Family, and they should act as they are, but they're normal really, aren't they' (interview 46).

There was no-one to put the opposing case, that 'really' they are born special, magical personages, completely unlike 'you' and 'me'. Instead, the split between the inner and the outer was accepted as common-sensical. The opposing view could be mocked as immature. The secretary, who was talking with her adult daughter, laughingly recalled that as a child she thought that royals did not 'have natural functions, not like we did' (interview 23). A fireman remembered when he was a child, seeing the Queen wipe her nose and thinking 'that can't be right, the Queen doesn't blow her nose' (interview 22). Adults know that royal noses need to be blown and bladders emptied.

Even so, bodily functions exert a continuing interest. The secretary and fireman were expressing a common joke of commoners, which strips the dignified of their dignity. Ziegler (1977), writing about crowds at royal occasions, records that 'speculation about the size of the royal bladder is one of the more common subjects of debate among the less reverent at every similar function' (p.95n). It is not only the irreverent, whose thoughts turn to the passing of royal water. A journalist, discussing royal visits, commented that 'everyone knows that it is the lavs that get done up, first and sumptuously, when the monarch intends a visit' (Gillian Reynolds, *Listener*, 3 February 1989). Carefully arranging the lavatory, polishing the seat and obtaining the softest of soft paper would seem to be acts of pure devotion. But these acts reduce regal dignity to the basest level. They suggest a kynical image: the royal seated defencelessly, ludicrously upon the toilet. Of course, 'their' bodies function like anybody else's. Or do they? That is the mystery; or, rather, it is the continuing joke.

MYSTERIES OF ROLE

Royalty seems to blur the distinction between the inner and the outer self. As the three mothers talked about the Queen's belief in her divine role, they depicted the royal job as more than a job (interview 54). It was not a role out of which the monarch could easily step: she actually does believe it; she actually *is* the Queen. The Queen, enacting her role, is imagined to be doing more than enacting a role. There is a further blurring: in the royal role, private and public realms become confused. As the *Daily Mirror* said, the royal business is a family business (14 December 1987). In fact, as will be discussed in the next chapter, their business is to lead a private life publicly. *[handwritten: Well]*

Robert Merton (1976) claims that most social roles are marked by 'sociological ambivalence': to fulfil the role adequately one must do more than fulfil the role. For example, to be a good doctor, one must be more than a doctor – one must appear to be a friend to the patient. This is part of the role. Thus, roles contain their own negations. This is particularly true for the 'royal role', which mixes the public and the private. To be a good royal, one must do more than act royally: one must be known as an individual personality. This means being distinguishable from the royal role. The paradox is that being such an individual is itself part of the role.

A husband and wife were discussing royal personalities (interview 10). The wife, an ex-barmaid, did not care much for the Duchess of York: 'I don't think she's a genuine royal, not really'. She was always acting inappropriately – 'I think what a silly girl'. Princess Anne was different, they agreed. The husband said of her that she 'now comes across as a very genuine royal, you know, something to be...proud of'. His wife praised the Princess for being 'sort of more down-to-earth'. A 'genuine' royal should be 'down-to-earth', a bit non-royal. That was part of doing the royal job genuinely well. By contrast, to be 'too royal' can be a criticism. The American journalist, Clancy Sigal, tells a story about a drunken actress trying to curtsey in front of a member of the Royal Family. The curtsey was poorly executed, and the unnamed royal delivered a chilling stare of disapproval. 'That may be "Royal" behaviour but it isn't very royal', commented Sigal (1986, p.150).

On the other hand, common-sense can argue that to be too ordinary is to be unroyal. 'What a silly girl', said the wife criticising the Duchess of York for her lack of dignity (interview 10). One person can criticise the monarch for believing in the Divine Right; another person can cite the belief as an indication that the role is being taken seriously. Common-sense provides the 'on-the-one-hand' and the 'on-the-other-hand'. Too royal – not royal enough; too public – too private; royal, but ordinary after all – ordinary, but royal after all: there is plenty to think and argue about. The debates

71

[handwritten: Use]

cannot be resolved if being 'genuinely' royal means not being too regal. The mysteries continue, courtesy of a cynical common-sense, which depicts the mystery as a role, and then mysteriously ensures that the role contains its own negation.

DEMYSTIFICATION AS MYSTIFICATION

According to Bagehot, the masses need to be protected from the truth about monarchy. Demystification would be a threat to their naïve faith. However, Bagehot did not notice that his own analysis was suggesting that the masses' naïvety might not be quite so naïve. In writing of the family upon the throne as 'an interesting idea', Bagehot commented, in a phrase which has become famous, that this interesting idea 'brings the pride of sovereignty to the level of petty life' (p.85). If the figures of majesty are reduced to the pettiness – or ordinariness – of being husbands and wives, then the great mysteries and the touch of divinity are that much harder to sustain. Even the masses would see that Her Majesty was a 'semi-retired widow'.

In talking of 'petty life', Bagehot was recognising that the family upon the throne offers a metaphorical invitation to its subjects to look behind the scenes. The majesty, which the theatrical displays were designed to uphold, and which Bagehot was so keen to protect, is not undermined by the demystification. There are several immediate reasons for this. First, the ordinariness of royals, rather than their extraordinariness, is a popular object of desire. Second, this desire is framed by assumptions of the extraordinariness of this ordinariness. There is a third theme, which is harder to identify, but which will emerge later. The majesty is accepted as display – it is an image. It is all the more real, rather than less real, for being such.

The desire for royalty's ordinariness is revealed in the way that people talk about contact with royalty – either the contacts which have taken place, or the contacts which are desired. Twice, the mother and daughter (interview 23) discussed when they had seen royal figures. They had been able to glimpse behind the public display. Ordinariness was unveiled but the magic of the occasion had been heightened.

The first occasion begins with a 'deviant case'. It is one of the few occasions when a royal person was described as a figure of extra-ordinary mystique. The daughter was complaining that the royals were too formal. The mother mentioned her friend, Pat, who 'follows the hunt and she often sees Charles'. The mother said that the Prince remembers Pat's name and talks to her 'just ordinary like'. She continued: 'He's better looking in real life than he looks on TV and the photographs'. There was something special about him: 'She said the old thing, whether it's true or not, that there is a difference; she feels there's a sort of aura about him'. The aura was special – 'not just a presence like you get with some people who have poise'. If it sounds incredible, well, Pat wouldn't exaggerate: 'I mean she's dead down-to-earth, Auntie Pat, I mean she'll call a spade a spade'.

The mother puts Auntie Pat's speech in *oratio obliqua*, just as she had placed 'God's name'. She gives a little disclaimer – 'whether it's true or not'. She indicates that the claim of aura might be 'the old thing' – a claim from a previous age and incredible to modern ears. Its incredibility calls for a testimonial: Auntie Pat is down-to-earth, not given to mystical flights of fancy. The aura is distinguished from other qualities: it is unlike 'poise', which exceptional commoners might have. Nor is the aura to be confused with extraordinary powers of conversation: the Prince talked to Auntie Pat about ordinary things. The aura is connected to the Prince as a royal figure. Significantly, there is little more to be said about it. The elaborate pre-modern discourse about magic touches and divine calling has not been preserved. The modern words run dry, except to say that it is 'the old thing'.

The common-sensical weakness of this mystical theme can be seen in what happened next. The daughter did not greet the story with scepticism. Far from it, she started to add to the mystical theme. 'It's true though isn't it?', she said, 'I mean when we went to Trooping of the Colour, it was as though they weren't real, they were china dolls they weren't real were they...they looked wax, waxworks'. The mother was quick to snuff out this nonsense: 'They probably were, I mean probably the make-up is like that'.

The mother's comment showed the vulnerability of a claim about aura. There is little to be said about it. Moreover, the claim cannot withstand the merest hint of a materialist explanation. The daughter withdraws her claim as soon as the waxiness of make-up is mentioned. The incident illustrates something further. The mother's demystification of this claim has not achieved a solid, down-to-earth material world, from which illusions are dispelled. The demystified world is itself a world of illusions, in which actors wear make-up, as if on the stage. Parts are being played, and 'we', the onlookers, observe. 'They weren't real', says the daughter. Yes, they were,

73

replies the mother. They were real people, with real make-up, like real actors. There is no register of disappointment, as if the adult had spoilt a childhood fairy story.

A second moment of demystification occurred during their trip to the Trooping of the Colour. The mother mentioned that they had 'got the biggest shock' when they saw the Queen Mother at close quarters. She seemed bald, with her hair pulled across her head and held in place with hair-grips, as if to cover 'a baldish patch'. The revelation might have been shocking, but it did not spoil the day out or diminish their affection for the Queen Mother. Another wife had also been to the Trooping of the Colour. She had noticed that the Queen Mother's face was covered with make-up, 'like a theatre mask'. Again, there was no hint of anger at attempted deception. Instead, there was sympathy for the old lady: 'Fancy having to wear that every day' (interview 36).

It is not easy to ascribe a mystical aura to an old woman who tries to cover her baldness with an elaborate arrangement of hair-grips. Pathos predominates over mythos. The spectators standing close to the participants at the Trooping of the Colour are like stage fans, who have been allowed a glimpse backstage: perhaps they have seen the star preparing for the performance in the dressing-room. The privileged glimpse heightens the excitement. There is the magic of hidden knowledge. Mother and daughter take home stories to tell of the special day and, in retelling the tales, they can recapture its uniqueness. They talk of receiving the biggest shock, but no beliefs have been shocked into disbelief. They can treasure that shocking moment when they saw the magic of something behind the magic.

JOKES AND TOFFEE NOSES

One reason why the moments of demystification do not destroy the illusion is that the ordinary side of monarchy is not wished away. The royal figures are said to be ordinary 'after all', and, if they fail to realise this in their demeanour, they will be criticised for being too remote. The contact with the Queen Mother had revealed just what the stratagem of hair arrangement was intended to hide: here is a frail old woman, whose body is in decline. And this was truly memorable.

It is the frail old woman, not her public uniform, which can be the object of popular desire. If people fantasise about contact with royalty, their fantasies wish away the ceremonial backdrop; they imagine one ordinary person meeting another ordinary person, who just happens to be royal. A few years ago, the author Brian Masters collected accounts of people's dreams about royalty. Frequently, the dreams involved meetings with royal figures, particularly with the Queen. Seldom was the setting a ceremonial one, but the dream-queen was dropping by for an informal cup of tea: 'If there is one activity which dominates the royal dreams of England, it is drinking tea' (Masters, 1973, p.17; see also Nairn, 1988, pp.84f).

Hardly any of the wide-awake family members wished to partici-pate in the great ceremonial occasions. The televised view of a royal wedding was sufficient for them. The preference was for the in-formal, chance meeting. Even so, there could be reluctance. A mother, son and daughter-in-law were talking about meeting royal figures (interview 60). They mentioned Prince Charles. 'Say if he came here and sat here, I mean...I wouldn't know what to talk to him', said the son, a school care-taker in his forties. Royalty was far too posh, his wife agreed, 'half the time they couldn't understand a word I said'. None of them would like to meet 'Fergie'. The mother, a retired cleaner, explained: 'She'd be a right lah-di-dah, she'd make you feel like a little kid'. But 'Di' would be different: 'She'd talk to us the same as we talk to her; yeah she knows how we feel'.

Another working-class family was discussing the possibility of the Queen visiting their council house (interview 56). 'If they came here', said the mother, 'I'd say "Do you want a cup of coffee? Do you want a cup of tea?" and, if she said "No", I'd say "Well, there's the door then, me duck, tarra, you're off"'. The daughter agreed with her mother: 'I wouldn't treat them different to anybody else'. 'No good treating them different' replied the mother, 'I mean they've got two arms, two legs, exactly the same'. If 'they' are going to act 'lah-di-dah', then the commoner would riposte by being determinedly common. The kynics would take their revenge.

Not that they expected all members of royalty to be so 'lah-di-dah'. The mother had seen Prince Charles on the television. 'He talks ordinary', she said. You could talk to him: 'Say an ordinary working-class like me, you could talk to him without putting on all your airs and graces; I don't know so much about the rest, I've never really took that much interest, but to me Charles looks the down-to-earth one out of the whole lot'. Not like Princess Anne: 'She looks a bit toffee-nosed'.

A working-class diffidence, related to speech, is apparent in such comments, as well as a refusal to be deferential. 'They', the upper-class, speak differently from 'us', making 'us' feel awkward. But we're not going to be condescended. No fear – tarra, on your way, me duck. It would be wrong to assume that this mixture of irreverence and imagined equality was exclusively working-class. The middle-class cannot claim equality with royalty. They too could speak diffidently about meeting the aristocracy, worrying lest their common speech failed to provide a common language with royalty. And they too could mock their superiors

There was the middle-class family whose arguments with the critical older son were described in the previous chapter (interview 41). They owned a converted eighteenth century cottage in a prosperous village. They were discussing the idea of meeting royalty. Neither of the two grown-up sons relished the prospect. 'I wouldn't know what to say', said the older; 'You've got absolutely nothing in common with them', said the younger, who was the royalist. The father turned to his wife and asked whether she would like to meet royalty. 'If it's a casual meeting, you just say "Hi how are you?"', she replied. But, she would not bother if it was 'a formal thing'. Language was still the problem, even for the middle-class: 'You have to talk and call them by the name "ma'am" and all that sort of thing'. She added, 'I wouldn't know what to say'.

A chance meeting would be best, she continued. She started dreaming aloud: 'You're walking along the road and you're suddenly face-to-face with Prince Charles, and he looked at you and you looked at him; the first thing you'd say is "Hi"...I'd say, "Don't you look like Charles" or something stupid like that'. '"Haven't you got a head like an FA Cup"', suggested the younger son. They all laughed loudly.

'Oh that's lovely', said his mother. She joined in the joke, toning down her son's imagined remark to the Prince of Wales: '"Do you know you're losing a few hairs on the top of your head, but you're still lovely"'. Still lovely, because one can imagine talking to him face-to-face, making rude personal remarks to the heir to the throne – there's no toffee nose in that imagined scene. Nor any humbled reverence.

Jokes about royalty are easily made. You've got a head like a football trophy; tarra out the door you go. They might not be talking about royal lavatories, but a similar irreverence is expressed. The joke reverses the order, depicting the commoner rudely in charge of the conversation, leaving the royal not knowing what to say.

Other joking reversals are possible. A conservative-minded father had worked up his tenuous brush with royalty into an oft-told joke (interview 1). When on holiday at the sea-side, he had happened to walk past the Queen Mother. In his account, she greets him by name: '"Hello, Jim" she says as she goes past'. The joke had become a family story: all the family join in to tell the joke.

Jokes might indicate wishes, as Freud asserted, but there is something more. By making the jokes, and by declaring to want only the informal contact, the speakers are making a claim about themselves. Despite the admissions of diffidence, they are claiming not to be overawed by royalty: I will show him the door, if he's snooty; I will tell him he's losing his hair. The claim is not only about an imagined event, which will never occur. It is also a claim about the present: I am joking about them; I am treating them with irreverence. It is the loyalist son, not the critic, who makes the remark about the FA Cup; the mother, even more keenly royalist, joins in. These are jokes for royalists told by royalists, affirming their lack of subservience. They are not the sort of people to bow-and-scrape in front of a man with an odd-shaped head.

JUST LIKE A NORMAL PERSON

Dreams do occasionally come true. As was mentioned in Chapter 1, the television news can headline a story about Prince Charles un-expectedly visiting a pub. The collectively shared wish to have a chance meeting with royalty makes the event note-worthy. A lucky customer has won the lottery. The dream is not to sample the magic aura, but to meet the special person ordinarily face-to-face. When the dream comes true, the kynical self seems to disappear. The father might have worked his most tenuous of tenuous contacts into a humorous joke, which is not told to be believed (interview 1). Others, with stories to be believed, talked differently. They did not talk of sovereigns being shown the door, or of princes mocked for their baldness. Zizek (1989) claims that people today have a cynical knowledge of things as they 'really' are, but they still behave 'as if they did not know' (p.31). This gap between thoughts and be-haviour seems to be recognisable in the phenomenon of royalty. Despite the cynical consciousness, the crowds will queue for hours. Face-to-face, and in the endless retelling afterwards, royalty can work a magic. Yet the retelling shows that the split between deeds and words is not so great: the magic is present in the words, which tell of the magical events.

The mother, who worked in the same secretarial office as her daughter, had a tale to tell about contact with Princess Margaret (interview 23). It involved three generations of her family: her own mother, herself and her daughter. Her daughter had been a baby when Princess Margaret had visited the row of terraced cottages in which they were living. The mother was standing there holding her baby, next to another mother who also had a young child. The Princess did not walk right past them. She stopped and, in so doing, provided a special moment in the family history – a story to be passed down to that baby, now herself fully grown and married. As the mother told the story, the use of 'you' indicated that she was retelling to the daughter as much as to the interviewer:

> 'Margaret turned right round and she waved and she said "What a beautiful baby", you know, just like a normal person would...Then, mum took you, didn't she, mum came round and she took you right into the front of our house, and, of course, the police tried to move us away, because she was going to walk along there; and we said "No, we live here, we're not moving off our steps." And she came right past and took hold of you'.

> (interview 23)

The tale is special because Princess Margaret noticed, praised and took hold of the baby. The daughter had actually been held, if only for a moment, in regal arms. As the mother said, the princess was behaving 'just like a normal person would'.

The phrase is significant. As Nairn (1988) points out, to say that royals are ordinary 'after all' is to say that 'really' they are special. Only because the mother accepts the Princess as extraordinary is the normality worthy of comment. No normal person would be described as holding a baby just like a normal person. The mother's tale has an additional theme: the police were attempting to move the family from its home. There is an indistinct echo from history. The monarch's bodyguards, armed with truncheons and whistles, rather than pikes and quarter-staves, are clearing a path for royalty: out of the way – out of your homes – Her Royal Majesty is passing – bow down with reverential awe. Nevertheless, the ordinary English-women stand firm by their houses, which, by common-sense right, are their castles. They are rewarded for their bravery. The royal personage does not sweep past regally. Nor does she demand deference. She stops and talks like a normal person. Extraordinary though it might seem, she turns out to have a wonderful aura of ordinariness. She confirms the rights of ordinary people to wait by their houses. She is on their side. Commoner and royalty are bound together in a shared moment, which is the stuff of dreams. The police must wait as onlookers. Normal time is stopped for an instant which will ever be remembered. And then the Princess walks on. The police resume their business.

REALLY EXCEPTIONAL QUALITIES

Common-sense does not provide an absolute matrix of thoughts, but its kaleidoscopic components can be arranged into different argumentative patterns. Claims about the ordinary person behind the royal role do not represent the only possible pattern of thinking. The elements of thought can be re-adjusted: demystification can reveal an extraordinary person, equipped with extraordinary talents. The hospital consultant, quoted at the start of the chapter, pronounced Princess Diana to have exceptional qualities of healing. Such a reversal does not upset the ideological assumptions. Nor does it necessarily entail a regression back to talk of older aura and sacral mystique. An example of a reversal – from the regally ordinary to the regally extraordinary – will be given. The ideological end-product of the reversal differs little from the original.

The example shows the power of the conversational touch with royalty, even with individuals, who claim to be immune from its glamorous allure. Life for the father and mother, who owned their small wool shop, was not easy (interview 3). They lived in a flat above the premises with their seventeen year old son and their severely handicapped daughter of twenty-one. The mother complained that, although she bore an equal share of the shop work, she had to do all the housework. For his part, the father felt constrained. He had given up an engineering career, so that he could remain on hand to help look after the daughter, who was now too heavy to be lifted by her mother alone. He did not find it easy adjusting to daily life in the wool shop beneath the home, rather than travelling to the male world of engineering.

Royal occasions had not provided moments for the couple to share together. The mother had watched all the weddings, but the father had not. He took pride in being 'the only person I know that didn't watch the Silver Jubilee celebrations on the television...it just didn't interest me enough to watch it'. What he was doing during those celebrations will be discussed in Chapter 7. His indifference to royal occasions contrasted with the way he talked about the brief moment, when he personally came into contact with a royal.

The family was discussing which members of the royalty should receive payment from the Civil List. The father strongly believed that only members of the immediate Royal Family should be paid. He criticised minor royals such as Mark Phillips. Then he casually mentioned that he admired the Duchess of Kent. The comment was not immediately picked up. Shortly afterwards, his wife cued him: 'You've met the Duchess of Kent, haven't you?'. 'Yes, I've met the Duchess of Kent, actually spoken to her for several minutes.'

Now he could tell his story. Whilst he had been working as an engineer, the Duchess of Kent had come to present the Queen's Award For Industry to his company. The employees were all lined up to meet her. The Duchess was walking past the line. Then, the miraculous moment occurred: 'I wasn't sort of meant to be introduced to her, but, as she walked along the line, she stopped at me out of about fifty or so, and stood talking to me for about five minutes'. He went on: 'From her voice and the way she spoke and the way that she conducts herself' he got the impression that the Duchess was 'someone of really exceptional qualities'. It wasn't fanciful: 'I can talk, I do actually know, you know'.

After the Duchess had walked on, he had been told by her Lady in Waiting that the royal party worked to a tight schedule. But, if the Duchess wanted to stop and talk to anybody, 'she completely ignored all time schedules, she did as she wanted to do'. A press photographer had recorded the historic scene: the father had a copy of the photo upstairs, if the interviewer wanted to see it. The wife started to move the conversation on to another topic. He interrupted, unwilling to let go of the moment and its retelling. He turned to the interviewer: 'I bet you haven't met many that's actually spoken to one for five minutes, have you?'.

Actually speaking to the Duchess of Kent mattered to this man who knew no-one less interested in royal occasions than himself. He had been selected by the Duchess, in preference to forty-nine others. In his imagination, the few brief words represented 'five minutes'. His uncynical behaviour is not left at odds with his cynical thoughts, but the gap is to be closed. There are further justifications and further claims of reality. The exceptional qualities, which he attributes to the Duchess, are not those of the aura, which 'Auntie Pat' was said to find in the Prince of Wales. He is talking of that very charm and poise – the conversation and the voice – which 'Auntie Pat' distinguished from aura.

The conversation was not extraordinary because the Duchess of Kent was royal, or so he was claiming. It was extraordinary because of extraordinary personal qualities, which the Duchess happened to possess. Poise and charm are qualities which talented non-royals might possess. In the father's depiction, the Duchess has earned the right to be called extraordinary. He mentioned that 'of course she does an awful lot of compassionate work'. So demystified has the Duchess been, that she is presented as a meritocratic achiever. She has been rendered ordinary – bourgeoisified perhaps – only then to be demonstrated as extraordinary.

The father might avoid most television programmes about royals, but he would watch something about the Duchess: 'I *would* sit and watch a television programme...about her'. His wife agreed: 'I think she's fantastic, isn't she'. 'Yes', he replied, 'I have a great admiration for her'. They recalled, both of them, watching a programme about the Duchess. On Jubilee Day, they might go their separate ways; but, a programme about the Duchess brought them together, side by side on the sofa, watching in shared enjoyment.

The husband, on the basis of a brief meeting, knows the Duchess of Kent and her personal extraordinariness. His wife is drawn by the very opposite. She mentioned that the thing which stuck most strongly in her mind about the Duchess is that 'she had that depressive illness...after she lost the baby'. She went on to say that 'that's the sort of thing (which) happens...to ordinary people...I think that sort of thing makes them more nice'. Before the wife could elaborate, the husband had interrupted once again to talk of his extraordinary meeting. One of them is struck by the Duchess's extraordinary poise, and the other by her depressive illness, which makes her seem so ordinary. The contrast could hardly be greater. Yet there was no argumentative disagreement between the two. She's fantastic, isn't she? says the mother. The father agrees. They both 'know' her. Together they admire the Duchess.

However, their paths of reasoning are not so dissimilar. The mother can find the Duchess's ordinariness appealing because she takes for granted the latter's extraordinariness as a member of royalty. The father seems to deny this: she is extraordinary by virtue of her personal qualities. There is an omission in his story, as well as an addition, which hints at the nature of the omission. He does not say why he was so easily overcome by such a small conversational touch from a minor royal. His tale has the structure of a romance. He was waiting for her. She looked at him, selecting him from all the other men. Their eyes met; they spoke; he was struck by her beauty, her poise. The whole world melted into the background as the two of them talked. It seemed like an eternity, but it was over all too briefly. He never can forget that moment, which she has probably forgotten already. He will love her till the day he dies.

It was not a love story between two individuals whose feelings transcend all barriers. The differences in class, and the essential royalty of the Duchess, cannot be wished away. They are the pre-conditions of the love story. This is betrayed in his proud addition: 'I bet you haven't met many that's actually spoken to one for five minutes'. To one: not to an individual of special qualities, but to one of the Royal Family. Royalty is the essence: the really exceptional qualities are the accident. He's been on speaking terms with a royal. That is far more magical than watching the televised weddings along with millions of others. Those private few words, whose content he does not reveal to the outsider, have worked their magic.

The power of the modern royal touch is not threatened by the themes of demystification. Sacral reverence can be put aside and its irrationality exposed. When ordinariness is discovered behind the extraordinary role, or extraordinariness within the ordinary person, the mystery is not dispelled. The Queen's mother may be balding; her sister may hold a baby like a normal person; her son's head might resemble a football trophy – none of this matters, or at least all of it does. Each comment, which seems to demystify the mystery, assumes and confirms the extraordinary position of royalty. It is the ground against which the figures play their parts. There is something else involved in the comments of respondents. They are also claiming their own selves, proclaiming their own rationality and their lack of subservience. Nevertheless, as they do so, they are claiming their position as subjects and as commoners. They desire egalitarian moments, when crown and commoner meet, with ordinary person talking to ordinary person. Differences of status seem to disappear from such moments of myth. But, here is the illusion, the mystification, or the forgetfulness. The inequalities must persist, in order to make those desired moments of equality so magical.

A TOUCH OF HYPOCRISY

All this suggests that there is magic in glimpsing at the private royal person behind the public royal display. It also suggests that the 'real' is assumed to reside in the private person behind the public 'job'. But that is not the end of the matter. The quest for the 'real' can be reversed, so that it is sought in the public performance of the role which is not quite a role. In this way, the private is not the only reality to be desired, but another 'reality', simultaneously more and less real, can also be desired. This is the reality of the 'public image'. The show, which Bagehot desired to be enacted for the masses, should now be performed for 'ourselves', who are not a naïvely superstitious audience. 'We' demand the reality of the image. This sort of demand, which simultaneously unmasks the unreality of the image and heralds it as a hyper-reality, should be carefully attended to. It has been claimed that post-modernist consciousness is distinguished from both pre-modern and modernist modes of thinking by this pattern of thinking about images (see Chapter 8 for more details).

Elements of this thinking could be heard in respondents from all social backgrounds. The retired cleaner was discussing with her son and daughter-in-law rumours about the marriage of the Prince and Princess of Wales (interview 60). The Princess should take care, she said, to accompany her husband in public: 'I think for the public image, she is the next Queen, she ought to think "Well, I really ought to stick by his side and stop all these rumours and stories in the press"'. It was the 'public image' which mattered. Even if the marriage was privately in tatters, the show must continue. The hair-grips must be held in place.

Even the religiously observant can be caught up in a secularised morality, which seems to justify deception in the cause of morality's image. This itself shows the strength of the desacralised common-sense, which, nevertheless, does not abandon all the illusions which it claims to be able to expose. The secular and religious themes, discussed earlier in this chapter, reappear. A middle-class mother in her late fifties said that she liked seeing the Royal Family going to church together as a family (interview 16). She was Church of England, but her husband was a Catholic, as were her four children, now adults. While her husband had taken the children to the

Catholic church on Sundays, she had gone to hers alone. How nice it was seeing the Royal Family worshipping together. In talking thus, the mother was not using a religious turn of speech. It was a discourse of family unity: it was good for families to do things together, whether holidaying, playing board games or going to church.

The father talked as if monarchy were a salaried profession: there were too many royals being supported and 'we should only pay for a limited number and those who...do their job'. He mentioned Princess Margaret: 'Why should we pay from the public purse if she doesn't want to do her job of work?'. It was a rhetorical question. His wife didn't supply an answer. She then complained of the immoral behaviour of some royals ('broken marriages, marrying divorcées'). God did not make an appearance, but 'images' did. She said 'it's spoilt the image that we've always had of pristine clean characters'. Her husband remarked that not all the old royals were that pristine clean: 'I mean old Edward the Seventh was a bit of a broth of a boy on the quiet'. But it had been on the quiet. There'd been no messy divorce. That was the way to manage things. 'Oh, I believe in a touch of hypocrisy', he laughed.

The terms of the conversation, far from being religious, were derived from the modern world of business relations: there were jobs to be done, salaries to be earned. There was the 'image', which royalty was paid to maintain. God's sight was left unmentioned, but the right image was needed for 'our' eyes. In this cynical world, even a religious believer like the father could suggest, with a smile, that the royal touch should be a touch of hypocrisy.

The same themes surfaced when those two secretaries, mother and daughter, talked of royal marriage and divorce (interview 23). The daughter did not oppose the idea of a divorce: 'What's the point in staying together to become king and queen and at each other all the time? I mean it wouldn't be good for us'. Her mother interrupted: 'I think it would be better for us not knowing that they're not getting on, them being figureheads and doing their own thing in private, like a lot of kings and queens have done before them'. In olden times, kings had kept secret mistresses. Better a touch of hypocrisy than a public divorce.

Such comments are curious. It is better for 'us' not to know what might be true. Bagehot's call for mass deception has been turned inwards by the people themselves, who have no image of 'ignorant others' to justify their own 'rational' enjoyment of the irrational parade. An outward display should be preserved for 'the public image', says a member of the public. 'We', the public, are calling for ourselves to be deceived, but the very idea implies a knowingness. The mother's defence of a mystified ignorance is far too late: already she and her daughter know too much about the Royal Family. They can talk about the very secrets which need to be kept secret. She cannot wipe from consciousness the words of her own common-sensical sociology. She commented on the unreality of monarchy: 'You do need that fairy story thing', she said, because 'you need to know there's something other than our everyday drudge'. She is simultaneously expressing the sociological voice of Durkheim, whilst claiming to be a member of the society, whose *conscience collective* the Durkheim is observing.

Demystification and mystification are proceeding in harness. She knows it's a 'fairy story', and she knows that fairy stories are not to be believed: that is what makes them fairy stories. Yet, she claims to believe in the fairy story. At the same time, she tells stories about the Queen Mother's barely hidden bald patches. Sloterdijk writes that 'in a culture in which one is regularly told lies, one wants to know not merely the truth but the *naked* truth' (1988, p.218, emphasis in original). Monarchy indicates a further turn. The cynical conscious-ness can demystify the image, in order to reveal the naked truth. But so it can reverse the process. In a culture, in which one might be regularly told the naked truth of the emperor's family, one also wants to imagine them as gloriously clothed. It is thought necessary to preserve the image, whose 'charisma' contains its own com-modity value. It is only an image, whispers one of the cynical voices of common-sense. Sssh, whispers another voice, just as cynical as the first. Sssh, it whispers, the image is the reality, which we need to know.

4

IDENTIFYING WITH 'THEM'

Judith Williamson starts her essay on the Royal Family with the statement that 'the key to the great significance and popularity of Royalty is that they are at once like us, and not like us' (1987, p.75). It is a mystery to be puzzled over: the Princess held the baby just like a normal person, said the mother in the last chapter, as if it were remarkable. According to Williamson, the institution of 'the family' is the key, for it provides 'the central structure of identification which allows us to feel they are like us' (p.75). The Princess didn't just hold the baby like a normal person – she did so like a normal woman, a normal mother. As Walter Bagehot predicted, having a family on the throne reduces majesty to the level of petty life.

There is a further reduction of majesty. As was seen in the previous chapter, people, including royals themselves, will talk of being royal as a 'job'. 'Royalty as a job' seems to express the cynical consciousness at its most cynical: it is 'just' a job, 'just' a family business. In these phrases, the mystery drops away. But that is not the end of the story. The idea of 'royalty as a job' leads on to other matters which are associated with ordinary jobs, such as rates of pay, the nature of the employers and the conduct of the employees. For the royal job, these matters are not straightforward.

'Royalty as a job' takes a familiar notion from ordinary life – 'having a job' – to describe the extraordinary life of royalty. To paraphrase Bagehot, royalty is rendered more understandably petty. Beneath the crowns and coronets are to be found 'mothers' and 'sons', 'working mothers' and 'working sons', just like 'us'. Faced with such similarities, it is tempting to use the psychological term 'identification', or, as Judith Williamson did, 'structures of identification'. Similarly, when the journalist, Katherine Whitehorn,

86

contributed a chapter to a volume, celebrating the Queen's sixtieth birthday, she wrote: 'It's ironic that we all want to believe in the fantasy of the dream-queen, but coupled with an ordinariness with which we can identify' (1986, p.13).

Because of its psychological overtones, the word 'identification' promises to offer an explanation for the popular obsession with the family upon the throne. There are reasons to be cautious, for the word may fail to deliver promised insights. Howitt (1982) points out that psychologists have used the word so loosely that 'the concept of identification...seems to be equal to *liking* a character' (p.35, emphasis in original; see also Barker, 1989, for a critique of the psychological concept of identification). One should not assume that there is a clearly defined psychological state of 'identification', nor that the 'structures of identification' can be unambiguously discovered. Instead, these issues are to be explored by listening to the ways that people talk about the similarities and differences between themselves and royalty. The claims of similarities and differences constitute the so-called 'structures of identification'.

In such talk, there is a feature, which is here called 'double-declaiming'. This is a concept which will figure in later chapters too, but a few general words of explication can be given. When people make claims in conversation, they are often doing more than making just a single claim. In Chapter 2, the 'tourist argument' was discussed. Claims that monarchy is an economically profitable tourist attraction were not simple: often people making such claims were doing a number of things at once. Double-declaiming refers to a particular sort of complexity. When speakers are making claims about others, they can also be making claims about themselves, either implicitly or explicitly. Thus, there can be a doubleness to their utterances.

When people make claims about the nature of the royal life, they are typically also making wider claims, for depictions of the royal life gain their meaning by reference to the non-royal life. This point was well expressed by Marx in a footnote in *Capital*. Marx wrote that a man is only king because others imagine they are subjects; and they 'imagine that they are subjects because he is king' (1915, p.66n). Thus, when people are imagining what the royal life is like, they will be doing so in relation to what they know about the non-royal life. As they speak about the royals, so they will be making claims themselves as subjects of royalty. As will be seen, speakers will often show double-declaiming by contrasting the extraordinariness of the royal way with the pettiness of ordinary life. As Marx suggested, the subject position is imagined to be in contra-distinction to the kingly one, and vice versa. However, double-declaiming does not depend upon claims of difference. There are also claims of similarity: 'they' can hold babies just like 'us'. In making such a claim, speakers are doubly claiming how 'they' are and how 'we' are.

The notion of double-declaiming will be used to explore the ideological aspects of talk about royalty – how our claims about 'them' involve 'us' affirming 'our' own ordinary lives as subjects. The details can be left until later. Nevertheless, there is one aspect to be mentioned now. People will be heard to say that it is royalty's job to set moral examples. The ideas of 'moral examples' and 'identi-fication' suggest that we may be dealing with something akin to the Freudian super-ego. However, this is not so, or so it will be argued. According to Freud's theory of identification in 'Group psychology and the analysis of the ego', people come to identify with the image of an idealised figure, who psychologically becomes the person's inner voice of conscience or super-ego. In this way, people defer with obedience to their figures of identification. Today, the Royal Family has not become the national super-ego in this sense. The cynical consciousness is not producing Freudian 'structures of iden-tification' which would demand deference and forbid open mockery.

Writing in 1941, Max Horkheimer, claimed that 'the father may still possess a super-ego, but the child has long unmasked it' (p.367). Fifty years on, these children are now entering old age. Their chil-dren and their children's children can be heard maintaining a cynical consciousness, even as they talk of morality. Once more, it is a case of mystification and demystification: there are calls for moral standards of behaviour to be set and to be exposed. People can be heard to unmask the masks and, then, to claim that it is royalty's job to mask this unmasking.

MORE JOBS

To begin with, a few examples can be given of the way that people speak of royalty 'doing a job'. Some examples were given in the previous chapter. For instance, there was the mother and daughter talking of the way that the royals promoted trade, especially in the fashion industry (interview 50). Several more illustrations from a large corpus can be offered. A twenty-five year old dental nurse and her husband, who worked as a clerk, were talking about the possibility of abdication (interview 62). She opposed the idea: 'There's nothing wrong with the job she's doing', she said of the Queen. Her husband agreed: 'No, no, she's doing an excellent job'. Monarchy was a job, and if the job is being done excellently, there is no need to change the personnel. It all seems so matter of fact, so mundane.

Across the generations, the same common-place way of talking can be heard. An eighty-seven year old wife and her husband, retired farmers, belonged to the generation which Horkheimer was depicting (interview 40). She was talking in the same tones as the young couple in their twenties. She discussed the events of the 1936 abdication. She had not been impressed by Edward VIII: 'I don't think that the country lost anything'. But it had been difficult for 'the late King and Queen Mother'. She said: 'I think it was pretty hard on them to have to take up the job at, sort of, a week's notice'. She then specified: 'He was a highly strung sort of man and he had this speech defect which must have been very difficult for him to take on a job like that'. The language again is down-to-earth. Becoming king was 'taking on a job', and a difficult job for a man with a speech defect.

The nature of the job which was required to be done was indicated in other comments. A mother, a nurse in her thirties, was defending Prince Charles against the critics (interview 28). He was 'entitled' to speak his mind about architecture. 'I suppose you could say', she went on '"Well, he's there to do this job, and that's that"'. 'What job's that?', asked her husband, a computing consultant. She replied: 'Well, he'll be our king one day...be our ambassador'. Later, her husband was saying of the Royal Family 'they all do a relatively good job'. This time it was the interviewer who asked 'What is the job?'. 'It's a sort of ambassadorial sort of role here and selling this country', said the mother. The father agreed, expanding on the Queen's 'role' to advise politicians. Again, it was jobs and roles.

A daughter and her boyfriend, both university students, were adopting the radical position against the rest of her conservative family (interview 35). She was challenging them with the language of 'jobs': 'Go on, tell me what job does Princess Diana earn a living from? What job does she do, eh? Go on tell me what job does Prince Charles do, eh?' 'He's an ambassador', replied her father. 'They're all ambassadors, and good ones, apart from Margaret', added his wife in support. The father was not finished. The royals worked hard at their jobs: 'They work on average on the job that they do, whether it be a public relations officer or an ambassador or whatever, they work more hours...and with a much more hectic schedule than the average man in the street'.

The question 'What job do they do?' is held to be in order: its very terms are not an affront to modern majesty. 'They' do jobs, necessary jobs, and 'they' do them well, discounting unfortunate exceptions. The jobs are those of representation, rather than jobs of production. The royals are ambassadors, sales agents and public relations officers. When praised for performing these jobs so well, the royals are raised to the level of commercial usefulness.

The 'pettiness' of ordinary private life is not left far behind. Nor can it be, for the job of being a Royal Family is to be a family. According to a Gallup poll of December 1988, eighty-five percent of the population agreed that it is important that royalty 'set a standard of good citizenship and family life'. The idea that royalty should set standards of family behaviour is by no means new. Linda Colley (1984 and 1986) points to the reign of George III for the origins of the quietly domestic image of the English Royal Family. This image was translated into a job specification by a leading article in *The Times* of 1859. To mark the coming of age of the Prince of Wales, the future Edward VII, the paper set out what was required of a future monarch: 'It is the happiness of a King of England that we require from him no brilliant military achievement, no extraordinary diplomatic legerdemain, no startling effects, no scenic pomp, no histrionic dexterity'. Nothing exceptional was necessary: 'He may be great without the possession of extraordinary talents, and famous without dazzling exploits'. Instead, his job demanded something much more homely: 'Let him set to his people an example of domestic life' (*The Times*, 11 December 1859).

No special talents were required: the apprentice must be able to lead an ordinary family life. But there was a catch. It was not sufficient to live the domestic life, but the domestic life must be seen to be lived as an example to the people. The private life, which is privately lived far from the public gaze, would set no public example and would not achieve the great domestic ordinariness to which the prince should aspire. To use Tom Nairn's (1988) phrase, the royal life should be 'super-ordinary' (see also Edley, 1991). *The Times* leader-writer was indeed describing a curious job.

While other Victorian trades have disappeared, this one has persisted. A hundred years later, the views of *The Times* are little

more than common-sense. Over and again, in the family discussions, it was said that royalty should set moral standards, especially those of family life. 'To me', said a fireman in his forties, 'they
are the sort of figurehead of the family life' (interview 22). Family
life, he went on, should be 'rock solid'. It was the 'foundation' of all
morality: 'I don't think anything can function without that'. A retired
toolmaker stated that royalty 'should set a moral standard' and his
daughter, a hairdresser in her thirties, was quick to agree: 'They're
put in the limelight and they've got the opportunity to set standards'
(interview 29). According to a civil servant in his early thirties,
people needed models to look up to: 'No matter where you are in
life, I think you always need someone to look up to, whether it be a
youngster looking up to the mother or the father, or somebody
looking up to the teacher' (interview 18). Without that you'll have
'anarchy'. His wife agreed: that's why royalty must be placed 'on a
higher plane'. The actions of the Royal Family affect 'the country as
a whole' – anything bad they do 'affects us all'. That's why, she
added, 'it was so tragic to the Royal Family when Princess Margaret
did become divorced'.

Divorce threatened the right image of homely domesticity. As
was mentioned in the previous chapter, the mother, talking to her
daughter, who worked as a secretary in the same office, could
advocate a hidden private immorality, rather than risk the public
display of a royal divorce (interview 23). She said: 'If the Royal
Family's crumbling apart, people feel frightened; I mean if they're
not going to make it, what chance have the rest of us got?'. An
eighteen year old motor mechanic spoke in the same way: 'You've
got to have someone to look up to, what's right and what's wrong
and that's what they are – they're figureheads' (interview 58). The
father, who had actually met the Duchess of Kent, claimed that it
was royalty's duty to 'set standards at the top' and, therefore, a royal
divorce was out of the question (interview 3).

These are tales of strict standards and obedience to moral views.
They are depictions of hierarchy: the royal figures at the very top of
society are placed upon a pedestal, to be looked up to. These are
claims about how 'they', the royals, should behave. They are also
claims about 'us': 'we' need the examples; 'we' need authority; 'we'
are weak. The speakers seem to be echoing Bagehot's statement, in
The English Constitution, that 'we have to regard the Crown as the
centre of our *morality*' (p.96, emphasis in original).

The remarks about figureheads and so on seem to be calling for something analogous to the Freudian super-ego. However, the call itself unmasks the super-ego. For Freud, the super-ego developed spontaneously, without conscious awareness. Freud, in fact, suggested that the sort of conscious understanding which psycho-analysis claimed to provide would be the undoing of the super-ego. Freud himself claimed to be beyond the reach of the irrational hero-worship: by psycho-analytic self-knowledge, he had freed himself from such unreason. And he offered the talking-cure to others. There is a similar rhetoric in the common-sense claims that 'we' need the moral example of royalty. The mere utterance of this thought indicates that 'we' claim for ourselves insights which are beyond naïve hero-worship. The speakers are not uncritically looking up to a 'figurehead', but in claiming that people need a 'figurehead', they are unmasking the mystery of the figurehead and its power over 'us'.

There is double-declaiming going on here. In talking about royalty, the respondents are talking about the psychology of the royals' subjects, and, thus, about themselves. In the previous chapter, the dialectic between demystification and mystification was seen in terms of a common-sense sociology: there were the common-sense Durkheims and the *conscience collective*. Now there is a psychological theme. In this common-sense talk, people are simultaneously claiming, as it were, to be Freud and to be his patient. 'We' need the figurehead, who is, after all, just a human doing a job. 'We' need to be diagnosed and 'we' diagnose ourselves.

UNFOLLOWED EXAMPLES

If the Freudian super-ego is unmasked, then what remains is something less than the stern voice of conscience. Royalty might be asked to set a moral example – to be, in Bagehot's words, the centre of 'our' morality, especially 'our' domestic morality. Nevertheless, this example has become symbolic, and is to be recognised as such. An engineer in his late forties said 'they've got a job in life' and 'they're the figurehead' (interview 27). In this, differences between 'them' and 'us' are emphasised. 'Their' job is to be a figurehead, but it is not 'ours'. There is no compulsion for 'us' to adjust our behaviour to match the behaviour which 'we' desire them to produce as part of 'their' job specification.

Many times the point was made that 'their' behaviour must be fit for 'their' public position. The mother talked about the dire consequences which would follow if royalty were seen to be immoral and their family life was known to be crumbling (interview 23). That was why she believed that 'they' should not 'be allowed to divorce'. A bit of hypocrisy away from the public gaze would be preferable. She was talking to her daughter, who herself had been divorced. Her daughter disagreed with her mother's stance against royal divorce: 'I think they should be allowed to', she said, contradicting her mother. 'No, I don't'. 'I do'. The mother then made an adjustment. She said that she was only talking about royals, not ordinary people: 'Ordinary folks, yes; but not them'.

This conversation might have had a specific edge, with the mother qualifying herself in order to avoid offending her own divorced daughter. Yet there was a much more general point: 'their' standards need not be 'our' standards. For a former factory worker, now in her fifties, it was part of 'their' job not to get divorced (interview 15). She specifically mentioned the Queen's position as the Head of the Church of England: divorce wouldn't be right for her. Not that divorce in general was so dreadful: 'Well, divorce now, it's nothing, is it really'. For 'us' it was nothing.

The difference between 'them' and 'us' was plainly stated by a middle-class couple in their thirties (interview 7). Their two young children sat quietly during the interview. At one point, the parents were talking about royal divorce. They agreed that Prince Charles and Lady Diana would never be allowed to divorce. As the wife said: 'if they're going to remain at the top...and get the respect, then they've not got to be seen to be doing what everybody else does'.

Even within the Royal Family distinctions could be made: what was permissible for the lesser royals might not be suitable for a king or queen. This was the view of a husband and wife, estate agent and nurse respectively (interview 42). 'They say', said the wife, 'Fergie lived with another man before she married him (Prince Andrew)'. It was alright for her to marry Andrew, said her husband, 'but she couldn't have married Prince Charles, definitely not'. 'Why not?', asked his wife. 'Because she couldn't have.' 'It doesn't matter to me', said the wife, 'I really don't care one way or other'. Her husband was not to be manoeuvred into the position of being the prude: 'Well, it doesn't matter to *me*', he said, 'yet I think it matters to them'. He amplified his point: 'You can't have the Queen of England sitting there and this bloke says "I used to shack up with her round my flat"'. His wife was laughing. Her father, a former electrician, added seriously: 'They have got to set a standard, haven't they, to the rest'.

His son-in-law agreed: 'Yeah, course they should'. Perhaps it was alright if they did things 'on the quiet', suggested his wife, 'to behave one way publicly, but in reality it's something different'. 'It's a very hard life', commented her husband.

The husband and wife were claiming not to mind personally, if the royal bride was not a virgin. Their own morality was not offended by the prospect, so they claimed. Nor did they mind the future king's brother being married to a woman with a past. Yet, it wouldn't be right for the king – you couldn't have it. Someone might say something out of turn. If it were kept quiet, it would be alright. But the job of the monarch demands a public display of strict morality. It's a hard life. An implied double-declaiming was being whispered: 'our' life is so much easier.

A former teacher said that if 'the Royal Family lost the sense that they had to keep up respectability...and had totally come off their pedestals, then I think there would be a lot more demands generally for the Monarchy to be abandoned' (interview 30). She continued: 'I mean it's only the fact that they try and keep themselves sort of special and very moral that people don't question them'. Again, there is the implication that 'their' behaviour has to be seen to be especially moral – 'they', and not 'us', are upon the moral pedestal.

The thought was expressed more forcefully, indeed more cynically, by an unemployed, computing student in his late thirties (interview 34). He and his wife were saying that royalty should abide by moral standards. If 'they' couldn't, said the wife, they should do their misdeeds 'when nobody knows about them'. It was the touch of hypocrisy again. Once more, preserving the image of morality was what mattered. 'People', said her husband 'expect moral standards of the Royal Family, but not necessarily look up to them and follow them'. He went on to summarise the position, as if instructing royalty: 'We expect you to behave yourselves, but we'll do what we like, thank you very much'. He laughed aloud.

It is a strange situation, which reverses the traditional notions of duty and moral examples. Royalty must set an example of ordinary domestic morality, which ordinary people feel little obligation to follow. The setting of the example is an end in itself. Or at least it is a means towards demonstrating that another obligation had been fulfilled – that a well-paid job was being satisfactorily done. Double-declaiming is at work. The talk about 'their' obligations acts as an affirmation of 'us'. A moral double-standard is to be applied. The cynical voice has turned the patterns of deference upside-down. 'We' can mock 'them': 'we'll' do what 'we' want, thank you very much.

These themes emerged in an interview involving a working-class family (interview 57). The whole discussion was conducted with humorous banter, with the mother, a domestic assistant, figuring largely and loudly. The daughters talked of copying the fashions of the Princess of Wales: they used to tie their belts in the Princess's style, 'do our hair, put all bands and stuff on' and then they would stand outside their council house 'pretending we were royalty'.

Fashions might be copied for fun, but there was no imperative to copy other codes of behaviour. They were all talking about the public behaviour of the Duchess of York. The eighteen year old daughter, who worked in a hamburger restaurant, mentioned the occasion when the Duchess reputedly shouted to a crowd 'Oh, go away you morons'. The mother added that 'Anne's been reported as saying things and all'. The father, a lorry driver, chipped in: 'She's very posh; she says "hecky thump"'. They all laughed. The mother sympathised with royalty's indiscretions; talking of Princess Anne's blunt speaking, she commented that 'She'd only say what we'd say'. She added the familiar phrase 'after all, they're only people'. But, of course, royalty is paid to be unlike 'us'. It was the elder daughter who added this counter-point of common-sense: 'Yeah, but the Queen's got to give that image, hasn't she'. The mother agreed, introducing the word 'example': 'Yes, the Queen has got to set an example, I'll admit that; but not that it'd make any difference, because nobody follows her example'. Warming to her theme, the mother continued: 'And I don't think they'd like the Queen to be loud-mouthed like me'. Turning to her younger daughter, she said: 'and, you agree with that, don't you Sharon?'. Amidst more laughter, Sharon made her evasive reply: 'No, I won't say no more'.

The Queen should set the example, or, as the daughter suggested, she should give the image of setting the example. No-one need follow this example. The mother was not criticising the followers who will not follow. She is amongst their number. She is not going to act like a queen. The talk might have been marked by the humour of irreverence, but the points were serious. A loud-mouthed queen is not wanted. It's right that royals should talk posh, but there is no corresponding obligation for loud-mouthed commoners to adopt posh royal tones. No-one is meant to follow the regal example.

The mother is challenging her daughter to criticise, but the daughter teasingly withholds both criticism and reassurance. The mother's challenge stays open. Would they want her to stop joking, to walk regally around the council house, declaring that the kitchen or the front-room are hereby open? Do they want her to take seriously the game of copying royalty which the daughters had played for fun on the front step? Is that what they all want? Not likely. Not bloody likely.

HUMAN FAILINGS

'They' should set standards – 'they' should behave better than 'us'. But it is not that simple. The stern super-ego is not about to be sneaked in the back door. The common-places, which demand the moral superiority of the royals, encounter in the kaleidoscope of common-sense opposing common-places, which stress 'their' similarity to 'us'. The mother was saying that Princess Anne shouldn't speak as 'we' might under provocation. There again, 'we' understand her lapses from strict self-control: 'After all, they're only people', she said.

The recognition of ordinary humanity, and, thus, a recognition of 'their' similarity with 'us', is not merely a matter of forgiving a failure to meet the exacting standards demanded of a royal. As was discussed in the previous chapter, the royal 'role' contains its own negation. The royals are to be seen as being human, after all: that is part of their job. The wife, whose husband met the Duchess of Kent, mentioned the Duchess's post-natal depression as a reason for liking the Duchess (interview 3). It was good, she was implying, to see royals coping, or indeed not quite coping, with ordinary problems, just like 'us'. The job specification of *The Times* in 1859 demanded, not a super-human saintliness, but an ordinary domesticity. Ordinary people fail to achieve standards of perfection – they get depressed, speak out of turn, fall in love messily and so on. 'We' can recognise 'ourselves' in such failures.

The two sets of common-places – 'they' should behave better than 'us'/'they' are only human like 'us' – pose a continual dilemma, which frames each royal action and each royal personage. These contrary themes provide the elements for perpetual argument and controversy. There can be justified criticism and critical justification. A secretary in her forties opted for the justified criticism (interview 26). She was talking of the Duchess of York, who had reportedly shouted back at journalists. She said: 'If I had been there, if I were her, I suppose I might have done the same thing, but...the Royal Family are on a pedestal and you've got to be very careful what you say and how you act *all* the time'. She was being critical, but understandingly critical. She might have behaved in the same way as the Duchess. But what might be permissible for a commoner isn't for a royal. The Duchess's job is to be upon the pedestal.

The same elements can be re-arranged from sympathetic criticism to critical sympathy. Another mother, a shop manager in her late thirties, reversed the rhetorical ordering, in order to present the case for the defence. She was sympathising with Princess Anne for reacting sharply to journalists: 'I think I'd tend to do it; let's face it, they're still human; alright they're supposed to set an example, but they're still human' (interview 2).

In these matters of ordinariness and extraordinariness, there always seems to be a common-place 'on-the-other-hand'. 'They' might be upon the pedestal, but it can be argued that 'they' should descend from the heights of the pedestal. A fifty-nine year old mother specifically criticised the Queen for her remoteness: 'She should try and be a bit more commoner...a bit more natural' (interview 59). For the Queen to fulfil the royal role, which contains its own negation, she should be a commoner. Another mother would have disagreed: 'I think they're coming down off the pedestal and that's not really a good thing' (interview 1). Her husband, with the support of their two teenage children, was ready to put the other case. 'Mind you, I think it was good', he countered, 'it shows to the public they are human, the same as us'. Up the pedestal – down the pedestal: both could be justified by common-sense.

The dilemma need not be expressed by different speakers putting one or other cases. As individual speakers thought about the dilemma, they could rehearse the opposing themes, voicing aloud the 'one-hands' and the 'other-hands' (Billig *et al.*, 1988; Billig, 1990a). A thirty-nine year old ex-market gardener was talking about the dilemma of royalty (interview 7). If 'they' became 'too ordinary', she was saying, then 'they' would lose 'that respect'. But 'they are only the same as everyone else'. She continued: 'But on the other hand...it's better if they're a little bit removed'. She concluded 'there's a fine line...I think they've got it about right really; I think you can still look up to them, but they're not so high and mighty'.

Such comments do not indicate a desire for the royals to be figures of perfection. 'Their' similarity to 'us' – a similarity which implies a failure to maintain the strictest of standards – can be visible. Jacques Lacan's (1977) point about identification is relevant here. He suggested that the people whom we select to identify with are those in whose gaze we imagine ourselves to be likeable. If royals were imagined to be paragons of virtue, 'they' would be imagined to be looking down upon 'us' from 'their' moral pedestals. 'They' would be imagined to be superior critics of ordinary failure: 'their' moral perfections would be a constant accusation against 'us' who did not follow the examples which were being publicly set (see also Zizek, 1989, pp.104f for a development of Lacan's point).

There was one figure amongst the royals who was talked about in the sort of glowing terms which indicate near-perfection. This was the Queen Mother – she could be praised as being the ideal grandmother, even great-grandmother. A sixteen year old school-girl was praising 'Fergie' for not seeming too royal; then she mentioned, also in praise, the Queen Mother (interview 24). Her mother picked up the point: 'She's a motherly figure, isn't she, and she's also a grandmotherly figure – people would like grandmums, and probably mothers, to be (like her)'.

People would like their grandmothers, and possibly their mothers, to resemble the Queen Mother. The praise is double-edged. It implies criticism of all those ordinary mothers and grand-mothers who fail to make the grade. The comment from the mother to her daughter whispers: if only my mother, your grandmother....

Occasionally the implicit criticism was made explicit. Two parents, who themselves were of the age to be grandparents, were talking with their grown-up, but unmarried, daughter (interview 16). The mother was a voluntary worker, aged fifty-six, and her husband, a few years older, was a retired deputy manager of a power station. They were full of praise for the Queen Mother. The mother had raised the topic: 'Going back to the image of the Royal Family as a family, I think the special relationship that they all have with the Queen Mother is lovely; this brings granny back into focus'. She went on: 'Nobody wanted happiness for Prince Charles more than the Queen Mother and if she could do anything to help any of the younger members of the Royal Family she would do it'. The praise continued: 'I think this is a good image of a granny, some-body tender and loving and caring, which, in these days when granny is a fifty year old blonde in a wig with painted eye-lashes and tight jeans, I think, yeah, I think we've lost something'.

As the mother sat there – a tall, calm and confident figure – she most certainly was not wearing the tight jeans and painted eye-lashes which she found deplorable when worn by others of her age. Her praise of the Queen Mother was a reproach to others. Again, the example, which royalty supposedly set, was expressed in terms of an 'image' – 'a good image of a granny'.

The image of perfection can be uncomfortable, for it indicates to others their own imperfections. Perhaps, if there is to be perfection, or the image of perfection, within the exemplary family, then it is safer that the figure be an elderly woman. How amazing that she is still working at her age, doing the job of promoting the image of the grandmother! Younger speakers need not be discomforted by the praise for a nonagenarian; and, as they voice the praise, they can craftily criticise their elders.

An elderly couple, both themselves in their late eighties, praised the Queen Mother, but in a different way (interview 40). They talked about her past contributions as Queen – the good impressions she made when touring the Commonwealth, her bravery during the war years and so on. The perfect grandmother was absent in the talk of these her contemporaries. For younger speakers, the frail old woman had reached the age when she could safely be held to present the perfect image. But the image of a perfect son or daughter – a perfect mother or father – constantly staring from the daily papers: that would be different. Such an image would surely be resented by ordinary sons and daughters, mothers and fathers, the length and breadth of the kingdom.

THE RIGHT IMAGE

The notion of 'image' keeps recurring. The Queen Mother is praised for her 'image'. It is not merely the image of herself, but it is the image of the ideal stereotype of grandmotherhood, which she is said to embody. As was seen earlier, a mother was talking with her daughters about the examples which royalty should set and which 'we' need not follow (interview 57). The word 'image' was used interchangeably with 'example': 'they' set 'examples', 'they' produce 'images'. The unfollowed example is an image of an example; this enables the words to be used interchangeably without misunder-standing.

If royalty is a job, then the modern job description stipulates that royalty should produce suitable images. What exactly constitutes the desirable image is a 'fine line'. Dispute and controversy might be inevitable, but few would disagree that 'images' are required. *The Times* of 1859 might have predicted that the personal conduct of royals would be commonly appraised as a topic of discussion. What it did not, and could not have, anticipated is that in the late twentieth century this talk would be phrased in terms of 'image'.

A sales manager was talking about the Prince and Princess of Wales (interview 7). 'She's been a sort of high profile figure', he said, 'and I think they brought a sort of more modern image'. After all, 'the Queen was probably seen as a little bit boring, a little bit dowdy'. A forty-eight year old barmaid criticised the Duchess of York: 'When we first saw her and she was interviewed, she seemed a bit sort of lairey to me...and I thought "Well, that's not the image, is it really"' (inter- view 6). A housewife in her fifties spoke similarly. 'She's not regal, she's not royal', she was saying, 'She spoils the image, I think, totally, I think she's a let down' (interview 5). Later, she started criticising the Queen's style of dress ('very old-fashioned'), then 'her hair-style and her spectacles'. Her husband agreed: 'She doesn't give a very good image'. 'I think the Queen Mother does a lot better, the way she dresses, the way she looks', put in his wife.

If 'they' must set higher standards in the ways in which they appear than 'we' need to, then there can be sympathy for 'them'. The familiar common-places of similarity and dissimilarity can be mobilised into their argumentative positions. A retired fitter, in his late sixties, was praising the Queen Mother for being 'the motherly and grandmotherly figure' (interview 52). His wife interrupted to agree: 'Yeah, she creates a loving image'. They then turned to assess Prince Charles.

(Interview 52)

Wife: Wherever he goes people tend to take him to their hearts (.) and he'll come and meet people and he'll, I think he's very sincere (.) I think he'd make a good king

Husband: Mm

Wife: I really do

Husband: The trouble is then he'll go and do some daft thing like (.) when they start reporting talking to flowers and plants (*laughs*)

Wife: Oh well that shows he's human doesn't [it

Husband: [Yeah but, it it it

does, but it don't do his image any good (.) you know he'll do
something good and then he'll do something like that daft
what people think a bit daft yeah

The wife is praising the future king – people take him to their heart,
she says. Her husband offers a qualification: the problem is that the
Prince then goes and does something 'daft', like being said to talk to
flowers. Back comes the familiar mitigation: it shows he's human,
says the wife. Yes, but it doesn't do his 'image' any good, countered
the husband. It was humanity against image. The husband then
indicates what he means by 'image': if 'people' think that the Prince
is doing something 'daft', then the image suffers. The image
depends not just on what the Prince might do, but, most crucially,
on what 'people' think about his doings.

In such talk, 'image' can refer to those standards which 'we' might
wish to see 'them' set, but which 'we' do not necessarily follow. A
thirty-two year old wife said, 'they can't be too ordinary...too much
is expected of them, I mean they've got too many roles and duties
to perform, they've got to live up to this image, they're not ordinary
people' (interview 33). The obligation to live up to the image marks
'them' from 'us'. A grown-up daughter was agreeing with her
parents' criticisms of the Duchess of York: royals should be 'rather
straight-laced, and, you know, you are conducting yourself to a
public image' (interview 16).

The notion of 'image' suggests a division between the public and the
private person, with the image referring to what the public sees. As for
Prince Charles, the husband (interview 52) was saying, the trouble was
not that he talked to flowers – the trouble was that the public thought
the floral conversations were 'daft'. Had the conversations been privately conducted and remained unreported, the image would not have
suffered. It is another form of the touch of hypocrisy. The outer image,
which 'we' the public see, is what matters.

However, the notion of public image also indicates a private
personality. The image of the Prince is not merely of a future ceremonial king, but of a family man and individual with certain tastes
and habits. One husband said that the Queen 'gives a frosty image
across', and that she should try to be like the Queen Mother: 'She's a
very warm person' (interview 10). His words slide without jolt from
image to nature: the Queen's frosty image is compared with the
warmth which is the Queen Mother. The public image suggests the
private individual, just as the public role contains its own negation.

101

The image could be said to be more than an image, but, this, too, could be said to be part of the image: the image of the personality.

In another way, the image is more than *just* an image, a *mere* image. As respondents talked about the royal job, they frequently used the terms of advertising and public relations. These remarks were not made to belittle monarchy but to justify it, for image-making was part of the royal task. A mechanical engineer in his forties said that Prince Charles 'needs to develop his image for when he 'comes king' (interview 14). In interview 35, the father was combatting the radicalism of his daughter and her boyfriend: yes, 'they' work hard and usefully, whether it be in public relations or whatever. A sales manager was justifying monarchy: 'One of the biggest things with the Royal Family is the image that they portray and obviously they're going to try and protect that' (interview 7). This was said by a Conservative man – a reader of the *Daily Mail* and *Daily Express*. The image should be protected, he went on: 'The role should be protected from tarnish, they do represent something that we want to keep in the country'. Far from the notion of image undermining monarchy – it's *only* an image – it is used in justification. The image was monarchy's passport to success in a world where public images represent commercial reality.

There is an implicit double-declaiming in the claims about 'their' image and the need for 'them' to maintain 'their' image. Such claims refer to the way that 'they' are to appear in 'our' eyes, and, thus, to 'us' as the assessors of royalty. What matters is not what 'they' do, so much as how 'they' are seen by 'us', the public. If 'we' assess 'their' image', then 'we' are assessing 'them' in terms of how 'we', the public, assess them. 'We' praise them for having 'a good image': this is to praise 'them' for being praised. Or rather, since the image can be all-encompassing, 'we' praise them for presenting the image of being praise-worthy. This image of images implies that 'they' are presenting 'their' images for 'our' benefit. Yet, at the same time, 'we', the cynical public, can distrust the image; 'we' can entertain, even approve of, the possibility that the image is touched with hypocrisy. And 'we' can search for the image behind the image.

THE BLOOD ROYAL

If it is the job of royalty to project an image, then it is an image of themselves as members of a family said to be royal. The job's description assumes the reality of both categories – 'royal' and 'family'. These categories would seem to set the frame for the patterns of similarity and difference. Being royal, 'they' are different from 'us'; belonging to a family, 'they' are familiarly similar. Yet, it is not so straightforward, for, in the talk about a Royal Family, assumptions are made both about the nature of royalness and about the family. In this section, 'royalness' will be considered. In the following section, the assumptions of family will be the topic.

'The Royal Family', as a phrase, is so commonly used that it ceases to be mysterious. In the newspapers, on television and in conversations, 'The Royal Family' appears again and again. It is a matter-of-fact that there is a family, which is royal. 'They' might be criticised for not acting in a royal way – for not projecting a suitably royal image – yet, there is an assumption of 'royalness', existing as a reality, beyond the image of royalness. Royals should act in a royal way because they are royal. A non-royal might act as if royal, just as a royal might act unregally. But only a royal can *be* royal.

What constitutes this royalness remains enigmatic. The cynical consciousness might claim to unmask illusions and might cynically call for the image to be the reality. But 'royalness' seems to be accepted beyond this cynicism. A grandmother was heard to describe how the lot of kingship fell upon George VI (interview 40). She talked in terms of a 'job', for which he was unsuited by virtue of a speech defect. She did not, for a moment, pause to suggest that he should not have filled the job vacancy.

As was discussed in Chapter 3, royalness no longer depends upon God's grace. The disappearance of the mystical elements has created a vacuum. There is no ready way of describing this quality of royalness, which ensured that only George VI – speech impediment or not – should fill the vacancy. The ordinary language of 'jobs', even of public relations and marketing, has little to say about the essence of royalness. Instead, there is a void, which was only partially filled. When the topic was raised, it could be seen that the mysterious quality of royalness has descended from heaven to take up a bodily existence. There was talk of 'blood', and, in this, a quiet, but insistent, whisper of racial nationalism can be heard.

What is taken-for-granted in 'royalness' is an acceptance of hereditary privilege. In the modern age of democratic equality, this privilege has lost its phrases of justification. Semantically, it is marooned in a meritocratic world of jobs and earnings. Royalness, as something handed down from generation to generation, cannot be earned. Without the possibility of describing this link between past and present in terms of spiritual qualities, a biological description could be suggested. For instance, one father asserted: 'You've got to maintain the blood line' (interview 3).

A royalness of blood was to be transmitted across history and into the future. This much was implied by the comments about foreign royals, cited in Chapter 2. There, the claim was heard that foreign royalty did not have the line possessed by British royalty. In Spain, 'some guy' just set himself up as king. That wasn't genuinely royal. On the other hand, the British Royal Family was genuinely royal – it was *the* Royal Family. The essence stretched backwards to the distant origins of national time. Moreover, this stretching back was its essence. And so was the vagueness of origins. Some guy didn't just set himself up. There was no arbitrariness: kings *were* kings, marked, even then, by their special blood. In fact, there can be no origins if the essence of royalness lies in biological continuity with the past. There is just a sense of the royalness disappearing back into a disappeared past.

As for the present, a royalness without this imagined continuity was unthinkable. A family couldn't suddenly become royal, at least not properly royal. The cynical consciousness of today would recognise no-one authorised to anoint a new royal line. No church leader could announce that God had made an awful mistake in selecting the Windsors, formerly known as the Saxe-Coburgs: and that the divinely royal task now fell to the Smiths, or the Jones or the Thatchers. History could be the only anointer. Each casual mention of the Royal Family affirms, if only by implication, the reality of this history of blood.

There is a paradox in this history. The more knowledgeable royalists are about the 'blood line', the more they will be tracing the foreign origins of the national family. Until the present century, royalty was the only truly international class. Offspring regularly married within their class and this entailed marrying foreign spouses. This sort of detail was usually the property of the keenly interested royalists. The mother and daughter, who worked in the same secretarial office, were cases in point (interview 23). They mentioned the foreignness of royalty several times. 'Ours isn't really the British Royal Family, is it', said the daughter with emphasis. Her mother agreed: 'It isn't English, it isn't British actually'. She went on: 'We always imagine the Royal Family to be English, pure English, but they aren't'. 'They're not', echoed her daughter. A notion of the 'pure English' was being invoked. It was a whisper, or susurration, of race.

In interview 16, the mother was talking of Princess Diana's 'royal blood'. She was tracing the Princess's line back to royalty of the past: 'She's the most royal of the royals'. Then, it was on to the foreign line. Prince Philip was a Greek. The grown-up daughter drew out an implication: 'Prince Charles, Andrew and Edward are fifty percent Greek and fifty percent English'. It wasn't even that straightforward, said the father: 'If you enquire further back, you might find there's a chunk of German and Spanish and Dutch and Belgian and goodness knows what in them'. A thirty year old secretary said that 'we always think our Royal Family, they're British...but they're not, they've got all this mixed blood; you can't really say they're an English Royal Family because they're not' (interview 60).

Critics of royalty can use this 'reality' as an argumentative weapon against royalty, so expressing their radicalism in nationalist terms. 'That's not true blood English, as we call English', claimed an anti-royalist father (interview 2). He cited Prince Philip and Queen Victoria 'and all them, that was Germans, you know, they're not true British, as we call British line'. It was 'we' – the pure, true British with 'our' British blood – against 'them' the foreign royalty.

Experts sometimes claim to offer precise calculations for the national purity of blood, which is pumped along the royal arteries. The editor of *Burke's Peerage*, the guidebook to the British aristocracy, specifies, to precise percentage points, the nationality of the royal corpuscles. In his book *Her Majesty the Queen*, Hugh Montgomery-Massingberd claims that Prince William of Wales, thanks to his mother's British blood, 'will eventually become the most 'British' sovereign since James I with 58.8 percent British blood (and 4.69 percent American)' (1986, p.233).

The precise claims about 'their' difference from 'us' are beside the general point. What matters is that the talk about royalty and its past can easily turn to talk about purity and blood. The concept of royalness makes this identification of blood matter-of-fact: it is unremarkable to talk of the royal blood line and to grade it in terms of purity. No-one objected when this was done in the conversations. Each claim about the national characteristics of royal blood rests upon a general assumption that blood can sensibly be spoken of in this way. To say that the royal blood is not wholly English is to assume the reality of the notion of 'English' blood – of the possible 'purity' of national blood. Even the 'radical' critic of inherited privilege found himself speaking in this way.

The claims about 'them' are double-claims, for 'we' are indicated too. The whispers about the foreignness of royalty bear an even quieter whisper about 'ourselves'. The critical father suggested that 'they' are not *true* English (interview 2). The wife talked about 'their' mixed blood (interview 60). There was a presumption of the possibility of unmixed, pure blood. In this way, the racist illusions of modern nationalism are being gently carried along in the royal parade.

V. Good

For the most part, these whispers – these susurrations of race – are unrealised possibilities, their themes undeveloped with the talk of royalness. However, in one aspect, the racial element is being realised, at least by a number of English people. In the dialectic of similarity and dissimilarity, occasionally the issue of skin colour was raised. There was no wish for the possibility that 'they', by dint of marriage, might come to have darker skins than 'us'. The desire to prevent this from occurring was expressed, but not entirely directly. Instead, the desires of the Queen were imagined. A mother and daughter were discussing whether a royal would be allowed to marry a non-white (interview 56). They were convinced that the Queen would forbid Prince Edward, should he wish to do so. 'Oh dear I doubt it', said the mother, a cleaner in her forties, 'they would...scrub the poor devil to get it clean'. A distinction between inner blood and outer appearance was made: 'You know, they'll marry different nationalities, but coloured no'. They used to marry 'into other Royal Families, didn't they'. She repeated herself: 'I think they'd scrub them to get them clean, bleach them'. 'I don't think the Queen would like it', said her sixteen year old daughter, a factory worker, 'I think she would put a stop to it'.

A middle-class family was claiming that the Royal Family had carefully vetted Prince Charles's choice of bride (interview 41). 'He's dictated to, as to who he can fall in love with and get married', commented the father. An unsuitable partner would not have been permitted. 'I don't think he would have married a black girl either', said the younger son. 'Oh, no', said the mother. 'Or a Chinese girl', said the younger son. 'Or a Greek', laughed the older son mischievously.

The speakers' own selves have dropped out of these conversations. *They* are not seeking to exclude blacks from the family upon the throne: it is the Queen not liking the possibility. They are confident of her wishes. The ingredients of projection are here. There is the racist desire that the idealised national family should be white. Then, there is the social pressure against articulating such racist themes directly (Barker, 1981; Billig, 1988c; Potter and Wetherell, 1988; van Dijk, 1987). There is the attribution of the wish to another person: the Queen. She would prevent the undesired out- come. And then there is the silence. No criticisms of this projected wish are to be heard.

More than this, the Queen is defended: she is not racist, so it is said. A husband, wife and her father all agreed that Prince Edward would not be allowed to marry 'a coloured person' (interview 29). The husband, a market researcher, said that 'if they found out he was involved with a coloured person, then I think she would slowly go out of the limelight, inasmuch as she would be approached and told to leave him alone'. They agreed with the grandfather that it wasn't prejudice: 'I don't think the Queen would be prejudiced'.

It would all be hushed up, said the school care-taker: 'Before it even got to holding hands...they'd be shipped abroad or some-where out of the way' (interview 60). He went on: 'I don't think it would happen, not because they're racist; I'm not saying they're racist, you know, because they do mix with the (.) um; I can't see it myself; I don't know why'.

He couldn't say why. How could royalty be racist? They mixed with the 'um'. Perhaps he too mixed with the 'um'. If royalty were accused of prejudice at this point, then the defence would collapse. The wish to exclude non-whites from entering the royal line, and from reproducing royal progeny, would be revealed as racist. With-out the defence, then the possibility of non-whites upon the national throne would have to be entertained, even if only in conversation.

There is another theme. The hesitancies of the son and his claims of ignorance ('I don't know why') speak eloquently of what is not being spoken (interview 60). His wife agrees with him, but her words give the game away: 'It's the public image, it's what's ex-pected of the royals'. 'Yeah, that's it, it's imagery, yeah', he replied, pleased that the mystery was being solved. He added: 'it wouldn't look right in the public eye'. Not marrying dark-skinned Britons was expected of the royals. Who is doing the expecting is left vague. The speakers talk about the public's eyes. They do not identify their own eyes as part of the public's eyes. Black-skinned citizens are invisible in this depiction of the 'public', which is demanding an image of the white-skinned royalty.

Once more, the royal image is put forward as the reality. The existence of desire – the public's desire, their own desire – is denied.

107

It's the public image, says the wife. Yes, he agrees. Realities must adjust to the image. If royals are to be figures of identification in whom ordinary people can recognise themselves, then these Britons are saying they could only recognise themselves, and recognise their nation, in figures as pale as themselves. A white 'we' rules out the possibility of being the subjects of a non-white monarch.

There is a projection within a projection. The desire to project the correctly pale image is projected on to the Queen, and then it is projected back onto the public. Queen and public are imagined to want the same image. Her gaze and the public's gaze are mirror images: each is imagined to be a pale reflection of the other.

HANGING ON TO ROYALTY

The question 'Who should be family?' is no less pertinent than 'Who should be royal?'. It is easy to dismiss the question as being so obvious that a reply is unnecessary. Talking of the similarity between 'them' and 'us', a mother said, 'Every normal family has its arguments', as if the notion of a 'normal family' were entirely natural (interview 23). Anthropologically, families can come in a multiplicity of forms, but people talking about the Royal Family have a particular form of family in mind. It was not the complex family structure which royal genealogists delight in tracing and whose interconnecting web of lines can be found on the inside cover of many popular books on royalty. That is not the sort of family which is required as an object of identification. Instead, it is something much closer to home – something which the ordinary person can identify as 'normal'. Edward Shorter, in his history of the modern family, described the nuclear family as 'a state of mind rather than a particular kind of structure or set of household arrangements' (1975, p.204). This state of mind can be seen in the way that the Royal Family is talked about.

The matter can be approached obliquely, by considering a category of royals, who, virtually without dissent, were the object of criticism. These were the 'hangers-on'. The phrase was used across generation and class. Royalists and critics alike could complain about 'hangers-on', who were royals thought to be receiving rich payments undeservedly. They were 'scroungers' – the objects of a moral anger, which is more often directed against those located at the lower ends of the social stratum (Edelman, 1977; Golding and Middleton, 1982; Taylor-Gooby, 1983). However, as will be seen, the category of hangers-on was not a simple moral category; it implied the nuclear family as a state of mind.

In essence, the hangers-on were accused of getting something for nothing. A retired cleaner complained about those who might be 'thirtieth in line' or whatever (interview 47). 'What do they do for the country?', she asked rhetorically. A secretary in her forties said: there should be support for 'the Queen and her family, but I think a lot of the others are just hangers-on, that really could make their own way' (interview 26). A twenty-six year old clerk was talking about the value of royalty: 'I think the Royal Family, the immediate family, are great for the country, bringing lots of money in, etcetera, etcetera, but I think that after that they tend to be hangers-on' (interview 62). He went on to specify: 'I draw the line at the Queen's sons and daughters, that's where I draw the line'. His girlfriend agreed. He continued: 'I say only the immediate family as far as I'm concerned...people like the dukes can very well look after themselves'.

There might be debate where the line was to be drawn, but not that a line should be so drawn. A lorry driver specified that only 'the immediate Royal Family' should be kept 'in the monies we pay in taxes' (interview 57). The family discussed who constituted the 'immediate family'. The Queen, said the father. Prince Philip, said the older daughter. 'Charles', they all agreed; 'because he's next in line to the throne' said the mother. The Prince's brothers and sisters also, said the eighteen year old daughter. 'Why?', asked the father, 'they're quite capable of going out to work like you and me'. They also argued about Princess Margaret. The line would not be easy to draw. Other families also discussed the same problem. The details might differ, but there was broad agreement about the principle: the 'immediate family' was to be distinguished from the hangers-on. The mother, who was talking at work with her daughter, defined 'the hangers-on' as 'the extended family' (interview 23). The immediate family would include the monarch and her children, as well as the future monarch's children. And, of course, the monarch's mother.

Loyalists could agree with critics on this issue of 'hangers-on'. A young, left-wing husband argued against monarchy in general. More specifically, he complained that 'we' are supporting 'so many members' of the Royal Family (interview 53). He said: 'We're supporting cousin of cousin of cousin of cousin'. His traditionalist mother-in-law was in accord for once. 'That's right now', she interrupted, 'I agree with you there, Stephen'.

Another critic of royalty was doing argumentative battle with his family (interview 41). His mother was citing the hard work of Princess Anne. This was money well earned, she said. '*You* wouldn't do it, Robert', she challenged her son; 'Bet you, bet you', she taunted. And he conceded: 'No, I probably wouldn't'. The argument was not over. Robert came back gamely: 'It's all these hangers-on that get on my nerves, all the dukes and duchesses and all the earls'. No longer was he isolated. The conversation hummed with expressions of agreement.

The criticism of hangers-on can implicitly justify the royals who are being hung on to. By indicating the undeserving royals, the speakers are implying that others, the more centrally royal, are deserving. In consequence, critics, complaining of the 'hangers-on', can find themselves implicitly tolerating the central royals. This is achieved through the notion of 'the family'.

If hangers-on are defined in terms of their family position, then hard-working meritorious, minor royals would still be classified as 'hangers-on' if they received payments. The disabled ex-upholsterer was complaining about 'all these hangers-on' (interview 15). Amongst the hangers-on, he listed the Duchess of Kent. 'She does a lot of good work', he said. But still he wouldn't pay her. The same thought was expressed by the father, whose precious meeting with the Duchess was described in the previous chapter (interview 3). The royal job was only for 'the close Royal Family'. Sadly he would exclude even the most admirable of the royals from the payroll.

The nuclear family as a state of mind is evident in such talking. The royal job was only required of the 'immediate family', regardless of whether its members were suited to the task, and regardless of whether there were better equipped royals on the outer fringes. Distant relatives might be touched by royal blood, and by the talent to do the royal job; but still there should be no royal job for them and certainly no royal payment. They were not part of that family, which is to be 'our' object of identification. The genealogies, which aristocratic families preserve and whose scope lies beyond the ordinary family, were irrelevant. The image of the family, whose role is to set the image of family behaviour, is a reflection of 'our' family structure, or, rather, of the family structure which 'we' imagine to be 'natural' for 'us'. Thus, the Royal Family, in order to create the right image of the family, is to be created in 'our' image.

110

THE GOLDEN STANDARD

A moral anger was evident in the talk about dukes and earls, or cousins of cousins, getting something for nothing. The language of doing jobs invites such anger, for it expresses a morality of work. The hangers-on were offending this ethic: they were accused of receiving wages without working or, at best, for working at a job which they should not be doing. Similarly, there is a continuing potential for anger to be directed against the central royals. The Queen and her family might be praised for doing an excellent job, but the praise would turn to criticism, should the job not be done. This much was made clear, again and again.

The royal job was to set standards, or to give the image of setting standards. As such, said one father, it was 'part of the job' that 'they have to behave themselves' (interview 3). It was like a contract of employment. A mother spoke as if the contract stipulated privileges in return for the public display of moral responsibility (interview 23). The royals had all 'the material things of life' and 'they' could do the very things 'that we'd love to do'. But there were restrictions; 'their' life was 'governed by rules and regulations' and 'that's probably why they're given the privileges'. And that was why 'we pay them'.

'If you have the advantage of either being royal or attached to the Royal Family by marriage', said a sixty-six year old wife, 'I think you have to keep up a higher standard' (interview 37). A younger woman made the same point, when, having criticised the Duchess of York, she praised the Princess Royal: 'I mean they've got a duty to us, haven't they really...I mean, they can't be silly because, well, I mean, we're sort of paying to keep them in that lifestyle' (interview 10). 'We' want a return for 'our' payment: 'I mean they owe us such a lot really'. 'They', the so-called objects of identification, have a duty to 'us'. 'They' are in 'our' debt.

If the debt is not paid, then there are intimations of threat. The menace could be heard in the comment of the wife quoted earlier: if royalty lost their respectability, people would start demanding abolition (interview 30). As another mother said, people would start wondering 'Why are we paying for this, when they're not doing anything' (interview 31). A fifty-two year old salesman made a similar warning (interview 26): 'The public money doesn't support them to just do what they want...they are paid public money for doing public duties really, rather than pursuing their own enjoyment'. So much the better for 'them' that 'they' put duty first: 'If

Charles had been a sort of chinless wonder, and just playing polo and drinking and generally haring after divorcées, I think that would help accelerate public opinion against him'.

Themes of personal and class morality were entwined: chinless wonders and polo-players were idle aristocrats. The threat was clear from this self-employed salesman – a bourgeois who must pay his own way in life. A higher standard of morality was being demanded of 'them', because this was 'their' job. And 'they' were paid handsomely for the job. There was a moral economy based upon a gold standard. Gold, which glitters beyond the scope of common dreams, is to be paid in exchange for a golden standard of conduct.

Respondents could talk as if the maintenance of general morality depended upon the examples to be set by royals. Bagehot, too, wrote in this vein, when he described the Crown as the centre of 'our' morality. However, the setting of standards by royalty, far from being the source of morality, is itself subject to the moral economy of jobs. Theirs is a morality within a morality. 'They' must set 'their' standards, or else there will be anger. Then, 'they' will be faced with redundancy. Thus, the figures of the super-ego are unmasked as employees. Or so it seems.

The golden standard, caught within the wider morality of jobs, is not without its ambiguities. A golden standard of conduct is not required so much as the image of a golden standard. Even this is not quite accurate. As was mentioned, people are not demanding moral perfection. There are common-places to excuse the lapses. 'They' are only human, it can be said; 'they' will show all-too-human failings. Their weaknesses can be endearing. Mental illnesses, speech impediments, occasional flashes of impatience – they all go to show that the high and mighty are reassuringly not quite so high and mighty.

There was one fault which was not to be condoned. 'They' must be seen to be earning 'their' golden payment. Taking the money and living a life of immoral luxury was inexcusable. There were no 'but they're only human' mitigations to counter this possibility. The retired fitter was fierce in his condemnation of certain royals: 'I mean, like Fergie and her husband and Princess Margaret's kids and all that, I mean, all they're out for is a good time' (interview 52). Neither he nor his wife added a familiar common-place of mitigation. Just being out for a good time was a serious offence. It affronted the morality of work.

The 'touch of hypocrisy' must be understood in terms of this moral economy. Royals, who might be presenting the public image of morality, while leading an immoral private life, would be performing the job of presenting images. Not to bother with the image – just to be out for a good time – was to show contempt for the morality of earning wages: it would be grounds for dismissal. The desired image is not that of perfect morality, but it is the image of working hard to produce the right image.

If 'they' are to deserve 'their' golden wages, then 'they' must be imagined to be working hard at a job, whose demands are beyond the ordinary. There has already been mention of the family discussing whether the Prince of Wales could have married a woman with a sexual past (interview 42). 'They' have to set a standard, the family agreed. Perhaps it would be alright, said the wife, if they did things 'on the quiet' but behaved differently in public. It was at this very point when the husband made his remark about the royal life – 'It's a very hard life'. A payroll clerk said: 'it must be a bloody hard job to do, I wouldn't like it' (interview 32). On what grounds the job is imagined to be so hard – so bloody hard – will be discussed in the next chapter. That it must be so imagined is demanded by the cynical terms of the moral economy. An easy job would not justify the golden wages.

THE PREMISE OF ROYALNESS

All this suggests that there is neither a simple, nor static, 'structure of identification'. Instead, there are complex patterns of ascribed similarities and differences. The patterns shift, so that there are continual royal dilemmas and controversies. How similar should their conduct be to ours? How different? The matter is not settled, but it is there to be argued about in future editions of the morning papers.

Nevertheless, there are regularities in the ascribed patterns. Most importantly, there is an absence of deference. 'They' should set superior examples, but 'we' need not follow. And 'we' sympathise if 'their' standards fall short of perfection – 'they' are human, just like 'us', after all. This similarity is affirmed, as 'they' are said to inhabit two familiar worlds: 'they' belong to the worlds of family and work. In this way, 'they' are not being construed as differently superior persons, to whom deference is due.

There is much that can be said about 'their' similarities with 'us', for the language of equality is ready to use. Nevertheless, throughout, there is a background assumption of difference. They are marked by an element of 'royalness', which distinguishes 'them' from 'us' and which uniquely qualifies 'them' for 'their job of image-making'. However, this element of royalness is hardly articulated – it is almost an empty category, which can only be revealed indirectly through images of royal behaviour. Royalness is not derived from God's grace. Sometimes it appears as a characteristic of biology and blood. Perhaps it is expressed automatically in the universal habit of not calling the Queen familiarly by her first name. There is Philip, Margaret, Charles and Diana but no Elizabeth – only 'the Queen'. This is a habit which no participant commented upon and none avoided. Royalness, being taken for granted, is beyond belief or disbelief. People do not talk about believing or disbelieving that the Windsors are royal, or that the Queen is queen. Critics may dispute whether 'we' want the Royal Family, but they do not question that the family *is* royal. That is the premise of the common-sense talk of royalty.

As always, the unspoken elements of ideology are as significant as those which are loudly voiced. In Chapter 2, comparisons were to be heard between 'our' nation and other nations. Monarchy was an essential difference, and a notion of the genuineness of 'our' monarchy was invoked. The reality of 'our' monarchy – 'our' imagined tradition and unbroken biological line – put 'us' above other nations, including those nations with their own, less 'real', monarchies. However, this line of argumentation, with its implications of superiority and inferiority, is not turned inwards. There is a virtual silence about royalness, when 'we' compare ourselves with 'them'. Possessing a Royal Family, with 'real' royalness, might put 'us', the British, above others, the foreigners; but this royalness is not said to put 'them', the royals, above 'us', the commoners.

In fact, the reverse thought is openly expressed. Chapter 3 discussed the common demand that 'they' should not think themselves superior to 'us'. Cynical jokes were to be told by the loyally royalist, bringing 'them' down to earth. The fantasy is to meet 'them' on an informal, equal footing. Differences between 'them' and 'us' are expressed through the equalising language of jobs: they have a special job, a difficult job, one of the hardest in the world of public relations. But as the specialness of the job is indicated, so is its similarity to other jobs. Yet, the premise for the jokes, for the

114

meetings and for talk about the 'job' itself is the premise of royalness – a premise of inequity.

It is as if the ordinary language of the democratic world leaves little to be said about royalness. The modern subjects, not wishing to imagine themselves as subjects, have a gap in their imagining of royalty. Sometimes the gap could be concealed by a reversal of the conditions of inequity. This ideological reversal is to be heard in the language of jobs, which implies a world of employees and employers. When applied to royalty, it has a surprising result. 'We' are imagining 'ourselves' to be in the position of command. 'We' are the employers – 'they' are in our debt. 'We' possess the gold, which 'we' pay 'them' for duties performed. 'We' talk of repossessing 'our' gold, should the royal product become alloyed. In these imaginings, 'we' are no longer subjects, but 'they' are subject to 'us'. In separate homes, for which mortgages and rents are being paid, the poor and modestly middle-class imagine that they are employing the wealthiest family in the land. In so imagining, they affirm the wider ethics of employment and inequality.

V .
Good .

5

SETTLING ACCOUNTS

The former British Prime Minister, Margaret Thatcher, once claimed that 'an overwhelming number of people in the nation regard the Royal Family as the greatest asset that the United Kingdom has and greatly admire everything it does' (*Observer*, 21 October 1990). Certainly, the public opinion polls support the first half of Thatcher's statement. As for admiring greatly everything that the Royal Family does, there is little evidence of this. In the talk about royalty as a job, there was a noticeable undercurrent of hostility. There were frequent complaints against 'hangers-on' and against royals not thought to be earning their money; there were threats about the consequences if the royal output failed to meet desired standards. The economic moralism, which demands value for money and which Mrs Thatcher herself so prominently advocated during her premiership, does not halt at the palace walls in a posture of blind admiration.

There is no denying that admiration exists, but so does criticism. Moreover, admiration can so easily flip over into criticism. This is illustrated by the tabloid press, especially those sections who greatly admired almost everything which Mrs Thatcher's government did. In early October 1988, the *Sun*, owned by Rupert Murdoch and uncritically supporting the Conservative administration, was glowing with joy at the birth of a new princess. To mark the occasion, it had published its special *Souvenir Royal Album*: 'From William the Conqueror to the Duchess of York's new baby – the complete story of our illustrious Royal Family, told in living detail'. The *Album*, in its history of monarchy, gave extra mention to 'The Wonderful Windsors'. The celebratory mood of admiration, continued, as the paper printed a 'scoop' photo: 'Exclusive! Fergie Baby With Her

Two Grannies' (13 October 1988). The photograph had been a private one and the Palace threatened the newspaper with legal action. The mood of the *Sun* suddenly changed. The Windsors were not quite so wonderful. The front page of 17 October contained an editorial, headlined 'Queen Clicks Her Fingers And The Cops Come Running'. The text, using a populist rhetoric, introduced a historical theme, not to be found in the 'complete' history of the *Souvenir Royal Album*. The paper cited parliament's historic struggles against monarchy, claiming that today's government 'is dedicated in bringing greater democratic power to the people'. In an oblique reference to the Glorious Revolution of 1688, the editorial claimed that one thing had not changed in three hundred years: 'The power of the richest families; the dominance of those born with a whole canteen of silver spoons in their mouths'. No longer were the royals wonderfully royal, but they were powerfully rich (see Billig, 1990b, for a detailed analysis of the episode).

This sort of quick shift indicates a royalism in which the possibility of resentment is continually present, even at moments of celebration. A sudden brush against royalty, and populist hostility against social superiors can spill out. If the surface of admiration is scratched, even superficially, then the angry cry of economic moralism can be heard. In this cry, there is something other than the uncritical admiration, which Mrs Thatcher, following Bagehot, depicts as the view of the masses, but which neither she nor Bagehot shares.

The question is not what might provoke such an outburst of populist anger, but how resentment is more usually contained. The unmasking of the super-ego is relevant here. According to Freud, the super-ego solves the problem of envy by providing an object for identification. Were it not for identification, so his argument went, the ordinary person would envy leaders for their powers of authority and for their privileges. Freud argued that 'what was originally envy' is psychologically transformed into hero-worship. Envy is repressed from consciousness and there is a 'reversal of what was first a hostile feeling into a positively toned tie in the nature of an identification' ('Group psychology and the analysis of the ego', pp.120–1). As a result, leaders, who might have been envied for their superior position, become transformed into figures, whose every act is greatly admired.

If the super-ego is unmasked, then the problem of envy reappears. There are no psychological forces to inhibit the expression of jealousy against the figureheads. No sense of guilt attends the sneers against royal privilege – especially if a tabloid newspaper equates its own interests with those of the government and can self-righteously see itself continuing parliament's historic battles against powerful sovereigns.

Envy depends upon comparisons, for the jealous person compares his or her own lot with that of the envied figure. This aspect is stressed in modern psychological theories of 'social comparison', whereby individuals and groups are said to compare themselves with other individuals and groups (Hogg and Abrams, 1988; Tajfel, 1981; Tajfel and Turner, 1985). For these comparisons, people tend to select others who are considered to be similar to themselves. If people feel comparatively, or 'relatively', deprived, then anger, and even rebellion, is likely (Gurr, 1970; Smith and Gaskell, 1990; Taylor and Moghaddam, 1987). According to such psychological theories, comparisons are unlikely to made against those who are accepted as superior. If royals are so considered, then they will be protected against envy. As Francis Bacon wrote in his essay 'On Envy', subjects do not envy their monarchs, because they see royals to be so elevated: 'Kings are not envied but by kings' (1906, p.26).

Once royals are seen to be familiar figures, 'just like us', then conditions for comparison, and thereby for envy, are opened up. The common-places of 'jobs' invite 'us' to compare 'ourselves' with 'them': 'they' do 'jobs', so do 'we'; 'they' behave like 'us', but 'they' should behave better; but 'we' understand if 'they' don't. The potential for envy is there, in ways which Bacon would not have predicted four hundred years ago. The economic moralism, which demands value for investment, can utter aloud in the cause of morality: why should 'they' have 'their' canteen of silver spoons when 'we' have so little? Cynicism might strip away majesty; it might unmask the super-ego. Having done that, it must contain those envious impulses, which are part of itself. There must be other thoughts and expressions to settle down the ordinary person into the ordinary life. There is an ideological job of settlement to be done.

THEIR CREDITS/OUR DEBITS

In the previous chapter, respondents could be heard to talk about the royal job as if a contract had been made: there were privileges exchanged for duties. A balancing of calculations is indicated. Such a calculating mentality is depicted in psychological theories, which

118

view moral judgements as being the products of calculations of 'equity'. Costs and losses are said to be computed, in a desire to see that an equitable balance of morality is attained in the world (Folger, 1986; Martin, 1986; Walster *et al.*, 1976). As regards the royal job, there was the gold standard to be calculated: golden payments in return for golden conduct, or, rather, in return for the image of golden conduct. 'Their' job, it was heard, might be well paid, but it was an unreasonably hard job to do. It is as if an equity has been accomplished and 'the just world' is realised, at least in the calculator's mind (Lerner, 1975 and 1980). Nevertheless, before examining the claims about debits and credits, two preliminary points need to be made about the general argument of this chapter. Both points, it is hoped, will be supported by later illustrations from the family discussions.

First, the calculations about debits and credits are not merely calculations: in fact, in a strict sense, they are not even calculations. In Chapter 2, the 'tourist argument' was discussed. This argument appeared to be based upon economic calculations: the cost of keeping a monarchy was financially outweighed by the income from tourists, or so it was commonly claimed. However, no actual calculations were involved. Moreover, the claims involved more than a financial balance-sheet: the claims also depicted the social world, or, to be more precise, they depicted a view of Britain's unique place within the world. Similarly, the calculations about 'their' pay involve depictions: 'their' life and the rigours of 'their' job are imagined. In fact, the depictions of 'their' life fix the outcome of the uncalculated calculations.

Second, there is double-declaiming. The claims about 'them' and 'their life' are double-edged: they also carry claims about 'our' lives – 'our' credits and 'our' debits. In this double-declaiming, envy is kept at bay. The uncalculated calculations of common-sense's double-declaiming can be used to compare 'their' misfortunes with 'our' gains. A little bit of envy – a little bit of sympathy – a joke here and a joke there – and ordinary people settle themselves down, expressing satisfaction with their ordinary versions of the good life. Speakers are to be heard depicting the pleasures of 'ordinary life' in general, and affirming, in a personal way, the credits of their own particular lives.

To begin with, the envious theme can be heard quite directly. Royalty has privileges, or credits, which mirror the debits of 'our' lives. The comparisons between 'them' and 'us' were evident in the comments of the keenly royalist mother, quoted in the previous chapter, who said that royalty has 'a better life...they have the material things of life and probably things that we'd love to do' (interview 23). 'Their' life is not a *good* life, in an absolute sense, but it is a *better* life than 'ours'. At least, it is better in a material sense; 'they' have opportunities to do the things which 'we' would like to do. She was speaking these words of comparison without anger. And certainly without shame.

The wealth of royalty is so incomparably greater than ordinary income that a comparison can be humorous. A fireman was talking about the royal way of life, when his wife interrupted to ask: 'Well, is the Queen the richest women in the world?' (interview 22). Her two sons answered together: 'Second richest'. 'Who's the richest, then?', asked their mother. There was a pause. 'Well, it ain't mum, I can tell you that', said the father. 'No', she said laughing, 'it's not me'.

But comparisons were not entirely ridiculous, for the credits in the royal life could be specified, as implicit reversals of the debits of ordinary life. The mother's question about wealth had interrupted the father as he was imagining the benefits of the royal life: 'I don't imagine Prince Philip goes out with a great thick wad of £20 notes in his back pocket, when he just happens to be hopping about the place'. The Queen's husband is spared all the bother of 'going to fill the car with petrol and having to write a cheque, because you've not got enough cash to do it'. The father went on: 'I've never seen the Queen in Asda (the local supermarket), doing the weekly shopping, or Prince Philip trudging around with a trolley'. He wasn't being envious, he stressed: 'I just accept that they are apart from it, and they are entitled to it and that's their way'. As he accepted 'their way', he was depicting his own life's discontents. He had the irritation of paying for his own petrol. He was to be seen trudging around the supermarket with trolley and wife. That was his life, revealed in his remarks about 'them'.

People can read into the royal life the negation of their own particular discontents. Those who are worried about money, can look to the immense wealth of royalty. Those concerned about their jobs, can regard the securities of the royal job. What 'they' have as privilege is what 'we' lack – and, in particular, what 'I' personally lack.

A test plant engineer in his late forties said that royals were free from the worry of having to make their own way in the world (interview 27). He spoke as a man who had left school without qualifications but, through the efforts of night-school study, had risen into the professional middle-class. He now worried about career prospects for his teenage children. His wife had just made a comparison, suggesting that Prince Philip, 'a nice man', had the 'normal responsibility' for family matters, just like 'we've got with ours'. Her husband responded, pointing out how the royal life was enviably different: 'They've got no problems about think-ing...(about) the children, getting them the right education (and) a job at the end'. Working towards such an end was 'the major sort of thing that...young people channel their efforts into'. He continued about young people: for 'so much of their life, they're really on the treadmill' and they've got to be 'keeping their heads down to try to achieve something'. He knew about all that, but the royals didn't: 'They have their job in life'. 'They' need not strive for qualifications, fearful of failure. He was speaking about the royal privilege in front of his two daughters. There was an implicit exhortation, lest his children relax upon the serious treadmill of bourgeois life.

Such themes were absent when a working-class family, living in a semi-detached council house, specified the credits of the royal way of life (interview 39). They were concerned with the disciplines of today's toil, rather than with the acquisition of qualifications for the future. The young daughter-in-law, who had previously worked in a factory but now looked after her small baby, was talking of the royal advantages. 'Their lifestyle', she said, 'is completely different to ours'. She continued her comparison, indicating her own lifestyle: 'They don't know what it's like to get up at six in the morning, work in a factory'. Her husband, a twenty-three year old plumber in a factory, agreed that 'they' didn't 'do a hard graft job': 'theirs' wasn't physically demanding work. His mother, then, mentioned the hardships of the royal life. She said that the royals couldn't relax in the evenings with their feet up in front of the television. She continued, without irony, claiming that 'they' might 'have to go out to a banquet'.

Within this same family, differences of discontent could be heard, as males and females double-declaimed about their lives and royal lives. Husband and daughter-in-law were in agreement as they countered the mother. 'No', said the father, 'what we're saying is, what we're talking about is graft, about working for your money, right'. His daughter-in-law was speaking at the same time: 'We're talking about working, cooking and cleaning, hoovering, ironing, polishing'. It was said as if they were speaking with one voice: 'what we're saying...what we're talking about'. But it was two voices: a male and a female voice.

121

The father was only talking of the hard graft in the factory – about physical work, masculine work. His daughter-in-law indicated factory work too, but she had additional grafts, about which his voice was silent. She continued about the royals: 'They ain't got to worry about getting home to the dinner'. The mother did not deny that this was hard work. The father continued to talk of the pressures of 'the normal man in the street'. He was silent about the pressures on the 'normal woman', rushing through streets after work in order to prepare the dinner for the normal man in the street.

If royalty's job is to present the image of the idealised family, then others can read their own discontents into this well-paid idealisation. Women, in particular, can note the absence of domestic labour and daily harassment. Wouldn't it be lovely, declared a mother, who worked as a domestic assistant, to be 'waited on hand and foot' like the royals (interview 57). Royals have nannies for 'their' children, said a mother, an ex-teacher: 'It must be lovely when you've got little babies just to have a bit of help' (interview 25). She went on to say that 'they're very demanding, babies and children...you get so tired'. People say about royalty '"How fresh they look", and I think: well, they've not had to get up in the morning and do the jobs I have to do before I get ready and go out, and worrying what are we having for tea...all they've got to worry about is whether they look decent'. Again, a comparison between their job and 'the jobs that I have to do' enables the envious thought to be said.

Ann, a single parent, was talking with her two married friends, Lynn and Sue (interview 54). They were discussing whether royals did 'ordinary things', such as having baked beans on toast for their evening meals. The speakers' own lives were continually present as they talked of 'them' and 'their' privileges. 'It would be nice', said Sue, 'having somebody else prepare food *for* you'. 'Oh, I'd love that', said Ann. 'Tastefully decorated and sit at a long table; it'd be great', commented Lynn. Sue continued: 'So you could just sit down and have somebody bring your food to you and feed the children; the nanny feeds the children'. 'And wipes the mess up', laughed Ann, 'yes I'd like that'. 'You sit there', said Sue, 'and you eat your meal, they drop it on the floor and somebody else cleans it up; I think that would be wonderful'.

Men tended not to stress this aspect of royal life, but, there again, royalty is unlikely to be envied for what is already enjoyed. Such assumptions were occasionally expressed openly. A fifty-nine year old mother said she'd like to be waited on like royalty (interview

58). Her teenage son then commented that it wouldn't make much difference to him: 'That's what mum does now'. 'He don't do nothing', retorted his widowed mother, 'he don't do a thing...I says to him "Just nip up and dust your shelves where your model cars are", and he don't'. A young dental nurse was talking about royalty's servants. Her boyfriend, with whom she lived, a twenty-six year old clerk, made a comment about servants. She laughed: 'Well, you've got me anyway, you've already got one' (interview 62).

As speakers talk about the royal privileges, they can express wishes which reverse the realities of their own personal lives. The women, who talk of royalty's leisured and graceful meals, are indicating their cramped kitchens – noise, children and the mess of baked beans. If a father envies royalty for the security of its profession, then he offers a glimpse of his own life's efforts. Similarly, when a young wife details the domestic tasks, which royalty escapes (the polishing, the hoovering, the cleaning etc.), she is reciting, before the men of her family, the tasks which fall upon her within the family house.

In this, the general themes of common-sense become personalised for individual use. It is as if common-sense provides a general coupon to be filled in by individual speakers to match their own personal requirements. This hypothetical coupon is like the entry forms for those competitions to be found in popular magazines and on tinned food labels: Write down what you would like best about being a royal and what you would like least; don't forget to add your name and address; fill in the coupon immediately and you could win the prize of being contented with your lot.

However, the answers are not entirely personal, and the personal selves are not entirely individual. Roland Barthes (1983) wrote that 'in each sign sleeps that monster: a stereotype' (p.461). The speakers, in making their claims about royal privileges, are using stereotypes of ordinary lives. Whether it is an image of baby-minding, purchasing petrol or rising early for the factory, these are ordinary activities because they are commonly shared. Each particular credit and debit is presented as having a wider application. Speakers know that others, in their turn, will identify their lives in the stereotype. As the three women spoke of royal meals, they recognise each other's lives and they are aware of this shared recognition. With their specific examples of dropped food and nannies, they are doing something general. They are constructing a metonym for those ordinary discontents, which royalty is enviably recognised to avoid.

SETTLING THE CREDITS AND DEBITS

If matters were left there, then envy of the royal way would be uncontained. In the absence of a super-ego, rhetorical means are required to contain the jealous wish. There are other coupons to be completed. Common-sense provides counter-arguments, which are to be recalled when the talk drifts to the royal credits. Those quoted in the previous section had more claims to make about 'their' and 'our' lives. There was an 'on-the-other-hand' – a common-sensical debit – to be added to the royal credits. This debit reflected an entry in the column of credits for 'our' ordinary lives.

As the columns of credits and debits are summed, so the accounts are settled to arrive at the conclusion that there is a 'just-world', at least so far as royals and commoners are concerned. 'Their' credits are well earned, and 'our' debits accepted. The conclusion is that the ordinary life, despite its debits, is really the good life. But the conclusion is also the premise of the calculations. Thus, there might be the outward rhetoric of computation – as if credits and debits are being weighed – but there is no actual computation. The accounting is based on uncalculated calculations.

The main examples of the previous section can be taken in turn, one by one, to show how the arguments for envy met their rhetorical counter-arguments, and that envious doubt was settled down by uncalculated calculation. The first example was that of the mother talking about 'them' leading a materially better life (interview 23). Her remark had been taken from its context. The expression of envy was part of a longer statement, which denied envy. She said that royals can do the 'things we'd love to do', but this was qualified, even as it was expressed: 'but I think they're limited'. She compared 'our' life favourably with 'theirs': 'Our life is governed nine till five; you're told what your work (is)...and after that you do your own thing...But their whole life...is governed by rules and regulations, which I would absolutely hate'. Envy has lost its sting. 'They' might have material possessions and some enviable opportunities, but, these are only particulars, outweighed by the general condition of 'their' life. 'Their' whole life is a debit – a hateful debit.

A similar self-qualification of envy occurred in the second example, when the fireman was envying Prince Philip for not having to trudge around the supermarket (interview 22). In describing the royal credits, the father had specifically signalled his acceptance of the situation: 'I just accept that they are apart from it and they are entitled to it'. When the conversation had turned to money (whether the Queen was the richest woman in the world), the older son made disparaging remarks about royalty – about 'their' money and 'their' frequent holidays. Mother and father were quick to put him right: 'They don't seem to have any freedom at all', said the father. Again it was the general – a total lack of freedom – offsetting the particulars: the avoidance of supermarkets and other daily irritations. An implicit image of 'our' life as the free life was being claimed.

The same sort of self-qualification occurred when the father was envying the royals for not having to worry about the careers of 'their' children (interview 27). There was an immediate self-qualification. After the envious comparison comes the on-the-other-hand: 'But they don't just have it all nice and easy...they're in the public eye most of the time'. Each credit could be set against a debit. 'They' might have their job in life ('what they're going to do'), but they don't have the freedom to control their lives, even the freedom to step on to the treadmill: 'But, I mean, they're just, if you like, like pawns, aren't they'. The father had summed up 'their' general condition of life and added it to the debit side of the unequal equation. 'They're' *just* pawns. We, by implication, are more than pawns.

When husband and daughter-in-law had jointly been pointing out the royals' freedom from graft, hoovering and ironing, it was left to the mother to supply the settling 'on-the-other-hand' (interview 39). The mother agreed that the royal life had its desirable sides. 'But' there was more to be said. 'Oh, yeah' she said, 'but it must be hard doing what they're doing'. Now, it was the father's turn to agree and then to qualify: 'It is, yeah, but they make up for it in other ways, I mean it's swings and roundabouts'. Here seemed to be a balance: credits and debits piled up equally, rather than the whole weighing down the part.

But that was not the end of the matter. The mother continued her account of the royal hard work. More particulars were added. The royals, she pointed out, had to go to film premières. She compared this to the ordinary life of husband and daughter-in-law: 'You can turn round and say "Oh, I don't really feel like going to the pictures tonight"; if they've got a film première, they've got to go'. Not only must they go, 'but they have to stand for hours shaking hands'. And, then, the mother drew the general point: 'I mean their lives aren't their own, their lives belong to the people'. Her son accepted the point: 'Alright, it ain't their life, but it ain't a bad one'. 'It ain't bad at all', agreed his father. 'Oh no, it ain't', conceded the mother, 'I shouldn't mind a helping of it'. 'This is the point I'm trying to make', said the father.

This was their agreed point. There are enviable aspects of the royal life. On the other hand, there is also the entirety of that life. The royals don't possess their own lives; the people possess 'them'. Quietly, the double-claim is made: unlike 'them', 'we' possess 'our' own lives. Even the adamantly royalist mother – a regular attender of the Trooping of the Colour – can voice particular envies: she wouldn't mind a helping of the royal life. But, who would want a life which was not their own? The part was outweighed by the un-enviable whole. Since it was part versus whole, the calculation could remain uncalculated – the final balance had been determined in advance.

The ex-teacher made the same point (interview 25). She had said that royals don't have to look after their own children. No wonder 'they' look fresh. It wasn't quite that simple. Envy was specific. She herself wouldn't like the life, being 'gawped at and always to do the right thing'. She felt sorry for 'them'. She hoped that they had 'a life of their own'.

Previously, the quotations from the three mothers, discussing meal-times, were cut misleadingly short (interview 54). The re-construction of their conversation ended before the qualificatory 'but' had made its rhetorical entrance. They agreed how wonderful it would be to be waited upon. Lynn supplied the 'other-hand': 'I wouldn't *really* like it forever', she said, 'but for six months'. Sue disagreed, 'Oh, I'd like it forever; I can't lie, I'd love it'. 'Oh no', said Lynn, 'you'd wonder what was happening to you as a person'. Sue still disagreed: 'I'm not made for clearing up mess'. Lynn persisted: surely you wouldn't like all the media attention, she asked. This time her friend hesitated: 'Yes, I think I'd have to be selective; I'd want the servants and the, um, money, and err, I wouldn't want much else'.

Earlier, the three had been discussing the same issues. Sue had agreed with Lynn about the royal life. The money couldn't com-pensate for the general condition of the life: 'It's a very hollow existence, really, it's horrible', Lynn had said. And Sue had agreed. They might like a part: six months or evening meal-times. Sue had tried to argue for more. But she had been forced to concede that she would be selective. The whole royal life was not desired. It wasn't a 'real' existence.

Over thirty years ago, Richard Hoggart, in *The Uses of Literacy*, suggested that working-class people thought superficially about royalty, and about other social issues. They would repeat 'cracker-barrel mottoes', which were frequently contradictory one with another. At first glance, something like this might be thought to be occurring with the debiting and crediting of royal lives. There are the stereotypes of royal privilege: 'their' money, 'their' servants, 'their' holidays. These are quickly followed by the 'on-the-other-hands', which themselves are also stereotypes. Hoggart cited such clichés, which are just as familiar thirty years on: '"They don't have to struggle with the kids when they're tired out"; they're "waited on hand and foot"..."It's a rotten job", people will say, "they get pushed around as much as we do"' (1958, pp.86–7).

Nevertheless, Hoggart oversimplified on three counts. First, this way of talking is not confined to the ways that the working-class speak about royalty. Working-class people might fill in the coupon with a particular set of credits and debits. However, this matrix – the coupon itself – cuts across class; and so does the gendering of some of the replies. Second, the repetition of the common-places does not necessarily represent shallow or confused thinking. Speakers have complex ways of arguing, debating and probing the ridiculous aspects of privilege. There was no lack of thought, and certainly not of humour, in the working-class discussions.

There is a third point. This pattern of thinking has a characteristic not specifically noted by Hoggart. The dialectic of envy and sympathy is leading to an ideological settlement. The calculation between part and whole is unequal: on the whole, 'their' life is undesirable. The caption on the coupon can be read backwards: on the whole, 'our' life is desirable. In this way, the depiction of 'their' life – 'their' whole life – confines the envy and settles down the speaker with an affirmation of the desirability of 'ordinary life'.

Reference to 'their' life can be used to block the jealous thought. A young couple – he, a technician, and she, a clerk in a building society – had just moved into their own house and were talking lengthily about the whole business of home-ownership (interview 44). It had been a struggle saving for a deposit and then furnishing the house. Of course, said the girlfriend, they had been lucky, being as she worked for a building society. For other young couples, it was so much harder. The interviewer interrupted their story, to ask whether they would like to be in the position of some royals, who owned three or four large houses. The question was an invitation for the jealous thought. The girlfriend answered, by ignoring the houses – the obvious object of an envious desire for those who were struggling to own their first house. 'I don't know', she began; it might seem enviable, but 'look at their other life, I mean they're like split people, I mean the things they have to do'. The boyfriend agreed. They had answered the specific question about houses – a question inviting envy – with general statements about the whole way of royal life.

As they talked about the royal life, and its undesirable hardships, the girlfriend commented, 'I would hate to be in that position'. Of course, it would be 'nice to have all that money', but not to perform all 'the public engagements' which the royals have to do. She went on: 'I would sooner have what I've got now, if you like perhaps a little bit more; but to have to *earn* it how they do, no; I don't think they have an easy life at all'.

A twinge of jealousy is admitted; there is no need to deny the obvious desire for money. But the image of royalty, 'earning' its golden privileges, rhetorically restrains the envy. 'Their' whole life is enough to make 'us' satisfied – well, almost satisfied – with what 'I've' got. The uncalculated calculation has been made and its expression is itself an act of ideological settlement.

THE JEALOUS BONE

Common-sense does not provide an absolute matrix of thought, which is, and must be, reproduced with exactitude. Its themes are to be personalised in infinite ways to suit individual lives and desires. Also, argumentative tendencies can be reversed. As the British psychologist, Sir Frederick Bartlett, wrote, it is possible to 'turn round one's schema' (1932, p.201). The debits of one's own life can be felt to be so pressing – so filled with suffering – that the commonplace argument can be reversed. 'Our' debits can overshadow the royals' debits, which, in turn, can be overshadowed by 'their' credits. Although envy might be expressed within such accounting, the effect need not be totally unsettling. The ordinary person might not desire to lead the life of royalty; instead, he or she might wish that the balance of royal pleasures and pains should be tilted downwards to match their own sufferings.

The widow, who could not get her eighteen year old son to dust his shelves, has already been encountered (interview 58). The two of them lived together in a council house on a large estate. Money was tight. Her husband, a steel worker, had died four months previously. Her two older sons lived away. It was just the mother and her youngest son, a mechanic and part-time bouncer. Throughout the discussion, she criticised royalty and talked volubly about the hardships of her own life. As she did so, her son would disagree with a mixture of embarrassment and exasperation. At times, he interrupted to disagree. Or he would ostentatiously bury his face in his hands. Sometimes, as his mother spoke, he would mutter 'senile, senile'.

In voicing her complaints, she shuffled between the discontents of her own life and her discontent with 'them', the royals. She complained that the Royal Family were 'spongers, I think they're scroungers'. She then appeared to make a concession: the Queen was a figurehead, and 'a figurehead we have to have, I suppose'. Immediately, without prompting, she qualified her concession: 'But, again, that's for the rich'. The son interrupted: 'You've got no idea, you ain't'.

She specifically, and spontaneously, compared immediate discontents in her own life with the presumed luxuries of the royals. Small irritations could become the metonymic representation of 'their' privilege. She had been reading the local newspaper, and her hands were black with the dirt of newsprint: 'The Queen has to have hers specifically prepared, so no black goes on her fingers; I mean look at me, I've been reading *The Post*'. 'Oh, shut up about it', said her son.

At one point, they were talking about royal divorce in general and about the state of Prince Charles's marriage in particular. The son started to use the familiar argument against royal divorce: 'You've got to have someone to look up to for what's right and wrong'. His mother agreed with him, saying 'I don't believe in divorce'. Immediately, her son changed his position. In contradiction to her and to himself, he now said he believed in divorce. As for the royal couple, 'if there is something wrong then they should get a divorce'. His mother argued back. The normal state of argumentative disagreement was resumed.

As the mother said why royals should not divorce, she talked about her own marriage. '*Real* love was everlasting', she said: 'I mean love, I don't mean err, I don't mean, err, the body, lust, the passion and what have you'. The son sighed. Real love should carry you through: 'I mean, God, there's times when I could have run a knife through my old man, but, I mean you don't, you counteract it and you get over it'. Problems are bound to arise – 'jealousy arises', 'lack of faith arises', she went on. In fact, not two weeks after her own wedding, there arose an incident with a royal theme. She recounted how she and her husband had been to the cinema. The news-reel had featured an item on the young Princess Margaret. Her husband remarked that the Princess looked nice: 'I got awfully jealous, awfully mad and I stormed out the picture house and I says "Well, have her then"'. 'Senile', mumbled her son.

He said that her marriage was irrelevant to a discussion about royalty: 'Dad, what's he got to do with it?'. In order to demonstrate the irrelevance of his father, he argued generally that royal marriage was different from 'normal' marriage: 'they' have to be separated for weeks on end and 'that's not a normal marriage'. As a result, royalty was 'bound to get lonely'. One should be sympathetic about the prospect of royal divorce, he concluded. His mother disagreed. She was going to talk specifically about her 'normal' marriage. Dad had everything to do with it. In a raised voice, she let her son know that royals weren't the only ones to suffer separation:

(Interview 58)

Mother: Well, that's what happened...when your dad left me with a baby then and had to go in the army and was in the army for a year (.) two or three

Son: Well, so (.) he had to go in the army

Mother: And I was here on me own

Son: It's different

Mother: I didn't say 'Right, I'll go with another man' and he didn't say 'right, I'll go with another woman'.

Son: Right, then, well, oh God you do me head in {sighs}, you really do me head in.

The mother was arguing for the similarity between herself and royalty, denying the essential difference claimed by the son. Her ascription of similarity did not constitute an argument for an affectionate 'identification'. Quite the contrary, the similarity was part of a critical moralism. Her son needed the argument of difference in order to argue for sympathetic understanding.

However hard the son tried, he was powerless to prevent his mother from continuing her story. Her husband, after coming out of the army, worked away from home, all over the country for twelve weeks at a time ('here we go', said the son). She carried on: 'There's been times when I've wanted to scream and scream and scream because your dad's had to work away and left me with three kids'. It had been dangerous work, but he had got extra money for working beyond a height of two hundred feet: 'If he went over that, he got sixpence an hour extra, the Queen gets bloody five, ten, hundred, thousand'. The son said: 'Senile old biddy'.

The mother's own life was providing her point of criticism against royalty. Her emphasis was on the need to accept the discontents of life. She had suffered – she had put up with things. And so should 'they', the figureheads. After all, 'they' are paid so much more, without the perils of working two hundred or so feet above ground level. But 'they' don't seem to put up with things. She specified the Duchess of York and her freedom from responsibilities: 'I think they get away with blooming murder, I do'.

The language of 'getting away with things' is the same language which Sennett and Cobb (1976) noted that working men would use against 'scroungers' and the 'work-shy'. Working-men, whose lives were restricted by the demands of labour, expressed hostility against those of their own class who seemed to escape such rigours. The mother's tone might indicate envy. But it is not an envy which threatens the social order. Her voice may have been critical, even radical: royalty is for the rich. Yet, there is something essentially conservative in the criticism.

Her life-story, as she tells it, is one of acceptance. She didn't think of taking another man; nor of striking out for freedom, despite the screaming voice within her. Now that freedom has come, imposed by death, it is empty and literally impoverished. She has suffered, and she continues to suffer. So should 'they'. If 'they' are a figurehead of hedonism – representing luxurious pleasures without pains – then her own life has yet another discontent to add to its lengthy list. When she voices her anti-royal sentiments, it is not to change society, nor to create a different life for her son. It is to conserve the morality, which justified the acceptance of her own fate. Her life, depicted as a tale of suffering and self-denial, is held up as the example, which 'they' should follow.

To explain away her complaints as jealousy would do her less than justice. She was not *merely* envious, as if all her dissatisfactions stemmed from a desire to have what royalty had. Quite the reverse. She desired 'them' to share some of the deprivations, which life had forced on her. It is a variant of 'sour grapes' (Elster, 1983). She herself would deny the charge that she was being jealous. It was not 'their' privileges which she desired. She was complaining about the diamonds and expensive clothes worn by the younger members of the family. 'You're jealous', intervened the son. 'Oh God Almighty, I'm not jealous at all', she replied. 'You are', he repeats. Back came the woman, who had stormed out of a cinema when her husband praised a princess: 'I haven't got a jealous bone in my body'.

CLEANING THE ORDINARY PALACE

The widowed mother, without the jealous bone, does not wish to be royal. Nothing in her comments suggests that she personally dreams of being magicked away to become queen of the nation. In this, she resembles those other respondents, who might wish for a few of the royal privileges, but not for the whole life. The collection of dreams about royalty, assembled by Masters (1973), illustrated this too: the fantasy was to meet royalty, not to be royal. In this fantasy and in the desire for the part, and not the whole, of the royal life, there is double-declaiming: the desirability of being an ordinary person is affirmed.

The double-declaiming ensures that, as envy is contained, so the ordinary self is retained. There are further themes in this containing/ retaining. For example, there is a paradox of desire. 'We' might desire the privileges, but if 'our' wish were granted 'we' would not be 'us': 'we' would be 'them', 'we' would be privileged. Zizek (1989), in *The Sublime Object of Ideology*, reproduces a paradox of Lewis Carroll: '"I'm so glad I don't like asparagus", said the small girl to a sympathetic friend, "because, if I did, I should have to eat it – and I can't bear it"' (p.174). Imagining ourselves to have different desires is to de-imagine ourselves – it is to imagine ourselves as other than ourselves. Recalling this can stifle the envious desire, and affirm 'our' own ordinary selves.

Previously, the young couple, struggling to own their first house, were heard to dismiss being envious of the royals' large houses (interview 44). The young woman went straight to the whole royal life: it was a hard life, for which several larger houses would be poor recompense. Another common response to the question was to imagine oneself – with present routines, obligations and desires – within the royal residence. And then to laugh at the incongruity.

If asked whether they would like to live in the royal palace, respondents, especially women, would often make the same joke. The forty-one year old wife of the fireman, who herself worked as a credit controller, replied: 'Me, no, not if I'd got to clean it' (interview 22). Her husband added that he'd like 'to live in one but not have the upkeep'. Of course, actual royals wouldn't be cleaning the place themselves, but a fireman's wife, in a palace, would do so, while her husband worried whether his salary from the fire-service would cover the maintenance of castle and grounds. They were refusing to imagine themselves as anything but themselves. A housewife, who also worked as a cleaner, said: 'If you've got the cleaning to do, you'd think twice' (interview 56). And the second thought was to affirm herself as herself.

By playing with the paradox, respondents are cancelling the envious desire. 'I' would like the house, but 'I' wouldn't like to be the sort of person who owns such a house; therefore 'I' wouldn't like the house. Sometimes the themes were unpacked, as laughter alternated with seriousness. A disabled ex-upholsterer and his wife, both in their early fifties, were asked by the interviewer whether they would want to live like the Queen in a big house (interview 15). 'No', answered the wife straight away, 'I wouldn't fancy cleaning it, I've got enough to keep this clean'. Laughter. The interviewer persisted: 'But you'd have the servants wouldn't you?' 'Oh, I couldn't sit down for long', the wife replied, 'I should have to get up with my duster and do something'.

Next, it was the husband's turn to take the serious joke seriously: 'You've got to be bred for that'. His wife agreed. He continued: 'You know, you've got to be bred into where servants are given orders and what-not, telling them what-not'. It wasn't his breeding, his life. The interviewer asked him whether he would want to live in the palace with the servants. No, he said, that was not how he had 'been brought up, because I'd be out with the boys'. He would be down the pub, and royalty isn't supposed to do that: 'It's not looked upon for royalty to mix with the workers'.

Here was the theme of class, following on his wife's theme of gender. Even in his imagination, he was not going to depict himself as being superior to people like himself – the king ordering the servants to serve the asparagus. Placed in a palace, he would still be having fun with the likes of himself; he would continue being his own unroyal self. Thus, he cancels the desire for the royal life. Similarly, his wife claims that she would continue to wield the emblem of her unroyal self – the duster. Even in a palace, she would not stop busying herself with the housework. This was said as a reason for not wanting to live in the big house. 'They' are welcome to 'their' palaces and servants; she will dust her small, modern, semi-detached home.

Laughter is not merely a response to the incongruous image of a suburban housewife, duster in hand, within the palace; or the king nipping to the pub for a pint with the boys. After all, there are enough publicised images of the royals in poses of suburban ordinariness. The laughter is also a means of affirming the unroyal self. With no restraining super-ego to demand humble deference, envy can be contained by mocking 'them' and 'their' ways. Mockery of the royal life is also mockery of the desire to be royal. It affirms the independence of the self – unbowed, irreverent, unimpressed by superiors. And, ironically, it confirms the privileged position of the superiors.

The reactions of a nineteen year old catering assistant provide an example (interview 50). The palace? 'Oh, I'd love it', she said, 'as long as I didn't have to clean it; I'd have the maids to clean it'. She laughed with her mother and sister. She paused and then added unprompted: 'I wouldn't mind being a maid actually'. Her mother was surprised: 'A maid?'. 'Yeah, just to be nosey, you know, and see what the house was like, not for long, you know, just for a couple of days...No I don't think I'd like to be a princess'. Nor would the mother like one of the palaces: 'I could do with a bigger house than we've already got', she said. 'And a bigger wage packet', added the daughter, 'but that's about all'. But not the house, went on the mother, 'not all that silver to clean, Lisa, no'. 'I wouldn't clean it', Lisa laughed, 'I'd get stainless steel'. 'Throw the silver out, Jeeves, stainless steel next time', said the mother. Mockery again.

The ambitions of the imagination have been limited to desiring to be a maid, who can spy on her mistress, and possibly mock her behind her back. The young woman imagines herself to be within the palace, as herself and only for a couple of days. Then she jokes about being royal. She wouldn't clean the silver. She'd get rid of it. Her mother joins in, mocking the voice of royalty, and ordering stainless steel cutlery for the palace. In effect, they are saying to royalty: 'we' will have your house and your wages, but 'we' will not eat asparagus off your silver plates, thank you very much. They will get the footmen to serve common food with common cutlery. That is the joke.

'I' wouldn't like to clean the palace, jokes the ordinary woman. Back can come the common-sense reply: you'd have servants. But then 'I' would be an employer of servants; 'I' wouldn't be myself; 'I' wouldn't be master/mistress of 'my' own home. There'd be no privacy, said a mother in her forties, who had just completed a course in typing (interview 31). There would always be somebody ordinary watching: 'There's *always* somebody around, isn't there, I mean footmen, housemaids and all that sort of thing; no, no, no, the only thing I'd like is a gardener'. The gardener would remain in the garden, outside the house. The mother, who said she would 'absolutely hate' the royal lifestyle, would like a big house (interview 23). On the other hand, she wouldn't want 'servants that live in, (but) I'd like a daily who would be there and not be seen'. Her daughter agreed. The mother continued about the unseen daily help: 'I wouldn't have to deal with her because I'm a terrible snob'. Snob – a curious word from a former cleaner, who was now embarrassed to contemplate being an employer.

The young couple have already been cited briefly, talking about servants (interview 62). The girlfriend was saying why she would not want servants around her house: 'I'd feel like it wasn't my house, I wouldn't be able to walk in and flop down'. They would always be there – in the kitchen. Her boyfriend added: 'They'd be in the kitchen when I'd want to go in the kitchen and make myself a sandwich'. Then, the girlfriend made her remark that he already had a servant to make his sandwiches. Better to be a servant in one's own house, than have servants in a palace. Again, the sounds of settlement are being uttered – this time, as a young woman is setting up the domestic routines for her own married life, and claiming, with her partner's connivance, the kitchen as hers.

There is nothing within common-sense to prevent a wish for servants. Such wishes have already been heard. For instance, the three mothers fantasised about graceful meal-times with servants in attendance (interview 54). But then they had argued whether that was 'really' what they wanted. Sue would like it forever, or so she said. Lynn, arguing against her, seemed to be edging her friend towards the paradox of desire. You'd wonder what was happening to you as a person, she said to Sue: 'You'd have to find something meaningful to do with your own life'. Sue stopped her friend. She made her assertion that her present self was not her true self: 'I'm not made for clearing up mess'. Even so, after more arguing, Sue conceded that she would only select bits of the royal life – the servants, the money but not much else.

The servants were now in the desired part, but not much had changed. Sue was asserting that it would be herself, sitting at the long table, receiving silver platters of asparagus – much more herself than having to scrape baked beans from her kitchen floor. It would still be Sue, sitting there in splendid elegance. She would not wish to be Queen. As she and her friends were imagining themselves enthroned in the palatial dining-hall, so they were laughing.

THE FREE LIFE

'The Queen, oh crikey, I wouldn't have her job for a million pounds', said the wife, just before making her remarks about big houses, servants and her need to wield the duster (interview 15). Such remarks doubly assert claims about the Queen's life and about ordinary life. Both ordinary lives and royals' lives are depicted, with the former proclaimed as the desirable life, whose benefits are priceless beyond riches.

Specific reasons are given to support the claim that the royal life is undesirable, as compared with the ordinary life. The royal life-style, it is said, is hollow; 'their' lives are not 'their' own. By contrast, such comments indicate the genuineness of 'our' lives. 'We' may not have golden fortunes, but 'we' have something money cannot buy: 'we' have liberty, and 'we' own 'ourselves'. 'We' can go to the pub with the 'boys', said the husband of the duster-wielding woman. An image of a free, spontaneous, undeferential self is being constructed.

Chapter 2 discussed the arguments of the middle-class family, in which the older son, a photographic engineer, was continually criticising royalty, whilst his parents and brothers offered defences (interview 41). As so often, the critic was emphasising the wealth of the Royal Family. It was wrong that 'they do have such a lifestyle when such a lot of people don't have anything'. His parents and his younger brother combined to argue against him. 'I feel sorry...for the Royal Family', said the critic's younger brother, 'because they've never had a choice, they've been born into it'. The father agreed: 'Charlie couldn't turn round and say "I want to be a carpenter" or "I want to be a bricklayer"'. Nor, said the younger son, could the royal prince say '"I want to go down the fish and chip shop"'. The father took up the point: 'He can't go walking down the road and do what everybody else does and go to the local and have a pint if he wants to'. The royal debits were the ordinary credits: the prince can't do what everybody else can do: 'It's not an enviable position', said the father. The younger son agreed. So did his politically pink brother: 'Oh, yeah, yeah, I'd go along with that, yeah'. As always, the concessions of the critic indicate the strength of a common-place. And so do the absences. No-one mentioned that 'we' never had the choice to turn round and say 'I want to be a prince' – the reality of royalness was taken for granted. In this regard, 'our' unfreedom was unremarked – 'theirs' was to be pitied.

A fitter in his forties said: 'They can't say sort of like "We'll nip off to the pictures tonight", or "We'll have a run"' (interview 55). It was as if he were imagining royals to live in a suburban home without the facilities for a private cinema and without an estate large enough for undisturbed runs. Similar themes were voiced by another family, when a school laboratory technician in his late fifties said: 'It must be horrible' (interview 42). His son-in-law, an estate agent, supplied the horrible details of the royal life. 'They' couldn't even sit in their own gardens without worrying about photographers. Worse still, 'they couldn't say "Let's go up to the pub for a drink"; they can't do that, can't even go shopping, can they'.

Here again is the possibility of coupon-filling. Royalty is claimed to lack the priceless freedoms which 'we' possess. 'We' can fill in the general matrix with illustrations of free moments from 'our' own lives. It could be the pub; the chip shop; the going shopping or whatever. 'We' are free to fill in the coupon, as 'we' desire. However, the listed freedoms, like the listed debits, are not purely personal, but they are emblematic. Similar themes recur again and again, as they depict the general condition of the ordinary life.

The fireman had talked about the royals not having to trudge around the supermarket (interview 22). The depiction of such credits called for the citing of the debits. The mother provided the on-the-other-hand: 'I don't envy them their lifestyle'. She continued: 'they're not free just to flit off up to the Peak District for the weekend or whatever; they've got certain engagements'. The father added different examples, and the gendering of desire was audible. He and his teenage sons liked to spend their leisure time at motor racing events: 'You don't see...Prince Charles or any of them at a motor race meeting or like, that'd seem quite normal to me'. He continued: 'You don't see Prince Charles on St Pancras Station train-spotting, or just nipping about on a motor bike'. It was because 'they' can't 'just up and do exactly what they want to do, they've always got to have it vetted or planned out weeks in advance'.

The father introduced the theme of balancing: 'The only way you can compensate for that would be to have a bit more money'. Then 'you could do the things that you were allowed to do in a better fashion'. However, the bargain would not be tempting. The financial part could not compensate for the alienated whole. As the father said, 'their' life was not enviable. The older son agreed: 'I couldn't live anything like they live; to start with I'd just want to do me own thing, that's all, that's it really'. Money could not really compensate for not doing 'your own thing'. The same argumentative structure could be applied whether your own thing was getting away to the Peak District, watching motor racing, or noting the railway engines pulling into St Pancras Station.

According to another father, the royals don't 'lead the family life that you and I would lead', for they can't say '"Well, I think I'll go to the races tomorrow", or "I'll go down the pub tomorrow"' (interview 3). The mother added other examples of ordinary family life: '"Or I'll have fish and chips for tea tonight, or something from the chip shop"; they can't do that, can they?'. If 'they' don't cook the meal after work, then they can't enjoy the spontaneous freedom of occasionally not cooking it. Nor can the ordinary, waited-upon male.

A mother and two daughters were talking about the lovely big houses in which royalty live (interview 50). As was mentioned previously, they'd like the big house and the wage packet; and that's about all. 'I'd hate to have to be on me toes all the time', said the mother. 'Di' can't even go shopping, to buy her husband's 'knickers in Marks and Sparks', suggested the daughter with a laugh. It was the 'going shopping' again, not the trudging around the supermarket. The mother added a qualification, concerning Princess Diana: 'She does pretty well really, she does have this freedom where she dashes out every now and again'. As a royal, you're doing pretty well if you can make the occasional brief dash from the palatial prison into the sort of freedom which 'we' are assumed to take for granted. All the royal cash hardly compensates for the ordinary pleasures of going shopping – of walking freely (but not trudging) around Marks and Spencer's. If only there was a bit more money in the ordinary purse – then all would be ideal.

A retired cleaner, her son and her daughter-in-law were chatting about the media and the royals' lack of privacy (interview 60). The mother commented that 'they can't go out and have a decent walk and a talk'. The son, a school care-taker, agreed: having 'the press behind me all the time, any time you went anywhere' would really 'get up my nose'. There was no 'neighbourliness' in the royal life, he added, 'nobody getting together, you know nipping round for a meal'. Later the son commented on the royals' lack of privacy at Buckingham Palace: 'Virtually near twenty-four hours a day, somebody's looking through that fence at the windows, what privacy have you got?'. The mother thought the royals must be 'bored stiff' because 'they've got everything done for them'. She added, taking up the theme of neighbourliness: 'They can't just stand on the gate like me and have a gas round...the street'. Nor, added her daughter-in-law, could 'they' pop out for a Chinese takeaway meal. The Queen would have to send a servant, said the son. Then the mother added: 'That's what I say, they couldn't say "Oooh, I'll have a walk across to the corner shop and have a glance round the shop"'.

The frequency with which the same examples recurred shows that the personal freedom is not personal in the sense of being particular to the person. It is a shared image of freedom, which ordinary people are presumed to recognise. Common metonyms of ordinariness were cited: the pub, the fish and chip shop, going shopping. Working- and middle-class can list these pleasures. The pleasure of shopping is not the purchasing of expensive goods, but the going. The eating of fish and chips was especially mentioned. Not only is the meal cheap; not only is it emblematically 'British'; but its eating constitutes a rebellion against formality. Chips can be eaten in the fingers, from the wrapping paper, in the streets. 'We' are free to break the very rules of meal-time, which 'we' imagine constrain 'them'.

The metonymic pleasures of ordinary life may be cheap or free pleasures, but that precisely is their point. More expensive pleasures would leave the ordinary life in envy. Money is the commodity which 'they' have. The ordinary person is claiming to possess a commodity more precious than money. The pleasures of ordinary life are presented as priceless. 'They' could buy whole shop floors, but 'they' cannot *go* shopping. Free pleasures, such as standing on the street talking or noting down the serial numbers of locomotives, are imagined to be closed to royalty. 'They' must eat 'their' asparagus from the silver platter with servants hovering.

As the good, ordinary life is depicted, so familiar phrases were used by different speakers. 'Nipping' was often mentioned: the ordinary person can 'nip' out – whether to pub, Chinese takeaway or friend's house. Nipping is claimed to characterise the ordinary life. There were indications that the pleasure is not located in the activity itself. The real pleasure is the spontaneity, or the sudden possibility of pleasures, which are free in both senses of the word.

It wasn't just that the royals couldn't do certain things. 'They' were imagined to be unable to say things, which 'we' can say to express our freedoms: 'they couldn't say "Oooh, I'll have a walk across to the corner shop"'; 'they can't say "Well, I think I'll go to the races tomorrow", or "I'll go down the pub tomorrow"'; 'they can't say sort of like "we'll nip off to the pictures tonight", or "we'll have a run"'. 'We' can voice the words of sudden desire, and 'we' can translate the words into action, if 'we' so choose. It doesn't matter what precisely the action is. Each nipping is equivalent in that it represents the same cheap freedom. In this way, 'we' proclaim 'ourselves' to be the fortunately free, fortune-free subjects.

THE ENVIABLE PRIVILEGES OF ORDINARY LIFE

The talk about the Royal Family's unenviable life is a variant of the general common-place 'money doesn't bring happiness'. The maxim offers reassurance to those without fortunes, in a society in which money is commonly valued and desired. The strength of monetary themes in common-sense arguments has already been seen. In Chapter 2, the 'tourist argument' was examined. The institution of monarchy seemed to be defended in terms of a cynical economics: the financial returns are greater than the monarchical investment. When the uncalculated calculations were challenged, the cynicism met its limits. A different appeal was heard: 'they' are priceless. The same appeal is made in relation to personal lives. 'Our' freedoms to nip are priceless: there is more to 'our' life than 'mere' money. The thought is settling: no, 'I' wouldn't want a golden fortune in exchange for 'my' priceless ordinary self.

If the image of the Royal Family is settling, with the envied parts constantly and cumulatively confronting the unenviable whole, then this settlement is accomplished through ideological imagination, rather than through calculation. The family discussions show how easily and confidently ordinary people depict the royal life. There are few hesitations in imagining the unfortunate life of the family claimed to be the richest (and, occasionally, the second richest) in the world. People make claims about the royal life, without claiming special knowledge. The privations of the royals are things which everybody 'knows'. In the next chapter, this 'knowledge' will be discussed in more detail.

As common-sense's settling terms are used, one can sometimes hear an older generation curtailing the imagination of the younger. Wouldn't it be lovely, said the mother, a secretary, to live in 'their' big houses (interview 24). She quickly added a settling qualification: 'if you've got to forfeit your privacy, I wouldn't want it'. No, agreed her daughter, 'it's not your own life anymore'. She continued: but if you could have the wealth and were 'able to do exactly what you want...that would be great'. That would be the ideal life. The father brought the daughter's imagined ideal firmly down to earth: 'Well, they can't do exactly what they want to do'. And, by implication, 'we' can't have exactly what 'we' want to have. It's not possible. It's not worth wishing.

In this settling down, envy is not merely rhetorically cancelled, but also, as part of the settling argument, it can be depicted and projected. Depictions of envy were described in Chapter 2. The rest of the world was imagined to envy Britain, for having a Royal Family. Being the monarch was not the envied position, but having a monarch was. As such, subjects of the Queen were depicting themselves as objects of envy. There is a further depiction of envy. Not only do foreigners envy 'us' for 'our' subject position; royals, imprisoned within 'their' unauthentic lives of restricting wealth, can also be imagined to envy 'us'.

The preconditions for imagining this envy have already been mentioned. There are common-places which seem to invert the positions of 'them' and 'us'. In *The German Ideology*, Marx and Engels wrote that 'in all ideology, men and their circumstances appear upside-down as if in a camera obscura' (1970, p.47). The language of jobs, described in the previous chapter, suggests that 'we' are the employers, handing over fabulous wages to 'our' royal employees. A further reversal is to be heard. The notion of 'privilege' can be brought down semantically from the heights of the royal castle to the ordinariness of the domestic house. 'We', not 'they', are the privileged ones, so it can be said.

The daughter-in-law had been envying the royals 'their' freedom from dusting and polishing and so on (interview 39). The mother and father had counter-balanced the envious talk with remarks about freedom; it was swings and roundabouts. The son, agreeing with his parents, but not with his wife, declared: 'I've got the only privilege, I've got, of doing, that is, I can walk out me front door and drive down town without fear of nobody trying to shoot me or press taking photos'. The ordinary, everyday freedom had become a 'privilege'. The fireman compared 'our' advantages to royal dis-advantages: 'Anybody such as ourselves, you can keep a private side to your life, if you so wish, or you can go out and tell everybody what you want to do; but they don't seem to have that privilege' (interview 22). Both times, this use of 'privilege' went unchallenged.

'We' can call ourselves privileged, and, as 'we' claim not to envy 'their' life, so the counter-claim of the imagination can be made: 'they' desire to live like 'us'. 'Ours' is the enviable life. A mother was saying that royalty could not lead a normal life: 'With all that money how could you be like a normal family, you couldn't, could you? never having to wash a nappy' (interview 3). Her husband agreed. They 'might like to be like one, but I don't think they'll ever be one'. 'They', the royals are being imagined to want to be like 'us', the normal family, which has to wash its own nappies. It was then that he made his remarks, already quoted, about 'them' not being able to say that 'they' would like to go to the pub or the races. Or the fish and chip shop, added the mother.

The unfreedoms of ordinary life can be momentarily imagined away in the imagining of the royal envy. One working-class family, living on a large council estate, provided an example (interview 56). The pavements outside their home were filled with litter from the nearby shops. Gangs of youths congregated on the street. It wasn't safe, said the daughter, for women to walk out alone after dark. In the evening they were imprisoned inside the small rented house.

Mother and daughter – cleaner and factory worker respectively – were sitting in their living-room, talking about the hardships of the royal life. According to the mother, royalty had been 'drilled' into its way of life. No-one would choose to live like that naturally. Familiar emblems of ordinary freedom and royal restriction were cited: 'I mean like the cutlery, I mean sort of how we'd enjoy a bag of chips, walking along the road, I mean you wouldn't see the Queen doing that'. Again, chips were the metonym of the free spirit.

As the mother and her daughter talked about the desirability of 'their' own life, the lines of common-sense were leading towards a thought which was so ideologically pointed, that it could only be uttered innocently as common-sense. Would 'they' – royalty – like to be able to walk along the road, eating chips?, asked the inter-viewer. 'I bet they would', replied the mother quickly. The daughter agreed. Immediately, and without prompting, she widened the particular into the general: 'I bet they'd love to live the way we live'.

'Ours' was the enviable life, the one which 'they' would desire to live. 'Our' imprisonments were momentarily forgotten, as the mother and her daughter, confined within the safety of their home, imagined the envy of the royals.

Outside the house, the gangs of the evening were gathering on the path to the chip shop.

6

DESIRE, DENIAL AND THE PRESS

The imagining of the royal job as a hard job is a major theme in the containment of envy. Time and again, it was said that 'we' wouldn't like 'their' life: 'they' have no freedom, no privacy, 'their' every move is watched. These thoughts were spoken with confidence, as if 'their' life was a matter of common knowledge. Yet, there is a paradox. 'Their' every move is watched – 'we' know this because 'we' are watching 'them'. If 'we' sympathise with royalty because 'they' are imagined to be watched, then are not 'we' imagining 'ourselves' to be the causes of 'their' hardship? If so, then how can 'we' offer 'our' sympathy? The themes of common-sense would seem to be beckoning towards matters which might not be easily admitted.

In 'Totem and taboo', Freud discussed the psychology of primitive kingship. He suggested that subjects unconsciously harboured feelings of aggressive jealousy against their monarch. According to Freud, subjects express this unconscious aggression in the way that they treat their monarch. As they pay their courtly homage, so they imprison the king: 'The ceremonial taboo of kings is *ostensibly* the highest honour and protection for them, while *actually* it is a punishment for their exaltation, a revenge taken on them by their subjects' (1964b p.51).

It is not too fanciful to depict something analogous in modern monarchy. The subjects want to imagine the monarch's life to be hard. Without this imagining, feelings of envious hostility would arise: the royal would be accused of getting away with unpaid-for privileges. Reporters and photographers of the media provide the ceremonial restrictions of modern monarchy. Royals cannot step forth without their every move being captured. Every day, the papers and television screens bear witness of this imprisonment.

Witnessing this reproduced evidence, 'we' can rest assured that 'their' life is suitably hard. However, all this cannot be admitted too directly. 'Our' sympathy for 'them' would be dulled, if 'we' exposed 'ourselves' as the persecutors who require this evidence: what, then, would 'we' imagine that 'they' think of 'us'?

In this chapter, the monarch's subjects are to be heard voicing common-sense complaints against the media, and, in particular, against the press for being the jailers of royalty. But, 'we' do not blame 'ourselves' as consumers of the media. There are strategies of dissociation and projection at work. Shameful desires are denied, and attributed to others. If this appears somewhat Freudian, then in one respect it is less Freudian than Freud, and, in another respect, it is more so.

It is less Freudian in that the shameful desires are not held in check by a rigid super-ego. All is nearer the surface, and closer to being cheerfully admitted, for the modern consciousness is more cynical about its own illusions. In another respect, all this has a more Freudian character than is found within Freud's own account in 'Totem and taboo'. When writing on kingship, Freud, un-characteristically for him, equated fantasy with reality. Not only did he assume that subjects unconsciously desired their king to suffer; he also believed that the king *actually* did suffer. The king's life was 'a torment and an intolerable burden'; it was 'a bondage far worse than that of his subjects' (1964b p.50). There is no need to assume this. It is possible to remain at the level of the imaginary. The subjects claim that the royal life is vexatious, and, by implication, they depict the comparative ease of their own ordinary burdens. Whether or not the royal life is quite so onerous need not be calculated here. The crucial issue is one of the ideological imagination: subjects are imagining the royal life to be unenviable. No more need be conceded.

PERSECUTION AND KNOWLEDGE

Opinion polls reveal the extent to which the press and the monarchy occupy opposite polar positions in popular estimation. For instance, Gallup asked members of the public to indicate which institutions in public life they most and least respected: monarchy and newspapers respectively were the frequent responses (Heald and Wybrow, 1986, pp.74 and 281). According to a Gallup survey of December 1988, eighty percent of the population responded that the press, TV and radio should show the Royal Family more respect. A MORI survey of January 1990 revealed that sixty-five percent thought press and TV pay too much attention to royalty; sixty-one percent thought that the press coverage of the Royal Family was on the whole unfair. The polls also show that the public thinks it knows the royal personalities. In the Gallup survey of 1988, only four percent of the population refused to assign a personality characteristic (i.e. 'arrogant', 'sympathetic', 'caring', or whatever) to the Queen or to the Prince of Wales. The vast majority felt no difficulty in doing so.

If the public claims to 'know' royalty, it does so at second-hand through the media, which it claims to distrust. There is a further point to this distrust. The British buy newspapers in greater numbers than any other nation apart from the Swedes (Baistow, 1985, p.7). There is here a complex of themes worth a further look. These themes concern the way that people talk about the press and royalty, and also the ways that they think of themselves as purchasers of newspapers, which are said to persecute the royals. To begin with, there are some typical examples of respondents claiming to know the royals and claiming to know that the royals are persecuted.

Knowing the royals

There was a sense of easy familiarity with royalty. Enough quotations have been given of remarks about 'Charlie' and 'Di', 'Andy' and 'Fergie'. As was seen in Chapter 3, respondents would fantasise about informal meetings with royalty, which would not be like meetings with strangers. A mother and her daughters were saying that they liked to know what the royals are doing and what they're wearing (interview 50). Being 'nosey' was how the older daughter put it. She and her sister laughed at their mother for being 'terrible' in that regard. She conceded: 'It is being nosey; it's the fact that the Royal Family seems part of you'. She went on: 'It's like if they said after the news "We're going to feature Tracey's Auntie Tricia opening a store in such and such"; you'd watch it because you feel they're familiar'. Yes, agreed her elder daughter: 'You feel as if you know them; and you could come in and could have a conversation with them'.

The analogy with one's own family was made by another mother: 'I mean, if something happened to the Queen, I think it'd be upsetting for a lot of people because it's like you know her and it's like somebody in your family' (interview 39). 'We' have family knowledge about 'them': 'we' share their births, marriages, illnesses and so on. But, of course, this knowledge is not direct. 'We' would watch 'Auntie Tricia' on the television, because 'we' know her off the screen. But, apart from a few exceptionally magic moments, 'we' only know the royals from screen or paper. According to MORI, February 1986, only ten percent of the population claim to have met and spoken to a member of the Royal Family.

As a secretary in her late forties said, in a statement quoted in Chapter 2, 'they're in the paper every day and on television, as I say you know them warts and all' (interview 23). She and her daughter displayed this knowledge throughout their talk. 'Harry's not as boisterous as William, a lot quieter', the mother said of the Queen's grandchildren and the daughter could echo agreement, 'he's a lot quieter'. The characters were familiar. 'I think Diana's gorgeous and I really love her', said the mother, 'but if she did anything to upset my Charles, she'd be in trouble'.

In such talk – and many, many more examples could be given – there is a sense of personal knowledge. Of course, the Queen and her children are not really members of the family, in the way that an Auntie Tricia is. Nevertheless, the royals are claimed to be known. This knowledge, which can be spoken with the immediacy of first-hand knowledge, is second-hand. It is the papers and the television which give 'us' the intimate glimpses – the royal warts and all.

Press persecution

There is a further set of common-place themes which suggests that 'our' knowledge of the Royal Family might be thought to have been gained illicitly. Freud's tales of courtiers restricting every kingly move have become tales of reporters and photographers. Speakers often criticised the media for denying royalty privacy. A few typical instances can be given. A cleaner complained that the royals 'can't have a bit of privacy', but there's always cameras 'spying on them and checking up', even when 'they go on holiday' (interview 56). A fitter, in his forties, said: 'they can't have a private life...even when they go to their holidays up in Scotland, they're plagued by re-porters, there's no private life' (interview 55). A nineteen year old shop assistant said that the royal routine was 'too much like hard work': it was a twenty-four hour a day job and 'where you go, you've always got the fear of there being a photographer behind you, no matter who you're talking to' (interview 50).

Often, the lack of freedom was seen as a deplorable modern development, which is compared with respectful attitudes of old. A mother declared that 'they can't even sort of gallop in the sea or lay in the sun like we all can without somebody spying through a hedge *now*...it didn't used to be like that, years ago, nobody crept around or looked out for them and watched for them, nobody ran after them in the streets, it's going to get worse' (interview 41). A fifty-nine year old retired school cleaner made the same point, and then, in an unfortunate conjunction of metaphors, she asserted that royalty can't even 'sneeze out of place...it's all blown out of proportion' (interview 47).

In such comments, and many more like them, the judgements are clear. Royal lack of freedom is not fortuitous. There is a reason why 'they' cannot nip out for fish and chips or wander around the corner shop: they will be pursued by journalists and photographers. 'We' are not the prying spies, but 'they', the press, are. The newshounds are infringing upon propriety: they are spying, plaguing, spreading fear among the royals, frightening 'their' corgis. It is disgraceful.

The press provided a major common-sense reason for not wanting to be royal and for being grateful for the ordinariness of 'our' ordinary life. In the previous chapter, the mother and her daughters were quoted, discussing the advantages and drawbacks of living in a palace (interview 50). The younger daughter had expressed envy and then qualified herself, saying that she would like to be a maid. There was more to the conversational exchange. She continued with her fantasy of living in a palace: 'Oh, just think of the parties you could throw'. She laughed, but her mother added seriously: 'You couldn't, because it'd be all over the front page of the *Sun*: "Princess Wendy Keeps Throwing All These Wild Parties"'. Immediately, Wendy conceded the point. She replied: 'No, I don't think I'd like to be a princess'. The envious impulse was over.

A small act of ideological settlement had been achieved, as the older generation talks to the younger. The mother brings her daughter back from unsettling fantasy to settled reality. The instrument for ending the daughter's brief dream was the spectre of the press: just imagine what the newspapers would say about you – just think of the headlines in the *Sun*. The mere mention of those modern demons, the newspapers, has cured the jealous itch. No, I don't want to be a princess.

THE CONTRADICTIONS OF PAPER-TALK

The papers were not only reproached for printing intrusive material, which they should not publish, but there was a further accusation: the papers were full of lies. The two themes – intruding and lying – often accompanied each other. A family was saying that Prince Edward's life would be ideal, if it were not for the press, who would 'dig the dirt', as the father put it (interview 41). Even if they failed to find a scandal, said the younger son, 'sooner or later, they'll make something up'. No-one disagreed.

Newspapers might be the means by which 'we' come to know the royal warts and all; but they are also the purveyors of deliberate falsehood. Discourse analysts have stressed that people do not typically possess a single 'attitude' on an issue, which is to be repeated unchangingly and unceasingly. Instead, there is variability, as different common-sense repertoires of speaking will be used on different conversational occasions (Gilbert and Mulkay, 1984; Potter and Wetherell, 1987; Wetherell and Potter, 1988). In this case, two different, common-sense ways of talking about the press and royalty are indicated: the papers as the source of lies and the papers as the source of knowledge.

On the one hand, there is a language of distrust – a common-sense version of what Paul Ricoeur (1986) calls 'the hermeneutics of suspicion'. According to this way of talking, the press is an object of suspicion. On the other hand, there is a language of warranting – the press can be cited as evidence about the world. One should not expect that there are two different types of people: those that condemn the newspapers as organs of untruth, and other people who will quote them as sources. Instead, both ways of talking will be used by the same people, as 'we' claim both to 'know' royalty and to 'know' that 'they' are being lied about.

The two ways of talking – or repertoires of interpretation – are more than ways of talking about the topic of the press – and, indeed, more than talking about the specific issue of the reporting of royals. They also permit the possibility of double-declaiming. Speakers claim themselves to be independent-minded egos, uninfluenced by the lies of the media. Also, in citing newspapers, they can also be claiming themselves to be knowledgeable and well-read. The two sets of claims and double-declaims can be brought into argumentative collision.

149

Just after the mother had ended her daughter's fantasy of being royal, she talked generally of the press (interview 50). 'I don't believe anything I read in the paper, well very little', she said. Her daughters agreed. 'Yeah, you don't know who to believe nowadays', said the younger daughter. Yet they were newspaper-readers. The *Daily Mirror* was delivered to their home. It's 'not too bad actually', said the mother, 'not like the *Sun* and the *Star*, oh my god, they're terrible; it's wrong really that they can print some of the things that they do'. The mother, who claimed to know the royal warts and all, had said that the papers print too much private information about the royals (interview 23). But you can't trust the papers: 'I don't trust any of them'. Except, she added, James Whitaker, the royal correspondent of the *Mirror*. 'I tend to believe him', she conceded. 'Well', said her daughter, 'he's a friend of theirs, isn't he'. Not really a journalist, more a friend.

A cleaner was talking about the gossip in the newspapers (interview 56). Some of them print material 'what the Queen's not agreed with'. 'Yeah, but the papers are lies', said her sixteen year old daughter. 'How much do you believe?', asked the interviewer. 'Not much', said the daughter. Not much, agreed her mother. 'I mean', said the daughter, 'anybody can make a story up about somebody'. Mother and daughter were agreed in their common-places of cynicism.

The rhetoric of global dismissal was easy to make: it's all lies, all 'paper-talk'. However, the cynicism was not total. The speakers were making qualifications, as they expressed their cynical distrust. One newspaper was not too bad, actually. There was a reporter whose views on royalty could be trusted. Well, he was a friend of 'theirs'. The warts could still be known; and the same speakers, who could dismiss the media as being full of lies, could also claim knowledge from the papers.

The mother might have agreed with her daughter that the papers are lies: there wasn't much which they could believe. At other times, the same woman cited the papers as a warrant for knowledge. She was talking about the man who broke into the Queen's bedroom. She added: 'even just lately, they've had some funny creatures working for them, gays and what have you'. 'Have they?', asked the interviewer, 'I'd not heard about that'. 'Oh, yeah, it was in the paper a few weeks ago'.

The mother and her daughters could claim not to believe anything in the papers; well, very little (interview 50). But the mother felt as if she knew the royals – as if they're a part of 'you'. She and her daughters were combining to tell a story about Prince Charles in New York. The point of the story was the rudeness which the Prince had to encounter. A newspaper was cited as the source. 'He went to New York', said the daughter, 'I've seen one of the papers'. 'Yes', said her mother, 'and somebody made a comment about his ears, didn't they'. She continued: the Prince had been at a wild-life park and 'they'd brought him this chimp for him to hold'. 'He says, "Hasn't it got big ears?"', said the daughter. And then this American announcer said: '"You'll notice the similarity in the ears"'. The mother said that the Prince chose to ignore the remark, but he did give the announcer a withering glance 'according to the newspaper report'.

'According to the newspaper report' can be an ambivalent phrase. The story about the Prince was told as fact, in order to make a point. Its source – the newspaper – is cited in support. However, the warrant for knowledge can be turned around into doubt. It was in the newspaper – it's only newspaper-talk. The one saying can challenge the other. For instance, a husband and wife, both retired, were discussing a story about Prince William (interview 52). The wife was saying 'I always remember somebody saying that little William stood with his father on the balcony and he says to his father "Look, daddy, look at all the peasants"'. 'Yeah', cut in her husband, 'but we don't know whether that's true or not'. She agreed: 'But then that's all just paper-talk'.

A mother, her son and daughter-in-law were complaining about paper-talk (interview 60). The press was always blowing things up, especially making insinuations about royal marriages. They've only 'got to see Di with somebody different', said the daughter-in-law, 'and they're just going to make two and two make five'. Yes, agreed her husband: in that very morning's paper 'Charles has been seen with somebody and they're inferring already that there's something going off'. The mother agreed: 'the press put more to it'. And so on. They were in accord about press fabrication and exaggeration. The stories were not to be believed.

But still they regularly bought their tabloids, with the mother actually buying two different papers each morning. There was information to be gathered from the papers. The mother was criticising the Queen's appearance: 'I mean she's never changed her hair-style since I can remember'. 'Well, I think she likes it that way', said her son, 'she's not one for change'. 'And she dyes it, she dyes it', went on the mother. 'How do you know?', challenged the son. 'She does', answered the mother, 'I read it in the paper'. The son laughed gently: 'Paper again'.

But even he thinks he knows that the Queen is not one for change.

MORAL METHODOLOGIES

The claim that the media are full of lies is also a claim about truth. As the son was claiming not to be fooled by the stories about Princess Diana's marriage, so he was making a claim about the truth of the marriage – he 'knew' that the stories were fallacious (interview 60). Moreover, he was not merely making a claim about the royal marriage. He was also making a claim about himself: he was not the sort of person to be misled by erroneous tittle-tattle. He was laying claim to being an independent, critical ego – the sort of ego which is celebrated in the ideology of liberalism (Henriques *et al.*, 1984; Macpherson, 1962; Sampson, 1977, 1988 and 1990).

Over referency

There were common stories told about the ways in which newspapers should be read or televisions watched, in order to escape error. In these stories, the 'hermeneutics of suspicion' are used to justify belief, so that the result is not a generalised, or alienated, scepticism. The stories also indicate something which is overlooked in current research into the effects of the media. A number of analysts have commented quite correctly that consumers of the media do not passively receive the messages from screen or paper; audiences discuss and try to make sense of the media (Jensen, 1990; Livingstone, 1990; Morley and Silverstone, 1990). People do more than make sense of the contents of the media, for they also give accounts of how they do this. They tell stories about their methodologies for extracting information. These accounts are not descriptions of how the papers are *actually* read or televisions watched. The stories are 'moral methodologies'. Speakers proclaim the virtue of distrust, and claim how they, by using critical distrust, have been able to evade error.

A common moral methodology was to proclaim the necessity of 'reading between the lines'. Lines of print are not to be uncritically accepted, but truths between the lines are said to be discoverable with critical effort. A housewife and part-time bar-worker in her late forties was talking about the newspaper coverage of the Duke of York and his amatory escapades: 'I think you have to read between the lines...because the press have a field day' (interview 6). A mother and father were talking about the influence of the Queen (interview 25). The father, a self-employed architectural technician, thought that the Queen was more influential than was commonly thought. 'Not as you would read from the media', he said, 'but I think if you read between the lines, as you might say, I think she's got more influence'. A mechanical engineer was talking about the politics of the Queen and Prince Charles (interview 10). He commented: 'you can read between the lines what they're thinking'. The truth was there, but special reading was required to extract it from the outward untruths of the media's lines.

Sometimes a two-stage process was described: the papers are read critically, and then an independent judgement is passed. According to one husband, 'I'll read through it and...form an opinion like same as everybody else...You know if somebody's trying to bring them down sort of thing, you know bit of scandal or something like that, I read it and form my own opinion' (interview 15). It is a tale of rationality versus fury, told by the free-standing ego, proclaiming its critical freedom.

Another methodology of the critical ego was to juxtapose different papers or newspaper and television. A sixteen year old factory worker expressed her distrust: 'The papers are lies...if you read one paper and then in another paper it's completely different' (interview 57). Her mother offered a maxim: 'It's like what I've always said with newspapers, seeing is believing'. On television you can see, but the family continued to buy, and to read, its *Daily Star* and *News of the World*. 'I don't believe anything they report until I've heard it on the news', said a twenty-two year old shop assistant, 'and then perhaps I might just start believing it' (interview 50). As a mother said, you read something in the papers, and then you see it on television and then 'you'd think, "well they did say that but you'd taken that right out of context, that's a lie"; and you start to question what you read...well, I don't believe any of it' (interview 23). Well, she did believe James Whitaker – and she knew the royal warts.

A husband and wife were denying an interest in matters scandalous (interview 1). According to the husband, 'we watch the news...but if there's anything about them that is scandalising, I just turn it off *mindwise*, it might still be on, because you don't know what else is coming on the news'. This mental discipline of turning off mindwise is claimed to guard the ego against error or triviality. Analogous strategies can be claimed for reading newspapers. A mother said that she distrusted the tabloid papers, which she regularly read: 'Something gets printed about somebody you like, say like the Royal Family, that I don't like, then I think "Oh well, I'm not reading that, you can't believe what you read in the papers"; and I don't read it and I don't believe it' (interview 57). The ego claims to decide not to believe what it does not wish to believe. The protection is accomplished by uttering to oneself the magic formula that 'you can't believe what you read in the papers'. Hey presto, the evil influence is willed away; it is a victory for common-sense.

These accounts should not be interpreted as literal descriptions, for they are moral, rather than empirical, tales. The mother claims that she does not read what she must have already read: 'Oh well, I'm not reading that' she decides on the basis of reading what she is not going to read. A retired office supervisor in her sixties offered two different methodologies, each of which seemed to contradict the other in a literal sense (interview 4). However, their moral sense was perfectly consistent.

The first tale was positively Cartesian in its advocacy of wholesale doubt: 'You hear all these stories and the media,...it's so strong now that papers and television, you don't know what's the truth and what isn't, I automatically disbelieve most of it'. This everyday tale of Cartesianism is worth examining. She doesn't know what the truth is, and to avoid error she automatically disbelieves. Yet, like Descartes, her doubt is limited, and the doubting has to stop (even before it is started). She automatically doubts *most* of the royal stories: not *all* of them. Some stories automatically escape doubt. Thus, the doubt reveals its opposite: some things are automatically trusted by the doubting mind. She doubts, ergo she believes.

It was not so simple, for this mother also had another philosophy, or psychology, of reading the news. She was talking about the Commonwealth and was expressing concern because 'you can tell that the Queen's worried'. Her husband interjected a note of doubt: 'It's only what you read in the papers'. The wife agreed and then reversed her Cartesian tale: 'Yes, that's what worries me...I think you can be brain-washed by media, that worries me really, I mean, I read as avidly as anyone else and I believe it at the time, and then I think "Well, is it true, are we just being brain-washed to think that?"'.

The tale has reversed the ordering of doubt and belief. Naïve belief comes first, to be followed by a doubt which is not crippling. Later, she and her husband were talking about the Queen Mother and King George VI. They never wanted to be King and Queen, said the husband. This time it was the mother's turn to add the

154

qualification of doubt: 'It's only newspapers and magazines, things you read'. This did not stop her from saying a moment later: 'I know Charles is very fond of his grandmother'. The well-known figures of royalty could still be known well by the self-proclaimed doubters.

Speakers, in making such claims were, in effect, saying that it is possible to intuit hidden royal truths 'between the lines'. A house-wife in her sixties said that 'the majority of people only know of them through the press and the media'. The press might tell lies, but still, added her husband, a retired chartered engineer, 'you develop a sixth sense...you can just pick out something what you think is false' (interview 37). A father in his early forties was talking about the media's views on Princess Anne (interview 11). The newspapers distort, but in interviews and on television 'something does shine through...you get a bit of the person shining through'.

There is an omission in these methodological tales of appre-hending truth through scepticism. The speakers do not say that the press stories, which they claim to doubt, typically claim to be hidden revelations. According to one royal journalist: 'One tends to read between the lines of what the Press Secretary tells you and what you have heard elsewhere' (quoted in Hoey, 1987, p.133). The readers are claiming to read between the lines, which themselves are claim-ing to read between other lines.

Ordinary people are claiming a special knowledge, by which supposedly they can intuit the true from the false. Subjects can imagine themselves to be on the same side as the royals. They are both combating the common enemy – the media which lies to 'us' about 'them'. 'We' sympathise with 'them', supporting 'them' in 'their' travails with the media, which provides 'us' with the material for these imaginings. 'Our' claimed scepticism seems to bring 'us' closer to that family which is almost part of the family.

THE PRESS AND THE IMPRESSIONABLE

The moral methodologies are tales of dissociation, for speakers are separating themselves from the press and its contents. It is not the self who wishes for the persecution of royalty, so it is claimed – it is the media which are to blame. However, there is another theme to be spoken about: the media do not operate alone, for the press has its readers and the television its viewers. Were it not for the readers, the papers would not print what they do, and would not make royalty's life such a misery – or so it can be said. Since most speakers

themselves are readers and viewers, they must do more than dissociate themselves from what they read and watch. They must also
distance themselves from other consumers of the media who are
imagined to believe uncritically, and, worse still, to desire to read
the scandalous lies. In short, others are to be accused of being
gullible and shameful.

In this section, the issue of gullibility will be discussed, and,
afterwards, the shameful desires will be examined. A church-going,
quality assurance manager provides an example of the accusation of
gullibility (interview 59). He was complaining about the press
reporting of royals: 'At least fifty percent I would say of what is
written in the papers is not true – it's just sensationalism'. The press
was 'a pack of lies...they're out to make money, exploit people...by
printing lies and hoping to sell the paper'. Thus, the readers were
implicated: 'Yeah, some people are gullible, they're very powerful
the newspapers'.

Such talk of gullibility is almost invariably talk about the Other or,
to be more precise, about Others. When, in the Platonic dialogue
Gorgias, Socrates attacked the sophists for claiming to make the
worse argument appear the better, he was letting his audience know
that he for one had not been persuaded by the sophists' base
rhetoric (Plato, 1971). Similarly, the father was implying that he
remained unfooled by the lies. 'Some people' were gullible; implicitly he excluded himself. After all, he had noticed that fifty percent
of the press was lies. The gullible others accepted it all as true.

The other's gullibility is being contrasted with the speaker's own
claimed self; in this sense the gullible other is a Contrastive Other.
There is the possibility for personalised coupon-filling. Common-
sense provides the coupon for complaining about the press and
impressionable others, but speakers can fill in the coupon to fit their
own purposes. Different speakers – indeed different groups of
speakers – can identify different Contrastive Others. Stereotypes can
be mobilised for the task. Those who do not buy tabloid papers
have a ready group of Contrastive Others – the tabloid readers.
Thus, the church-going father could identify the readers of the *Sun*
or the *Mirror* as his gullible others.

Some intriguing episodes of identifying Contrastive Others
occurred, when the Other, far from being distant, was in the same
room. In family conversation, general stereotypes, particularly those
of age and gender, can be invoked to pursue close-to-home business. The impersonal stereotype can suddenly appear to swoop

down and hail a particular individual sitting there. The speaker could claim all innocence: who me? I was only saying that....

The family in interview 50 were tabloid readers, but, as the mother said, they disapproved of the *Sun* and the *Star*. 'I think it's *wrong* really that they print some of the things that they print, because I think there are lots of people who read it and think it's true'. It was others who were the gullible readers. Her nineteen year old daughter agreed, immediately personalising the general: 'Well, my grandma and grandad do, don't they, they believe everything they read in the paper'. The mother then gave a reason for the grandparents' gullibility. For them, if something was in the paper, 'it *has* to be true...because, I mean they're seventy-six, seventy-seven, and that's how it used to be'. The young and the middle-aged were pointing to the elderly. Age was the reason for gullibility.

The older generation can use the coupons of common-sense to fire back argumentative bullets at the younger. A grandfather, a retired toolmaker, was arguing with his daughter and with her husband (interview 29). The older man was saying that the press boosted their circulation by printing distorted stories about the Royal Family. He himself wasn't interested in that sort of thing: 'I don't want to know'. Having established his own credentials, he pointed the moral finger: 'There's an awful lot of women, middle-aged women, that'll go and buy that paper to read about it'. There it was: the Other, identified by age and gender, separated from the speaker's older, male self.

His thirty-six year old daughter, a market researcher, did not rise to the challenge directly. She mentioned the 'type of papers that print anything...the gutter press...the *Sun*'. She dissociated herself from such stuff. It was her husband, a hairdresser, who confronted the old man: 'I think more men buy it than women quite frankly'. Yeah, I was just going to say that, said his wife. Her husband continued his defence of women: 'I think women actually are more discerning about their reading'. He did not mention which sort of men were less discerning: he did not specify age, as he looked back at his father-in-law.

The older man back-tracked, shuffling categories of class and gender to suggest a further Contrastive Other: 'Yeah and also a man, a working man will buy a paper according to his station in life, if he's a labourer that sweeps the floor or something, it's the *Daily Mirror* or *Star* or *Sun*...if you're a little bit higher up...then you probably go for the *Express* and the *Mail* or something like that, but if you consider that you're one of the privileged then you probably buy the, um, err, the *Guardian*.

His daughter was the next to speak, locating herself safely on her father's ascending social scale: 'The only newspaper I ever read is the *Daily Telegraph* and that's because Mike buys the *Telegraph* every day...I would never buy the *Sun* or anything like that'. 'You're a snob, then', her Mike retorted. A moment later, he added that he bought the *Telegraph* 'because I like to read the news and I'm not a snob about the papers'. The champion of women's superior discernment chooses the paper for his wife to read. He has other claims to make. Had his wife chosen the same newspaper as himself, that would have indicated her snobbery. His choice arises from quite different reasons: he wants the serious news. A contrast between his own serious self and a snobbish Other on the same sofa has been quickly made. The notion of women's superior discernment has served its purpose in the argument against the father-in-law, and it has now been put away. His wife now sits accused of inferior discernment. She keeps silent.

Examples have shown the old and the middle-aged being selected as the gullible Others. The young do not escape. A middle-class mother used the rhetoric of the bourgeoisie to condemn 'the uneducated' who purchase the tabloids (interview 41). She went on to describe 'youngsters these days' as 'empty vessels'. They refuse to learn at school and they uncritically accept the 'rubbish in the newspapers'. Her twenty-seven year old son described the young, gullible others: 'There are a lot of youngsters who read the *Sun* and watch the odd programme on telly and read the *Sunday Sport*, probably see the Royal Family as...load of yuppies who gallivant round the world ... laying on exotic islands in bikinis'. Such youngsters, courtesy of the tabloids, would have the wrong impression of the hard-working royals.

These stories about the lies of the media demand the figure of the gullible Other. If this figure were omitted, the tale would be a different one: it would be a tale of ineffectual newspapers without followers. However, these are tales of the press's dangerous powers – the power over readers and the power to persecute royalty. In telling such a story, the speakers can perform all sorts of family businesses. Capture, escape and re-capture could be heard in the quick interchanges between the retired toolmaker, his daughter and son-in-law (interview 29). In another interview, there was one incident in which the dynamics of family power were particularly marked: a member of the family was presented as the gullible Other. In order to maintain the story, the words of the Other were ignored by an act of collective deafness (interview 38).

This interview involved two sets of grandparents, aged between fifty-nine and sixty-six. The mother and father in interview 28 were their respective children. Also taking part was the eighty-seven year old mother of one of the grandmothers, and great-grandmother to the young children who had played quietly during the interview with their parents. Both sets of grandparents were lower middle-class: the grandfather was a retired bank clerk on one side and Presbyterian former army NCO on the other. The great-grandmother lived alone down on the south coast in a council house; she was visiting her daughter. There she sat on the antique-style furniture, as a remnant from a disappeared working-class life. Her contributions to the conversation were often interruptions, as she told jokes or reminisced about poverty before the war. She even broke into song once: 'I'm 'Enery the Eighth I am', she sang. For periods, she remained mute, while the not-so-elderly got on with their nimble conversational business. She had lost the ability to enter the rapid exchanges of the others. It was their world now, or rather it was already passing from them on to their children. Certainly, it was no longer hers.

On several occasions, the grandparents complained about the treatment of the royals in the press. 'It's absolutely scandalous', declared the old lady's son-in-law. His wife – her daughter – said that 'what they write in the papers today is a load of rubbish'. She added, with a little laugh, and with the voiced agreement of her husband, that 'mother believes everything'. The old lady said nothing.

Later on, the topic was raised again. This time the great-grandmother was brought into the conversation by her daughter, who at fifty-nine was the youngest person in the room, apart from the interviewer. Were women more interested in royalty than men, the interviewer had asked. 'I should think so, Mum you read all about the Royal Family don't you?', called out her daughter. 'Yeah', said the old lady. Her daughter continued: 'In the *Sun* and the *Mirror*, and it's all true', she said with ironic emphasis. This time, the old lady was not invited to reply. Nor did she. She was being presented as a specimen object, the Contrastive Other.

The irony in the speaker's remark was heavily stressed to ensure that the other listeners, especially the interviewer, received the message. She was distancing herself from elderly gullibility, and, by contrast, was marking out her own comparative lack of age and her own social betterment: she, the wife of a retired bank clerk, was not the sort of person who believed the rubbish of the tabloids. She, her husband and her son-in-law's parents were all of them above that sort of thing.

There was another exchange, which occurred in between those two quoted examples. This time the great-grandmother talked spontaneously about the press. She disrupted the conversation to talk of the past, her past. Years ago she used to work in the print-works for the *Argus*. Yeah, it was terrible, 'all lies they used to tell down that paper', she laughed. She worked for four shillings a week to start off, during the First World War: 'That was only a penny then, it was very cheap, the *Argus* was; they still do it now, but they tell more lies than ever'. She laughed again. It was the turn of the younger generation, the not-so-hard-of-hearing, to show deafness. None of them asked her about her first-hand experiences of the press – experiences which, for all their confident judgements about newspapers, they did not possess. No-one appeared to notice that she had switched from her past to the common present: today the papers tell more lies than ever, she was saying.

The daughter persisted in presenting her mother as the gullible Other, helplessly unable to sort out today's fiction from fact. Was this how she wanted her mother to be seen, a helpless object beyond her time? How they all wanted to see the old lady? And did their deafness to her words arise from this desire? There can be no definite answers, only interpretations. The old lady herself did not protest. Perhaps she did not notice. Perhaps she did.

PANDERING TO COMMON DESIRE

The Others – those uncritical consumers of the media – are not only depicted as innocent victims, who naïvely believe the untruths of the press. They can also be depicted as sharing the guilt, for they desire what should not be desired. Again, the accusations parallel the classical condemnations of rhetoric (Vickers, 1988). Socrates in *Gorgias* attacked orators for 'pandering' to the base instincts of their audiences. They aim 'merely to gratify hearers' and they treat 'their audience like children, whom their only object is to please' (Plato, 1971, p.110). The accusation assumes that the hearers have desires, which ought not to be gratified. So it is with accusations against modern newspapers. They are gratifying, so it is said, the desires of their readers – or, at least, the desires of their other readers.

Thus, it was claimed that the papers were responding to a demand. There was a market force of shameful desire. 'Who wants to know on the front page of a newspaper', demanded the radical nineteen year old daughter, 'that Sarah Ferguson looks fat in her new dress?' (interview 35). She continued with her rhetorical questions: 'Who wants to know that Lady Diana can sunbathe on the beach?' Do people really want to know? Of course, they do – father, brother and mother were quick to answer – look at the sales of the *Mirror* and the *Sun*. 'Obviously the newspapers think they do', said her father, 'otherwise they wouldn't print it, would they'. 'This country's so ridiculous', retorted the daughter.

She had conceded without an argumentative struggle that there were many who wanted to know about the ridiculous royal matters. It was common-sense that newspapers made money by pandering to their readers. As a twenty-seven year old financial assistant said, 'the newspapers have got to print what the people want to read about' (interview 41). It's all 'going to get worse', said his mother, 'if people don't say "We don't want that sort of news"'. But people do want it, replied her son, 'this is the problem...people still carry on buying the *Sun*...It's a sad reflection on this country'. 'Oh, it is, I agree', said his mother.

A fifty-six year old mother used similar words: 'I think this is a sad reflection on society today' (interview 16). She continued: 'People are very indiscreet, people do not respect the privacy of others; if there's a bit of scandal that the press, the media or anybody can stir up, they seem to get great pleasure from it'. And they get money too: 'They'll make so much money out of one photograph', complained her daughter. There was an economy of desire, with royalty as the victim of scandal's market-place. 'The media's getting worse', said a sixteen year old daughter, 'they've got nothing to write about so they pick on the royals' (interview 24). As she said, 'a bad story's a good story for the paper, it makes people want to read'.

These claims about the media and pandering also dissociate the self from Others. The speakers are claiming a high moral ground for themselves. All the remarks which have just been quoted contain linguistic devices of dissociation. Who wants to know about Sarah Ferguson's weight, the radical daughter had challenged her royalist family. The absence which followed her question was revealing. Not one of the royalists volunteered 'I do'. Instead, 'they' –

newspaper readers, other readers – were indicated. As has been remarked by linguists, small pronouns can speak so eloquently (Maitland and Wilson, 1987; Seidel, 1975). In the examples just cited (interviews 41, 16 and 24), it was 'people' who want to read the shameful stories; 'people' are indiscreet; 'people' don't respect privacy; 'people' will continue to buy the *Sun*. 'We don't buy it', said the mother specifically, lest the interviewer misunderstood her son.

If speakers were interested in knowing about the royals, then they needed to make contrastive distinctions between their innocent interests and the immoral desires of others, to which the papers pandered. The mother and daughter, who worked in the same office, were cases in point (interview 23). Really, said the mother, 'you want to know the nice things about their life'. Her daughter agreed: 'I mean some of the things they put in the paper, I mean, as though people are interested in it'. 'Yeah, but people are', replied her mother, 'that's what sells newspapers, especially papers like the *Sun*'. 'Yeah, I suppose they are, yeah', conceded her daughter. A quick change of grammatical subjects underlined the moral contrast. 'You', who want to know the nice things, included mother and daughter. 'People', and 'they', who want the nasty things, excluded the speakers. The substitution was done neatly, quickly.

If the speaker can claim to read a morally improving newspaper, then the contrast between the self and others can be easily achieved. We don't buy the *Sun*, said the mother, disclaiming the disgraceful desires of others (interview 41). More work of dissociation needed to be done, if the speakers themselves read the very papers which they accused.

An example occurred with the working-class family, where the mother and father read the *Star* during the week and the *News of the World* on Sundays (interview 39). The recently married son and daughter-in-law took the *Sun*. Familiar themes emerged as they talked about the press and royalty. None of them approved of press intrusion upon royal privacy: 'The private side of their life, the same as anybody's, should be respected', said the father. Then he specifically dissociated himself: as for 'the private side of their life, well, I particularly, I don't particularly want to know'. But 'Why do the papers print these details?', asked the interviewer. 'It sells papers', answered the mother. The others agreed: 'It sells papers and they're out to sell them', said the daughter-in-law. The son-in-law amplified, linking desire with profit: 'Yes, it sells papers, but people buy them, somebody obviously wants to know about it'. The 'people', or 'somebodies', who 'obviously' want to know, didn't include himself. Then, he made a further move: 'Yeah, but you don't necessarily buy it for the cheap sensationalism that you get in the paper'. 'You', which included himself, don't buy the sensational papers for the sensationalism. But others do, obviously.

Sometimes tabloid purchasers gave explicit reasons for their choice of newspaper. A grandmother, her son and daughter-in-law were talking of the disgraceful content of the tabloids, disapproving of the way they printed details of the royal private life (interview 60). 'It's got nothing to do with the country', said the grandmother. Yet she admitted to reading the tabloids regularly. Her son eased his mother over the potential embarrassment: 'Mum likes the *Sun* and the *Star*, because of the bingo, don't you'. 'Yeah', she replied, 'because I've got nowt else to do'. She added that she also bought the *News of the World*, 'but I only have it for my bingo, to be honest'.

The ex-fitter, and his wife who had worked as a cleaner, were criticising the press (interview 52). The interviewer asked them which papers they took. Embarrassment. 'I get the *Sun*', said the husband. He paused: 'Err, err, I think it's a terrible newspaper as a newspaper'. His wife agreed. He continued: 'But what happened is...'. He told an involved story about taking the *Daily Herald* many years ago; when that paper folded, changing its character to become the *Sun*, he continued reading it for 'the racing coverage'; but, 'as a newspaper, it's bad, it's bad'. 'You can't believe what they write, can you', agreed his wife. They criticised it lengthily: '...bad, bad, bad reporting...they just don't care...as a newspaper, it's a bad 'un'. But its racing coverage was good.

It has been observed that, in families, men tend to exert greater control over the consumption of media, buying the newspapers and controlling which television channel is watched (Morley, 1986). The exercise of male power offers a rhetorical opportunity for women. They are absolved of responsibility for purchasing the disapproved tabloids. Freed from such responsibility, they can more easily admit to reading the contents. As will be seen in the next chapter, a greater interest in royalty is ascribed to women than to men. The interest can be protected, if the men are blamed for buying the papers which are said to pander shamefully to such interests.

The mother, who knew the royal warts claimed that 'I read papers that I wouldn't choose; I don't buy newspapers but my husband has these papers and he buys the *Sunday People* and the

News of the World' (interview 23). If it was up to her, she wouldn't have such papers: 'I am given the *Daily Mirror* to look at, but I'd choose to buy *Today* newspaper'. She'd like a more serious paper. Yet she was full of praise for James Whitaker, the royal correspondent of the *Mirror*. A forty-seven year old cleaner complained about the exaggerations in the press and the way that journalists hounded royalty (interview 49). When asked specifically about what paper she read, she said, 'I don't really look at them, but Trevor (her husband) buys the *Sun*'. Neither her husband, nor that of the mother, who was given the *Mirror*, were present to make their disclaimers.

In another interview, both husband and wife were present, and complementary dissociations could be heard (interview 3). Husband and wife condemned the press treatment of royals as sensationalism. 'I mean they're looking for things to sell papers, aren't they? It's sensationalism', said the husband. 'They seem to embroider everything', added his wife. 'It's to sell the newspapers', he repeated. They were daily readers of the *Daily Mirror*. The mother, when questioned, almost admitted that she was no different from its other readers: 'I'd be just like everybody else and I'd read it all, but I don't think I like all this sort of trivial thing, no'. 'I'd' read it, she says – not I do read it. Straightaway she made a dissociation. She does not buy the offending paper. If it were up to her, they would buy something different, 'not too high up, because, I mean, some of them, I can't understand anyway'. But, 'we aren't allowed to change from the *Mirror*, because he likes it better...but it's not a very good paper'.

The father now offered the sort of self-justification which Hewitt and Stokes (1975) have termed 'credentialling'. He was not attracted by the sensationalism, he claimed. He volunteered a safely neutral, and rather familiar, reason for his choice of paper: 'I have the *Daily Mirror* because I think it's got the best racing page'.

The husband and wife could both dissociate themselves from those who buy the scandal-filled newspapers. The purchaser disclaims desire for the gossip: 'I'm not particularly interested in the Royal Family...I personally skip those bits'. The non-purchaser admits: 'Yes, I read *all* of it about the Royal Family'. But she absolves herself from responsibility: she wants a different paper. The two of them – the admitted reader and the claimed non-reader – have their respective alibis. They are not part of the economics of shame. Others desire the undesirable. Others are guilty.

TEMPTATION AND THE OBJECTS OF DESIRE

The cynical consciousness is not entirely shameless, for the tales of dissociation indicate that there are matters which are considered shameful. The desire for intimate knowledge of the royal life is a case in point. Even if the desire is conceded, it was hedged with embarrassment. 'I must admit I'd love to be a fly on the wall', said a mother, recognising that the desire was not quite proper (interview 2). At best, it was something to be confessed. And often it was to be denied and attributed to others.

Barthes (1983) has written of 'the author as an object of desire'. A reader can be fascinated by the author as an individual: 'If an author interests me, I may want to know the intimacy, the *small change* of his time, his tastes, his moods, his scruples' (p.481). In this sense, royalty is an object of desire. The portrait upon coinage of the small change is not the formal figure with coronet, but a body, which is all too nakedly human, after all. And the desire for the intimacy of this portrait is seen as illicit. But where there is shameful desire, there exists the possibility of temptation – especially when the desire can be excited for the price of a daily newspaper.

The interplay between desire and denial could be heard, as shameful temptations were talked about and the delights of hidden knowledge were denied. A husband, in his early fifties, complained of press photographs of 'Fergie or Princess Diana': 'You know how women get out of a car, they show a bit more leg...you've got always a photographer there...there always seems to be one there taking a picture, aah, a bit of a thigh' (interview 15). He continued: 'That's just a load of garbage, you know, I'm not interested'. He was not interested, but he had noticed. Not just once. There 'always' are these photographs.

'Do you read the gossipy bits?', asked the interviewer. 'Mum does', replied the twelve year old son (interview 17). 'No, I don't', his mother answered. She does, repeated the son. His fourteen year old sister added: 'And then she says "Oh this is such rubbish"'. The mother conceded that she might look at the *News of the World* or the *Sun* 'on an odd Sunday afternoon', when visiting her mother-in-law. She continued to justify herself: 'You always wonder why you bother reading it, frankly don't you, even if your eye's just gone along the line'. 'After you've read it for about half an hour', said her son. Then, her daughter added: 'Auntie Jane does that, she reads it, then she goes "I hate these papers that print these stories about the royals" and she's read everything'.

165

She's read everything – the eye has been drawn along the line – the bit of thigh has been spotted. And it's rubbish – uninteresting – hateful. But something leads the spectator towards the object of guilty desire. A respectably bourgeois family gave an example of the hidden attractions of the disapproved newspapers (interview 41). Their various members have already been heard condemning tabloid papers. It was the mother who complained about youthful *Sun* readers being empty vessels. Her younger son had specifically criticised *Sunday Sport* readers for believing that the royals were idle yuppies, lazing on beaches in bikinis. Yet, there was a family episode with the *Sunday Sport*, the most tabloid of all the tabloids.

The mother started the story: 'I picked up a newspaper the other day that I've never seen before, and I hope I don't see again, and it had the crazy title of the *Sunday Sport*'. The younger son knew exactly which paper his mother was talking about: 'Oh, yeah, yeah, it's got a little bit of sport on the back of it'. 'Oooh, oooh', the mother exclaimed. 'And a nude on every other page', laughed the father. The disapproval was marked, not by tight-lipped moralism, but by hoots of fun, in which they all joined. The mother told her complicated story about chancing upon an issue of the *Sport*. She had been visiting a friend, a farmer's wife in a market garden. And there it was – a picture 'propped up against a flower-pot, there was this great big fat man'. She continued her story: 'I said "What on earth is that?"; "Oooh", she said, "we found it in one of our old bags of papers"; she said, "Do you want to have a look?"; and I said, "Not really"; she said, "it's the most disgusting"'. But, together with her friend, she had looked at the object of disgust.

At this point, she was interrupted. Her sons had their tales to tell about the awfulness of the *Sunday Sport*. 'I bought it by accident the other week', said her older son, 'I meant to buy the *Post* but I bought the *Sunday Sport* instead on a Wednesday'. He did not explain how he could have mistaken the tabloid, with its lurid headlines, for the local evening paper. He had not returned to the newsagent to rectify matters. The father had seen the *Sport* too: 'I couldn't believe it'. He did not describe the circumstances of his encounter. They all joked about the paper. 'The headlines of last week's...were "Elvis Lives In My TV"', said the younger son. The mother laughed. 'Anyway', went on the younger son, 'this is the news that people want'. 'Yeah', agreed his brother. 'Well, evidently this fellow was fifty stone and he wanted a woman', the mother said, trying to continue with her story about the paper's story. 'Fifty stone women please reply', laughed her older son. 'Well', said the mother, 'I can tell you what the remarks were that were flying around the staff; so we're really getting down to the fact that our poor Royal Family is treated just like fodder for the crazy news people'.

The family members dissociate themselves from the *Sport*, as they express their disapproval. It's what 'people' – other people, the employed staff – want. Their own contacts are purely accidental, or so it is claimed. The mother chanced upon a picture; the son intended to buy something quite different. The mother never wants to see the paper again. But she wants to talk about it; and she overcomes interruptions to tell her story. The *Sport* might not be present in the living-room, but its contents are reconstructed in detail. In this form, it is welcomed into the family home.

Leith and Myerson (1989) suggest that stories are never merely stories, but 'there is a 'point' to storytelling' (p.28). The mother finishes her story with a moral conclusion. 'Our' poor Royal Family is the victim of other people's craziness. 'We' are sympathising, and others are persecuting. Any desire on 'our' part is denied.

Occasionally, in the course of argumentation, the self can be revealed to have the shameful desires which are claimed to be the property of others. When the mother made her confession about wishing to be a fly upon the royal wall, her husband, a fierce critic of monarchy, mocked her interest: 'Do they have separate bedrooms? I mean do they see each other at night?', he jeered (interview 2). His daughter conceded that 'you' shouldn't want to know, but 'people are curious'. She suggested that people are interested in royalty's private life, but not in that of ordinary people:

(Interview 2)

Daughter. But people out there don't say 'Ooh do Dave and Jan sleep together? {*Mother laughs*} Do they have separate bedrooms? Do they watch telly together? Do they do this?'

Mother. Yeah, but your dad came in tonight and said their {*the neighbours*} bedroom light's been on all the time {*Father laughs*}, there you are see, that's curiosity, isn't it {*laughs*}

Daughter. It's nothing to do with him

Father. Well, of course it hasn't; but, these, these, you've just, no the statement was made: do you think they're an ordinary family?

Some very close family work is being done, as it must be when a daughter brings the parental bedroom into the living-room conversation. Laughter punctuated the exchanges.

The father has claimed the high moral ground, damning his wife's interest in the royals as voyeuristic, even salacious. His daughter has agreed that people shouldn't want to know about the private life of royalty. Royals alone are the victims of the prurient gaze, she suggests. Strangers aren't interested in the secrets of the ordinary bedroom, for instance her parents' bedroom. They don't ask whether Dave and Jan – her father and mother – are sleeping together.

Not so, rejoins her mother. Take your dad: just tonight he comes in and says that the neighbours' bedroom light has been on all the time. It's got nothing to do with him, says the daughter. Her father, caught out, admits his guilt: of course, it was none of his business. His shameful curiosities – the very same ones he had mocked in others – have been exposed. He had wished to be a fly on someone else's bedroom wall. He flusters and changes the subject.

THE SUBJECT OF DESIRE

In one crucial respect, the royal as an object of desire differs from the author as an object of desire. According to Barthes, if someone takes an author as an object of their desire, they might 'even go so far as to prefer his person to his works, eagerly snatching up his journal and neglecting his books' (1983, p.481). For royalty today, the distinction between the person and the work cannot be maintained: their persons are their works. As was discussed in previous chapters, the 'job' of royalty is said, *inter alia*, to involve projecting the image of familial domesticity; it is to be a public image of private life. It might be true that the public will eagerly snatch up any book published by royals, but authorship is extra to the main work of appearing as a living journal. In fact, the royals' most eagerly snatched books have been journals, such as Queen Victoria's *Leaves from the Journal of Our Life in the Highlands* (1868); or *Queen Alexandra's Christmas Gift Book: Photographs from My Camera* (1908), designed to resemble a private snap-shot album.

An invisible royalty would not be doing the job of projecting the correct images of private life. But intrusion upon 'their' private life is criticised. 'We' might know them warts and all, as the mother in interview 23 said, but then this knowledge can be a matter for censure, and even guilt. One might turn the issue around, to talk not of the 'job' of royals, but the requirements of subjects. The loyal subject will 'know' the royals – almost as if the royals were part of the family. This knowledge and interest is a sign of loyalty. Yet, the loyal subject will be caught in the dilemma of knowing what should not be known.

The mother, who knew the warts and all, illustrates the dilemma (interview 23). She and her daughter displayed detailed and confident knowledge. For instance, their remarks about the Queen's grandchildren have already been quoted. Yet, at other times, knowledge was talked about differently. The papers were to blame, 'because you're told too much nowadays', said the mother. Her daughter agreed: we shouldn't be told 'about all these wild parties and arguments on doorsteps and things'. It was none of our business, said the mother. The daughter had a solution to the problem: 'I think they ought to have the official photograph every year at Christmas and then we don't want to know anything from them for the rest of the year'. Her mother hesitated: 'Um, well'. Then she admitted: 'it's nice for me to know, because I'm nosey, but I mean, I don't really want to know but'. She laughed, and the laugh finished her sentence.

She knew the royals intimately – warts and all – but she ought not to know them this way. She didn't want to know. There again, she did want to know. One official photograph wouldn't satisfy this desire. But she ought not to desire.

The mother ascribes the desire for knowledge to 'nosiness', as if it were an individual quirk of personality. But she is talking about the requirements of subject and of monarch. Royals would not be seen to be earning their wealth if they posed but once a year. Moreover, the cynical consciousness, which can advocate a display of hypocrisy, would know that the stiff, formal poses of an official picture are not to be trusted. Official lines are not to be accepted deferentially, but the spaces between the official lines are to be examined. The mother specifically criticised the journalists on women's magazines: 'They creep around, they're sycophantics'. More than deference and an official photograph are required to assess whether 'they', the royals, are satisfactorily doing their job of setting 'us' the correct examples. The royal private life is the public concern.

If the moral examples of the exemplary family are to be assessed, they must be examined. The more seriously the mother took monarchy, the more her talk probed for private knowledge. She and her daughter argued at length, assessing the moral personalities and dilemmas of royals. The daughter liked Princess Diana as much as she disliked the Duchess of York. She constantly made comparisons between the two royal wives, the failings of one being the virtues of the other. 'Fergie' was an insincere person: 'it's all false', 'she's not genuine'. On the other hand, Diana 'means what she says and what she does'; 'she's very genuine and straight'. And so on. The daughter, having claimed to have seen through the media's lies, could see through false royal personae. There was a double hermeneutics of suspicion.

Such claims often constituted judgements about fundamental matters of contemporary morality. Mother and daughter were discussing the rights and wrongs of the Duchess of York leaving her young baby in the care of a nurse, while she visited Australia. To discuss the particular case, they talked of wider matters. How should mothers behave? How should wives behave? Which came first – the responsibilities of wife or mother? The daughter argued against the Duchess. Her mother put the other side: 'Her husband should come first and foremost, even over her children'. From the general, she proceeded to the particular: 'They've not been married that long and they're obviously still *in love*'. But there were other considerations, other speculations: 'Of course, you don't know what demands he might put on her, he might be a man that might look elsewhere, if his wife isn't there; you just do not know and...she may need, they may need each other physically'. She too was looking at the window of another couple's bedroom.

Here was a loyal royalist, who read much about royalty and expressed distaste for the tabloid persecution. As she defends the Duchess, so she talks of the royal sex life. This is not just nosiness, as if the details were desired for their own sake. The father was caught gazing at his neighbours' bedroom window (interview 2). It's none of his business, his family declared. When mother and daughter are speculating about the private life of the Duchess, they are discussing how wives and mothers should behave. These married women are assessing the performance of one who is paid to represent that behaviour. The mother cites intimate, all too human, details to defend the Duchess. It is her business. And, yet, somehow it seems that it isn't.

Speakers might claim that there is a distinction between what should be known and what should not – between information about the grandchildren and information about the wild parties. Even so, the same speakers are drawn to estimating the royal character and the royal image. In the complexities of desires and denials, there is a dynamic which favours sympathy. It might be thought that the more that is known about the royals – the more the mystique is stripped away – the more faults are revealed. That might be so, but the possibilities for discovering the personal faults lead to reasons for sympathy. The outlines of the argumentative drift can be reconstructed. The more that is known of 'their' lives, including the warts and all, the more 'their' life is known to be known. The more it is known to be known, the harder 'their' life is imagined to be – the more 'we' sympathise with 'them' and blame the prying of others. The possibility for censure can tilt into sympathy: no wonder, 'they' fail to produce perfect behaviour. And in expressing sympathy for the hard life which they have to lead, 'we' accept our comparatively fortunate position as subjects. Even a slight tinge of guilt might accompany our acceptance.

There is a further point. The theme of the nation is never far removed from that of royalty. The talk about the media includes a number of depictions. There are the royals as victims, 'ourselves' as rationally critical, 'others' as gullible or shameless, and the press as villains. There is also a depiction of the nation. As several speakers claimed, the press treatment of royalty is a sad reflection on the country.

Benedict Anderson has claimed that newspapers have played a crucial role in the imagining of communities which are nations. He writes of the newspaper-reader 'observing exact replicas of his own paper being consumed by his subway, barbershop, or residential neighbours' (1983, p.39). In this way, a sense of a shared world is imagined. However, it is not that simple, for the imagined community is not imagined as a harmonious unity; but it is a fractured and morally corrupted community which is imagined. As speakers spoke of the newspapers and royalty, they imagine gullible, shameless others, reading what should not be read, whether in barbershop, on the train or at home. The self distances itself from these others and from the contents of the papers, which are being read. However, the self does not imagine itself to be alone in a land of shameful desires. The subjects can imagine that royalty thinks likewise. In this way, the subjects can imagine themselves drawn closer in sympathy with the family which is claimed to symbolise the imagined community. But this further imagining does not restore the imagined community to an imagined unity. There still remain the sad reflections in the imagination.

7

A WOMAN'S REALM

In the discussion of desire and denial, there was a theme which kept rising to the surface, bobbing along for a few moments, and then sinking from view. This was the theme of gender. If the notion of 'family' is integral to the phenomenon of modern royalty, then so must be gender. This much is contained in an anthropological point, made many years ago by Lévi-Strauss. In his famous essay on the family, Lévi-Strauss (1985) argued that all known family structures involve gendered divisions of labour. Thus, an interest in a royal family cannot but be an interest in a highly gendered phenomenon. However, what has bobbed to the surface has been more than this. The interest itself might be gendered, with women being said to be especially concerned with royal matters.

Increasingly, in the previous chapter, women's voices were to be heard. It was women who were saying that the royals seemed as if they were almost part of the family. Towards the end of the chapter, it was a mother and daughter who were heard discussing the intimate details of a princess's obligations as mother and wife. Other analysts have remarked on the feminine dimension of interest in royalty. Rosalind Coward (1983) notes that women's magazines constantly are referring to royal issues. According to Coward, the drama of 'The Royals', in common with most soap operas, attracts a disproportionately female audience, because it 'addresses choices faced by all women' (p.170). Diana Simmonds (1984), in her breezy but sardonic account of *Princess Di, The National Dish*, argues that princesses, as virgin brides and mothers of kings, are the key figures in the modern mythology of royalty. Moreover, Simmonds assumes that this mythology has a special appeal to those subjects who share the same gender as the princesses.

172

The public opinion polls tell a similar story. For instance, MORI, October 1987, indicates that twenty-five percent of women are prepared to describe themselves as 'very interested' in news about the Royal Family, as compared with eleven percent of men. Lack of interest does not indicate republicanism. Over half the male respondents (fifty-three percent) declared themselves uninterested in the Royal Family, but only seven percent said that Britain would be 'better off on balance' if monarchy were abolished. The differences between males and females, found on the question about 'interest', virtually disappeared on this question about the abolition of monarchy.

Gendering of interest should neither be treated as haphazard, nor as an obvious 'fact' of nature. Such gendering is connected to the nature of the 'job' which is commonly expected of royals. As has been discussed earlier, the 'royal job' is said to involve the public presentation of private, domestic morality. Nancy Fraser (1989), in her perceptive critique of Habermas's *Theory of Communicative Action*, argues that in the contemporary world the very division between private and public life is gendered. She suggests that the world of public affairs is a male world, whilst the private sphere is typically conceived to be female. The phenomenon of royalty cuts across the distinction between public and private worlds. It is that part of public life which is the presentation of the private. Therefore, it is, potentially at least, a feminised area in public life.

There is a curious feature about the role of the modern monarch. Alone, out of all the major roles of public life, it is the one for which women, despite the discriminatory customs of primogeniture, are held to be as fitted, if not more fitted, as men. In modern British history, the reigns of Victoria and Elizabeth II have been notable successes. The public does not look with dismay upon the prospect of a queen. In fact, the reverse might be the case. If the monarch is to represent domestic virtue, then a mother, indeed a grandmother, on the throne offers reassurance that the sovereign is not going to be too gamey a figure. A woman, whose job is to represent the family, is doing the traditionally female job of being wife or mother. On the other hand, a man, whose job is bound up with the family, is in the awkward position of not having a 'proper', public man's job. This, of course, marks a distinct difference from former times, when the sovereign might have been expected to be a warrior or politician whose prime responsibilities lay in the world of men.

The gendering of interest in monarchy can be examined in a number of ways. Male and female responses to questionnaire items could be examined for differences. The popularity of individual royals could be assessed, to see whether royal women are more likely to be the 'stars' of the show. However, the present tactic is to explore something much more simple, yet more fundamental. This is to examine the common-sense assumption that interest in royalty is gendered. As will be seen, both males and females will confidently say that royalty is a female interest.

An advance example of this way of talking can be given. A working-class woman of fifty-seven was speaking of her interest in royalty: 'I'm interested in the younger ones...whether Fergie's having another baby and in gossip really...I think that's what I'm interested in, just general gossip...I like to know the Queen's alright' (interview 52). She continued: 'I just generally like to know...just general gossip, I should think, just like a woman really'.

As she expressed her interest, so she downgraded it as 'just' gossip. In the previous chapter, an interest in gossip about the royals was seen to be open to the criticism of being intrusive, even salacious. The mother was specifically indicating that she did not desire that sort of gossip. It was 'general' gossip. She had the interests of the Queen at heart; she wanted to know she was alright; and whether another royal baby was on the way. Yet, it was still gossip, she acknowledged. There is a second theme in her comments. She attributes her desire for gossip to gender. Gossip, according to common stereotypes, is often held to be the preserve of women and it is branded as an unworthy form of communication (Aebischer, 1985; Fiske, 1987). This woman claims to like gossip about royalty, 'just like a woman'. The stereotype accompanies the downgrading and vice versa.

In these themes, there is ample scope for claiming and double-declaiming. Claims about the nature of royalty can be made, and about the nature of those who are interested in royalty. If the latter claims are gendered, then these will involve further claims about what it means to be male and to be female – what it means to be 'just like a woman, really'. As such, speakers will be making claims about their own gendered selves, as they depict the royal realm as a women's realm.

THE CONSTITUTION OF THE ENGLISH MALE

Before examining such themes in the interviews, it might be useful once more to glance backwards to Walter Bagehot. Such glances provide a corrective against the assumption that all is new in contemporary patterns of thinking. There is a particularly famous paragraph in *The English Constitution* in which Bagehot introduces the idea of the family upon the throne as an 'interesting idea'. The paragraph has been much quoted. Parts of it have already been quoted in previous chapters. The paragraph contains one theme – that of gender – which has largely passed unnoticed. As Bagehot developed his argument for the usefulness of a popular constitutional monarchy, he cited the nature of women and their interests in royal weddings. The whole paragraph is worth citing:

> A *family* on the throne is an interesting idea also. It brings down the pride of sovereignty to the level of petty life. No feeling could seem more childish than the enthusiasm of the English at the marriage of the Prince of Wales. They treated as a great political event, what, looked at as a matter of pure business, was very small indeed. But no feeling could be more like common human nature as it is, and as it is likely to be. The women – one half the human race at least – care fifty times more for a marriage than a ministry. All but a few cynics like to see a pretty novel touching for a moment the dry scenes of the grave world. A princely marriage is the brilliant edition of a universal fact, and, as such, it rivets mankind. We smile at the *Court Circular*; but remember how many people read the *Court Circular*! its use is not in what it says, but in those to whom it speaks.
>
> (Bagehot 1867/1965, pp.85–6)

Several points can be made about Bagehot's paragraph.

Women and weddings

Bagehot's train of thinking goes straight from the interesting idea of the family upon the throne to an interest in weddings. *The English Constitution* was published only four years after the marriage of the Prince of Wales. The wedding, as well as that of the Princess Royal in 1858, had attracted popular interest in ways which no royal marriages of the previous century had. In a vivid phrase, Bagehot calls the royal marriage the brilliant edition of a universal fact. He then makes another leap – the leap of gender. Women are particularly interested in royal marriages, because of their interest in marriages generally. Bagehot does not consider it necessary to

175

justify these claims. He merely refers to human nature – 'common human nature'. Thus, the claim about royal weddings depends upon a claim about the nature of women. All these claims are made rapidly within a few sentences.

Unity and division

The paragraph oscillates between images of unity and of division. Ostensibly, Bagehot is talking about the whole nation (identified as England), united in its affection for the sovereign and for the sovereign's family. Yet, in depicting national unity, he switches from talking about the whole of mankind (not just England) to talking about 'one half of the human race', namely women. The princely marriage might rivet 'mankind', but it is womankind which is especially riveted. Thus, a division of gender is visible within the supposedly united nation and a common human nature. There are women who care fifty times more for a princely wedding than for affairs of state. And there are men whose enthusiasms are more tempered, leaning perhaps towards the serious affairs of state.

Downgrading the womanly interest

In depicting the womanly interest, Bagehot downgrades it. As an urbanely tolerant liberal, he does not do so crudely. There is a juxtaposition of themes. Nothing could be more 'childish' than the interest in royal weddings, he writes. In this sentence, 'the English' in general are being childish. The juxtaposition allows the general childishness to be unpacked. The clue is given two sentences later. Not all people are drawn equally to childish pleasures. Women in particular care fifty times more for marriage than they do for the serious business of politics. Childish women, frivolous women, caring far more about private than public life: it is all there to be inferred, but not quite said directly.

Claiming the male constitution

As he writes of the nature of women, Bagehot is also affirming the nature of men. He is making claims about himself as the writer, and, in this context, his claims are implicitly gendered. Bagehot dissociates himself from the childlike sections of the population. He slips from 'they', who enjoy the royal marriages', to 'we' who

176

appreciate important matters. 'We' smile at the *Court Circular*, and he conspiratorially includes his readers in this band of high-minded brothers. 'We' – a serious, but tolerant 'we' – are told to take the *Court Circular* seriously, not for its contents (heaven forbid!), but for its usefulness. The intrinsically frivolous publication, like the intrinsically frivolous interest in weddings, accomplishes a serious end: loyalty to the English state. The frothy-minded, wedding-loving women are loyal women – not that it is stated quite so blatantly. But, it would be hard to make the mistake of believing that Bagehot's paragraph had been written by a woman. The words dissociate the author from women. 'The women' is the phrase used. 'Men', and most certainly 'the men', are absent phrases. 'We' are present, of course, educated, amused and amusing – and implicitly masculine.

A DEFINITE DIFFERENCE

In the modern talk of the family discussions, there is a similar tendency to gender the interest in monarchy. There are also claims that weddings are women's business. There, however, is a difference from Bagehot's paragraph. Bagehot was producing a monologue – a male monologue. 'Women' and their childish enthusiasms were only represented in his text through his voice, and then only as an aside. In the actual discussions, women were present to add their voices to the argument. And sometimes, with interesting consequences, male voices were entirely absent.

Women participated in disproportionate numbers, for the topic of the research had attracted more women than men. There were four wives who had been left to discuss the matter alone with the interviewer, because their husbands were unwilling to participate (interviews 21, 47, 49 and 51). By contrast, there were no solitary husbands. Similarly, there were groups of mothers and daughters, but no groups composed only of fathers and sons. In one case, as will be seen, there was a male lurking upstairs, unwilling to venture downstairs because of the topic under discussion (interview 50).

When the question of men's and women's interest was raised, respondents typically had little hesitation: of course, women, more than men, were interested in the Royal Family. Both males and females would imply that this was so obvious that it needed little justification. For instance, this was seen in the family discussion of the mother and father – secretary and engineer respectively – and their two teenage daughters, aged nineteen and sixteen (interview

177

27). It was a middle-class family, living in an old rural cottage. The appearance of conventional respectability was disturbed by the younger daughter's spiked hair, make-up and clothing – all heavily coloured black in the 'goth' style. The family had been talking about interest in royalty. The younger daughter had said that her own friends showed no particular interest. The father was sitting quietly as the three women chatted among themselves. The interviewer asked whether women were more interested. The three women, whether conventionally or rebelliously attired, were of one voice:

(Interview 27)
Interviewer. Are women more interested than men?
Mother.   Oh yes [I should think so, definitely, yeah
Older daughter.   [Oh yeah
Younger daughter.   [Yeah

None had any doubt. The obviousness needed no explanation. The interviewer persisted: 'Why is that?'. The younger daughter, the rebel amongst the country bourgeois, answered: 'Well, women just like to look at the clothes, don't they'.

Such an exchange was quite typical. The theme of clothing, which escaped Bagehot's attention, will crop up again and again. The cast of speakers can be changed – male for female, worker for bourgeois, old for young – but a similar script is repeated. A retired upholsterer and his wife, herself a former factory worker, are speaking (interview 15). Both are in their fifties:

(Interview 15)
Interviewer. Do you think women are more interested than men
     in hearing about them?
Husband. I think so, more, yeah [definitely
Wife.   [Yeah yeah, I think yeah, I
     think women are more interested in it than men

There is the same word of certainty: definitely, they say.

On another occasion, the interviewer asked 'Are women more interested than men in things like weddings?' (interview 50). The mother, a cleaner, and her two daughters all answered at once. 'Oh, they are yes, yes', said the mother. As she was saying this, both the daughters said in unison 'Definitely'. The mother repeated 'Definitely'. She then illustrated male lack of interest by citing the case of the nineteen year old daughter's boyfriend.

'Oh, yes, yes, definitely, yes', she said, 'I said to Wendy's boy-friend something about the Royal Family and he says "Oh...I'm going upstairs, because I don't know anything at all about them"; I said, "Well, you'd know the Queen if she sat next to you on a bus"; he says "Oh I doubt it, I don't know anything about it, I'm going upstairs"'. They all laughed at that.

The mother proceeded from the particular story of the boyfriend to a general conclusion, which is the 'point' of the story: 'They're not interested, are they? Well, most of them I don't think are'. The telling of the story enables a bit of family business to be done. The women mock the boyfriend's claim not to recognise the Queen. And they mock his flight to a royal-free, female-free zone of the house. The joke is enjoyed in the male-free zone – the father and thirteen year old son are absent at a football match. The mother's switching between the general and the particular ensures that the women, in laughing at the boyfriend, are laughing at men in general.

Other comments also suggested that royalty was a female topic. A nineteen year old daughter, a sales demonstrator, thought that it was women who bought books about royalty. 'I wouldn't have bought one for Dad', she said 'and I wouldn't have bought one for my boyfriend' (interview 5). She went on: 'I might have bought Mum one, I don't know whether you'd appreciate something on the Duchess or Lady Diana, or something'. Neither the father nor brother protested about their exclusion from the royal gift list.

Her brother expressed his lack of interest in royalty several times. Once, his father had asked him 'Do you ever talk to your friends about the Royal Family?'. He answered simply: 'No'. His sister asked whether the girls, whom he knew, were interested. After an initial denial, and after further probes from his family, he conceded that the girls might talk about royalty among themselves. His sister recalled her own school-days: 'I mean, I never talked about it to other boys at school, but yet we would have talked about it among ourselves'. Royalty was being marked out as female business. Mothers, not fathers, would be interested in royal books; girls, not boys, would stand in the playground chatting about the Royal Family. It was a picture which the family was jointly constructing.

In order to assess the strength of a common-place it is always advisable to look for those 'deviant cases', when the common-place is challenged. Two incidents can be given, when there was an argumentative challenge to the common-place that women are

179

more interested in royalty than men. Both cases reveal the strength of the common-place.

The first occurred in the only discussion to feature an all-male household (interview 19). This took place in the home shared by a ladies' hairdresser and his friend, a teacher. They were aged twenty-nine and thirty-one respectively. This atypical household produced an uncommon response to the question about women and interest. Instead of the rush towards definite agreement, there was reluct-ance: 'I don't feel able to comment on a question like that', said the teacher. He was supported by his friend: 'I think it's a very difficult question to answer because you start getting into the, um, the dangerous area of making generalisations'. This was the question which mothers and daughters, husbands and wives, found so easy to answer. 'All women are individuals', continued the hairdresser, 'and I think it's a very difficult question to answer really'. At this point, the two male friends were uncomfortable with the common-sense stereotypes of men and women.

Their reluctance to link interest in royalty with women did not arise because they themselves were greatly interested in royal affairs, and, in consequence, might fear being thought feminine. In fact, they distanced themselves from royal matters. The hairdresser was talking about the day after Prince Charles's marriage. He went back to work and 'and it was all like, you know, wedding, wedding, wedding all day'. He himself hadn't watched the wedding: 'It was like there was something wrong with me because I wasn't interested, you know, looking forward to this day, where I'd sit and watch the television and (say), "Didn't she look lovely, isn't her dress nice, you know"'. As he said the last bit, he mimicked a simpering female voice. It was not his interest, not his voice, not his gender.

His tone was providing a partial reply to the very question which he had been reluctant to answer. He was suggesting that interest in royal weddings was a female interest. As a male working in the female culture of a ladies' hairdressing salon, he felt out of place the day after the royal wedding. Still, he did not explicitly use the stereotypes of gender. In fact, he protested against the conventional stereotypes, claiming himself to be excluded by them. He said that advertising was aimed at white heterosexual men. 'Gay people and black people' felt excluded by the images of white families 'on the billboards around the city'. It was the same with the image of the Royal Family. Most of his close friends, he said, 'don't live as the stereotypical family unit that everyone thinks that we should live by'. Excluded by the stereotype, nevertheless, he could not escape it, especially on the day when it was wedding, wedding, wedding.

The conventional stereotype about women and interest in royalty was also challenged in the family whose general conservatism was upset by the radical daughter and her boyfriend, both of whom were fresh from university (interview 35). Mother, father and brother continually argued with the student pair. In the previous chapter, the rhetorical challenges of the daughter were quoted: 'Who wants to know on the front page of a newspaper that Sarah Ferguson looks fat in her new dress?'. Lots of people, responded father and brother, turning to cite the popularity of the popular press. The daughter then changed argumentative course, and, in so doing, she introduced gender. Royalty was promoting traditional values and gender stereotypes, she argued; royals threaten 'the modern view that women can go out looking scruffy or that woman shouldn't be like totally skinny'. The interviewer asked whether it is 'mostly a women's thing to be interested in the Royal Family?' and the daughter, loyal to the honour of her gender, fiercely resisted. 'No', she replied, pointing to her father, 'he's *far* more interested than I am'. The father defended himself, suggesting that his interest was not a womanly matter: 'I'm just a traditionalist'. Anyone could be a traditionalist, male or female.

Scarcely had the father made this comment, when the daughter rescinded her denial of women's interest. She did this of her own accord, without argumentative challenge from anyone. Her accusation that men in general – and her father in particular – were more interested in royalty crumpled as she qualified herself: 'I think it is', she said, 'like you get all these little old women buying the *Realm* or whatever it is'. Just like her own grandmother: 'Gran's really interested, isn't she', she said. 'She's patriotic', said her brother, pointedly re-interpreting the ascription. His sister ignored him. Again he said: 'She's patriotic'.

The daughter has contested that piece of common-sense which says that women are more interested in royalty than men. But her argument is not sustained. She is not defeated for want of suitable masculine examples. Her father does not deny his own interest. 'I'm just a traditionalist', he says. Her brother says that the grandmother's interest is likewise a sign of patriotism. The feminist critic of gendering resists these argumentative moves, which dignify the interest in royalty by describing it in ungendered terms. She is not going to be drawn along the patriotic path. Instead, she turns back, only to head towards the common-places of gender, thereby finding herself in a thicket of stereotypes. She indicates the little old women, reading *Women's Realm*, but distances herself from them. They read the '*Realm* or whatever it is', she says, using the same formula of dissociation employed by the mother, who talked about the 'Archbishop of whatever' (see Chapter 3). Dissociation or no, she has conceded the existence of the women's realm. She has re-directed the accusing finger from males, and from her father. It is now pointing towards her own gender, to the little old women, to her own grandmother. Brother and father can afford a smile.

WEDDINGS, DRESSES AND WEDDING DRESSES

According to Bagehot, interest in the brilliant edition of the royal wedding is to be explained in terms of more ordinary interests: women are interested in ordinary weddings and so they will be all the more interested in the royal nuptial. Maurice Bloch (1987) has argued, on the basis of anthropological evidence, that the power of royal ritual lies in its relations to the rituals of everyday life. He cites the ritual bath of the Merina king, which resembled the baths more ordinarily taken by his subjects in Madagascar. In Bagehot's terms, it was the brilliant edition of the universal bath. In the same way, interest in the royal wedding is said to be derived from interest in ordinary weddings.

There is a further interest, which Bagehot overlooked. This is the interest in clothing. The common-place that women have the greater interest in royalty was often accounted for in terms of women's interest in clothes. The royal fashions, as the brilliant edition of ordinary clothing, were drawing the attention of women, or so it was claimed. The younger daughter, dressed in her unconventional manner, specifically said that women want to look at the royal clothing (interview 27). The hairdresser mimicked women talking about the wedding dress: doesn't she look lovely, isn't her dress nice. By implication, men's comparative lack of interest in ordinary weddings, dresses and wedding dresses was indicated.

In depicting the interests of women and the non-interests of men, speakers would sometimes move easily from an interest in weddings to an interest in clothes, as if both interests were part of the same syndrome. One family had been talking about the Coronation when the interviewer asked whether women were more interested in royalty than were men (interview 3). In answering, the husband, like Bagehot, went from general interest to the specificity of weddings: 'Yeah, all women are', he answered with confidence. He proceeded to justify his sweeping statement: 'We live here at the shop and we're like opposite the church, so we see lots and lots of weddings and you always see a congregation of women, but you never see any men with them, so definitely women are more attracted to weddings than men'. His wife took up the point, speaking personally: 'I would think so, I don't think I miss a single wedding every Saturday nearly'. If the interest in weddings was given as a justification for a general womanly interest in royal matters, then the mother gave a further explanation: 'I always...try and have a quick look, so I think perhaps, it's just that you want to look at the fashions, don't you'. The interest in fashions was cited in explanation of the interest in the ordinary wedding, which was explaining the interest in the regally brilliant edition.

Similar styles of accounting were produced by another husband and wife (interview 52). The husband agreed that women were more interested in the royal weddings, and he gave a reason: 'because of the dresses and things'. His wife added that a royal wedding 'is very, very, very moving and...a woman tends to sort of shed a few tears'. Her husband, a retired fitter, talked generally of weddings as women's business: 'In normal life...if it were left to the bloke that were getting married, I don't think there'd be half these big church services and things like that; I think ninety percent would be in a registry office'. Again, there was a quick step from the gendering of interest in the royal occasion to a gendering of interests in ordinary life. The royal spectacle refracts and amplifies the glow of those more homely female concerns, as identified within common-sense. These latter interests, and their corresponding male lack of interests, are presumed to be so common-sensically 'natural' that no further explication was spontaneously offered.

What it means 'to be interested in royalty' was normally considered quite straightforward. Mostly, if people were asked whether women were more 'interested', they could answer without hesitation, as if the notion of 'interest' was quite clear. Occasionally, there was dispute about 'interest', as in the family where the father, a vociferous anti-royalist, continually argued against the royalism of wife, son and daughter (interview 2). The interviewer asked them whether they were 'interested' in the Royal Family. The mother and daughter said they were interested. The father had problems with the question. He, more than anyone, read the royal items in the papers: 'I do read it, but I'm not interested'. The son then claimed: 'He reads it to get wound up'. The father again denied it: 'No, I don't read it to get wound up...I'm not that interested, no, I just like to know what's going off, and what's happening'. 'So you're interested', said his wife. 'No, I'm interested in what's happening', he replied. 'You *are* interested', said son and mother in unison. And so it went on. Yes, he was interested – he liked to know what was happening; no, he wasn't interested – he had no sympathy in 'them'.

The father's problem with the word 'interest' throws into relief its unproblematic uses. Normally, someone taking trouble to read about, or watch, royalty would be said to be 'interested'. The interest would not merely be assumed to represent time spent absorbing information about royals, but also to indicate a set of motivations or feelings. The 'interested' person is expected to be drawn by sympathy, enjoyment or, in the most general sense, by desire. An analogy would be a hobby. A stamp-collector's 'interest' in philately implies both time spent in the activity and an enjoyment of the activity. The philatelist is not expected to read the catalogues and to affix the stamps in albums in order to get 'wound up' at the very idea of stamps. Some sort of 'love' for the object of the activity is expected, whether that object be fashions, princesses or postage stamps.

The gendering of this 'love' for fashions, and its demarcation from an assumed male stance, was illustrated by an exchange between a wife and her Polish-born husband (interview 37). The wife was saying why women were more interested in royalty. She claimed that 'women are more interested in people'. This general interest in people included an interest in what they wear. She then spoke personally: 'I'm interested in what they do and what they wear and what they say, I'm quite certain Joe couldn't care less what Princess Diana wears or the Queen wears or anybody else wears'. Her husband was being depicted as a typical male – uninterested in royal fashion. However, Joe, a staunch defender of his adopted nation's monarchy, objected: 'Correction, I like to see her nicely dressed and don't make a fool of herself'.

But that wasn't what the wife meant: 'Yes, but you don't, you wouldn't read avidly all about them, would you'. He agreed. They had sorted out the matter between them. It was true that he did care, but only in a minimalist way: he cared that royalty should wear appropriate garments. This wasn't an 'interest': it lacked the passion of avidity. The belief that users of the postal service should affix stamps to their letters does not make one an avid philatelist.

The vocabulary of 'desire' is not out of place when it comes to speaking about interests. Lynn, a married teacher was talking with her two friends: 'I love it...I love to see what she (Lady Diana) is wearing, I love that' (interview 54). As common-sense informs, this is a woman's love and it can be used to explain the interest in the royal occasion. A Conservative voter in her late thirties declared of women in general that 'they like to see the fashions, (even) if they're not interested in what they (royalty) are doing, they like to see the fashions' (interview 7).

If these comments are indicating a women's realm of interest, then, by implication, this territory is foreign to men. A male lack of interest in royal events could then be explained by a more general male lack of interest in fashion. The mother had described her daughter's boyfriend stomping up the stairs to avoid the royal discussion (interview 50). The interviewer asked why men weren't so interested in the Royal Family. The mother replied: 'Well, they're not interested in the fashions'. None of the women present challenged this. The absence of the boyfriend was confirming the common-sense, which was explaining that absence.

Some men might retreat upstairs lest they be drawn into the women's world. Others might catch a glimpse of it, only to find it alien. A seventeen year old apprentice electrician was talking about watching the wedding of Prince Charles and Lady Diana (interview 36): 'It seemed more like a fashion show...they were saying so-and-so's got a pink dress on with a funny hat or whatever...it just seemed to be mainly explaining what everybody was wearing...it started early on in the morning which seemed a bit strange, just describing what everybody was wearing'. His mother laughed. She explained the strangeness. It was a matter of gender: 'Especially women will sit and watch the fashions, they probably like to know...,what so-and-so's auntie and great uncle and great-distant-cousin are wearing, it's, you know, it's interesting for them'. He had been a stranger in a foreign land.

As the mother explained this to her son, her words seemed to hint at a personal dissociation. It's interesting for 'them', she said, as if excluding herself. In her next breath, she showed her interest. She talked of Lady Diana's wedding dress: how it had looked creased at first but 'when actually she got out and moved along a bit it all fell into place'. This was familiar territory for her, and she could act as native guide for her son.

In depicting what women like, the mother was depicting what women are like. The son, having had the strangeness of the televised commentary explained, does not then ask why women might be interested in fashions. It does not occur to him to view the gendering as strange: his mother had told him that women like these things and he accepts her words. No elaboration was necessary. It was just common-sense, just 'natural'.

The implication that these interests were 'natural' was occasionally made explicit. Father and mother – a fireman and credit controller in their forties – were agreeing that women were more interested in royalty (interview 22). The father mentioned the coverage of royalty in women's magazines. Such magazines 'are geared up for women', who like the 'glamour and princes and princesses and things that go along with that'. He mentioned *Women's Realm*: 'There isn't a *Man's Realm*'. His wife laughed at the very thought. He added: 'Well, it's just the way we are, isn't it? I don't know that you can do much about that'.

It was the way 'we' are; nothing can be done about it. The 'we', to which the father referred, could be interpreted to be all-encompassing; it could include males and females. But it was not a unitary 'we', for 'our' ways were being described as being fundamentally different. Husband and wife, mother and son, father and daughter, were separated. There was a realm of women's interests, naturally distinct from men's interests. In this way, ordinary families were united in the belief that they were naturally divided by their interests.

'STUPID THINGS THAT WOMEN THINK OF'

If there are male and female realms of interest, then it is not to be expected that they will be considered of equal status. Bagehot was downgrading the woman's area, and, already, a woman has been quoted dismissing her interest in royalty as being 'just gossip'. Social scientists have claimed that dominated groups tended to be marked out as conspicuously deviant, while the dominant majority disappears into the 'naturalness' of the social landscape. In particular, maleness is taken for granted, while femaleness becomes conspicuous (Guillaumin, 1972 and 1986). Male interests will be treated as 'obviously interesting' and not specifically male, while female interests will be marginalised. For example, the coding categories of an established American survey into daily activities distinguish between 'Hobbies' and 'Ladies' Hobbies' (Robinson, 1988). 'Ladies' Hobbies', one can predict, will carry the lower social cachet and are likely to be related to the private sphere. Angela McRobbie, in her analysis of magazines for teenage girls, writes that 'possibly the only hobbies which are deemed truly suitable for *Jackie* readers are fashion and beauty' (1981, p.122).

Sometimes, contrasts were made between the ways that males and females might be interested in royalty. These contrasts tended to indicate realms of male seriousness and female frivolity. A young couple, not long married, were talking about women's interest in royalty (interview 32). The wife, in her early twenties, spontaneously mentioned fashion and then went from fashion to weddings: women were 'more interested in the fashion side of things, such as the weddings, interested to see what they are all wearing and what the wedding dress is'. She had a particular curiosity, having just celebrated her own wedding. She said: 'Women tend to...be more interested in weddings in general, don't they'. She turned to her husband: 'You'd perhaps be more interested about what Charles had got to say on the buildings'. 'Yeah', he responded, 'rather than what he was wearing'.

This newly wedded couple were fitting their own selves to stereotypes of gender. Their comments were suggesting that women royals were to be objects of gaze, whereas male royals were to be listened to. In this, there are the familiar stereotypes of female decorative passivity and male public activity: Lady Diana should wear beautiful clothes, while her husband speaks seriously about serious issues. But there is more than the gendered stereotypes of royals, for the speakers were indicating something about their own selves. The women subjects would gaze at the clothes while the males would listen to the serious words, each directing their attention to the royals of their own gender. In making claims for themselves, and for each other, the young couple were in close agreement about what divided them. At an early stage of their married life, they were claiming conventional stereotypes for themselves and for each other.

Another husband and wife were far beyond the newly-wed stage (interview 26). He was in his early fifties and she in her forties. They used the common-places of gender to mock each other. The interviewer had asked the question about women's and men's interests in the Royal Family. They answered the general question personally. The husband said that he did not read the 'gossipy' articles, specifying a particular columnist in the *Daily Mail*, which he did not read. 'Oh, I read that', she said. 'There isn't an equivalent in the

Independent, he said of his newspaper. He preferred to read about Prince Charles and architecture. As he was talking thus, he heard his wife say something under her breath. He broke off: 'What did you say?' She replied: 'I said, "Obviously, big snob"'. She laughed.

He laughed too, but he was unable to let the joke stand unanswered: 'Well, no it's nothing to do with being snobbish, I mean, it's, it's um...'. He went on to say how admirable Prince Charles was. Again, a particular, and personal, contrast was given in response to a general question about interest and gender. On the one hand, there was female interest in gossip, openly acknowledged. On the other hand, there is the male interest in serious things which are seriously said by royalty. Once again, family members were using the general stereotypes to describe themselves, and using themselves to claim the truth of the stereotype. So the kaleidoscope is turned one way and then back the other; the resulting patterns remain familiar.

Towards the beginning of this chapter, a wife was quoted, talking about her interest in royal gossip, 'just like a woman really' (interview 52). Gossip, which is downgraded as trivial, is marked out as female. The interviewer asked a married couple, both civil servants in their early thirties, about gender differences (interview 18). The wife answered that women were probably interested in 'the gossipy side of it, they're probably more interested in the clothes they wear'. Gossip and fashion were being combined as similar, and 'they' was indicating a familiar dissociation of the self. The wife then qualified herself, citing an exception to the general rule of gender. Her father was 'a great royal fan'. Then, she specifically distinguished her father's interests from the gossipy interests ascribed to women. Her father was 'a big history fan'. She drew a general conclusion from this single example. Perhaps it wasn't true to say that men were less interested, but maybe men were 'more into the history side of it'. Once more a serious, masculine interest in public affairs – this time an interest in history – was being contrasted with womanly gossip.

As so often, the 'deviant case' can highlight the assumptions behind the general common-sense. The husband and wife in their mid-forties were discussing interest (interview 10). He was a mechanical engineer and she had held a variety of working jobs – barmaid, shop assistant, factory worker etc. The husband, rather than the wife, expressed an interest in gazing at royals and their clothes. He said that he liked 'to catch a glimpse of what they're wearing and, you know, how much leg they're showing'. The wife immediately offered an account of her husband's interests. She did so in a way which specifically proclaimed his masculinity: 'But you've always liked ladies, haven't you', she said. For the benefit of the interviewer, she clarified the point: you'll 'find Ray in women's company'. She turned back to her husband: 'You do enjoy the company, because they're not so serious'. He followed where she had been leading: 'I think they're less serious, I don't like too serious people, I tend to think women are less serious'. The themes have come together: royal clothes, women's interests and lack of serious-ness. Together, husband and wife affirm his masculinity. He is the male relaxing in the women's company, flirting with the not so serious. He says something which women avidly interested in the royal appearance do not say: he likes to know how much 'leg they're showing'. He is not so much looking at the clothes but at the female body underneath. Just like the man, the ladies' man, which his wife is helping him to appear.

A direct downgrading of women's interests appeared as the middle-class family with the left-wing adult son spoke (interview 41). The mother and father were talking about watching royal cere-monies. The left-wing son had mocked the pageantry. The father said that only ex-servicemen like himself could really appreciate it. When he heard the brass band playing a march, he would remember the camaraderie of the forces. 'And that's when your dad cries', put in the mother. 'That's right', said the father, 'it's nostalgia'. This was military interest, with manly tears shed over manly company.

At this point, gender had not been directly mentioned, but the wife then made a contrast: 'I mean, women go for it to see what the Queen, the people, are going to wear, what hat Maggie Thatcher's going to wear, what dress Lady Di's going to wear'. She started to dissociate herself from the womanly interest in hats and dresses by ascribing them to other women. 'I don't think I fall into that cate-gory', she said, then adding a qualification, 'although I do find myself saying "Oooh she could have had her hat a bit off her face, you know"'. She added: 'Stupid things that women think of, but I don't do it a lot, but every now and again I find myself doing it'.

Her husband's tears had not been called stupid, nor had they been specifically marked out as men's business. But her occasional interest in fashion was different. It was stupid and it was womanly. Despite her better self – her apparently ungendered self – she finds herself uttering these stupid things that women think of. As the only female in the family, she apologises for her brief excursions into the woman's realm.

ABSENT FRIENDS AND PRESENT CRITICS

If the women's interest in royalty is claimed to be derived from ordinary interests, then the way is open for disclaiming the special attraction of the royal dimension. It is the ordinary which makes the brilliant edition so compelling, or so it can be claimed. One wife has already been quoted as suggesting that women like to see the royal fashions, even if they are not interested in royalty (interview 7). A successful young couple were asked whether women were 'more interested than men' (interview 33). They both answered the general question in terms of their own selves. The husband, a European marketing manager, said that he was not interested himself. His wife said: 'I like to watch the royal weddings, I mean, obviously because the clothes are spectacular...and apart from that, I don't really take that much interest in the Royal Family'. It is as if a Madagascan had claimed that the ritual of the royal bath was fascinating because bath-times generally are so interesting.

Previous analyses of royal events have not specifically discussed gender (Jennings and Madge, 1987; Shils and Young, 1953; Ziegler, 1977). However, the great events, which supposedly unite the nation and its families, might be celebrated differently by males and females. Specifically, the association of royal days with womanly interest in clothes opens up an intriguing possibility. Women, who might be critical of monarchy, may still be drawn as spectators. On the other hand, males, who might be conventionally loyal in their monarchism, may feel out of place in the women's realm.

First, the present critics can be considered. There was a small number of women who were vigourously critical of royalty, but who admitted that they watched with interest the royal weddings. The daughter-in-law was heard in Chapter 2 arguing with her parents-in-law, as she outspokenly criticised the royals (interview 39). At one point, she and her mother-in-law were talking about royal weddings, while their respective husbands sat quietly. The mother-in-law, a keen royalist, had many more royal weddings to remember, but the younger woman also had her memories: 'When Charles got married to Diana, I'll never forget that day'. She remembered watching the ceremony at a neighbour's. She talked about the long aisle, down which the royal couple had walked. Several times she claimed that she would always remember the day. Her voice was no longer critical. She might not join her mother-in-law on the annual coach to see the Trooping of the Colour, but she willingly joined in the female reminiscences of ever-memorable royal weddings.

The widow, whose bitter comments were recorded in Chapter 5, was forthright in her anti-royalism (interview 58). However, she had watched and enjoyed the royal weddings. She attempted to deny the royal dimension: 'I watched, of course, Charles and Diana's wedding and Margaret's I watched...the interest is there because I think it's the pomp more than it's royalty, the clothes, the colour... I'm not bothered by the fact that they was royalty'. 'Of course' she watched, the phrase indicating how natural this interest appeared. Her son, who argued with her continually, did not pick up this point. He seemed to accept as unremarkable that his anti-royalist mother would watch all the royal weddings. By contrast, the mother assumed that her loyalist son would not have watched them. She said as much:

(Interview 58)
Interviewer: Did you watch anything of the weddings or anything on TV?
Mother: Oh yes, yes, I, well, I did; I don't, I don't think he did
Son: I watched Prince Charles's wedding
Mother: [Did you?
Interviewer: [Did you?
Son: I had it on all the time

He had watched, but she had not expected him to. She knew of his views about royalty. Even so, his watching, but not hers, was the surprise. The interviewer, too, seemed surprised.

Neither the ex-teacher nor her husband, who declared himself to be a communist, were in favour of monarchy (interview 30). Monarchy was an anachronism, she said, and the country would be better off without it. She had watched the weddings: 'Yes, little bits of them, yes little bits, like looking at the dresses and things like that'. Her twelve year old daughter spoke about women watching the events: 'Some of us watch because they're glamorous and the men don't really take up with this sort of thing'. 'You mean like the dresses and that sort of thing?', queried the mother. 'Yeah', said the daughter. The father had not watched. Of course.

There is the contrary pattern of loyalist men who avoided the royal weddings, as the widow had expected her son to have done (interview 58). The case of the critical daughter-in-law and her loyalist father-in-law is instructive (interview 39). She would always remember the marriage of Prince Charles, so she said. He had watched a number of royal weddings, but none had been memorable: 'I mean there may be a vague recollection but...there's nothing that sticks in me mind to say "Ah, I know what happened when they got wed"'. One royal wedding, however, did stick in his mind: 'I can remember when Charles and Di got married, I did an extra four hours that afternoon at work and I got twelve hours double time for that and, oh, a day off in lieu'. He went on in detail: 'I mean I'd got to work anyway, I was on the early shift, and at that time we did four hours extra in the afternoon, so it was my turn to do it, so I made the extra four hours at double time...and a day off because it was a bank holiday sort of thing; that sticks out in my mind'. He remembers the day well. The detailed calculations of extra wages are readily recalled, but royal weddings actually observed have slipped from memory.

The father, who was proud to have met and spoken to the Duchess of Kent, was discussed in Chapter 3. He was almost as proud not to have watched the Silver Jubilee ceremonies on television: 'I just mowed the lawns all day and did gardening' (interview 3). He said that he was the only person he knew who didn't watch it: 'It just didn't interest me enough'. His wife watched that ceremony, the other royal weddings, and all the weddings in the church across the road. Her husband's gardening was no protest against monarchy; he was as theoretically royalist as his wife.

When in another interview the interviewer asked whether women were more interested than men in watching royalty on the television, the mother, a district nurse in her fifties, answered immediately: 'I would say so yes' (interview 42). Her husband mentioned 'the weddings' and said to his wife 'you were watching the whole of the morning...where I think I went outside in the garden, I think I was gardening'. His wife cut in: 'And you said, "Oooh not that again"'. Again, a royalist man does the gardening during a royal wedding. And, again, the particular episode is held to be an example of a general difference between men and women.

A similar pattern occurred in the family whose son found the television coverage of Prince Charles's wedding so strange (interview 36). The father had not watched specifically: 'I obviously saw it on the news, because it was on so many times, but, I mean, as such, a wedding doesn't particularly interest me'. He had not joined the rest of the family around the television on the big day. He couldn't quite remember what he had been doing. His wife reminded him: 'You were painting the outside of the house all day'. 'Yeah', he remembered now, 'I was painting the house, yeah, yeah'.

Male activities were being substituted for the watching of the royal occasions: working an extra shift, mowing the lawn and painting the house. The father of the household was outside the house doing manly things, whilst the womenfolk were taking over the home with their womanly interest, which the occasional male could find strange. The gendered pattern cuts across class differences. It was a middle-class lawn which was being mown and a middle-class house which was being painted. The shift, so memorably worked, was a working-class one. In different households, masculine selves were being claimed, as the masculine activities were being recalled.

Exceptions can be revealing; one man mentioned non-masculine activities as his substitute for watching the wedding of Prince Charles. The hairdresser, who lived with his male friend, said that while the rest of the country ('the complete country') shut down and watched it on television, he had felt apart: 'It was almost like making a statement really by not watching it' (interview 19). The interviewer asked what he had done instead. 'Did the washing, I should think', he replied and laughed. Then he added: 'No, I can't remember what I did'. His joke was not one made by the men who painted their houses or mowed their lawns. They didn't do the washing, although it might have seriously helped their wives, had they done so. Nor did they joke about the possibility. The hairdresser depicts himself as an isolated figure, doing his washing, and possibly that of his male friend, while the rest of the country gathers together in families to celebrate the royal marriage. He feels excluded from the Durkheimian event. He makes the statement that he was almost making a statement by not partaking in the celebration.

Contrary to the hairdresser's belief, the rest of the country was not joined together in their family groups. Some men were doing other activities, but these often confirmed their familial identities, their masculinity and the general stereotypes of gender, from which the hairdresser felt excluded. By their absences, such men were enacting the ordinary family life, which royalty was so brilliantly representing.

Often, the theme of gender was not made explicit, when discussing the male absences. Occasionally, it was, as when, for instance, a husband and wife in their early sixties talked of royal weddings (interview 59). As they sat together on the sofa in their council house living-room, the wife tended to defer to her husband, a solid masculine figure. They had not been sitting there when Prince Charles had married Lady Diana. On that public holiday, they had gone walking in Derbyshire. The father recalled: 'I remember very well, because we walked over Kinder, we went from Edale to the Snake Pass Inn and they'd not laid any extra facilities on, because they'd thought everybody would be at home watching the television and the wedding'. He found this incredible and he had told the staff of the pub so: 'I said "You must be mad because it's an ideal day for a man to leave his wife watching the wedding on the television, while he gets out and does his own thing"'.

His wife sat silently, whilst he continued his story. The bar 'was packed with disappointed men'. There was a cafeteria but it hadn't been opened on that day of all days: 'Of course everyone was queuing up at the one bar and very disappointed, because they'd not been offered this extra facility...the general feeling among the men was they must have been mad not to have anticipated the hundreds of men up there; it was a gorgeous day; oh, it was a fantastic day'.

Ideological effects are being worked within these patterns of presences and absences. Critical women can be drawn towards the royal event. As such women gather around their television sets, their critical impulses are momentarily blinded by the brilliance of the occasion. It is only the clothes, they can reassure themselves. It's not monarchy. The reassurance glosses over that it is the essence of monarchy in the modern age to be the brilliant version of the ordinary. Meanwhile, menfolk might be off elsewhere, avoiding the business of women. Like Bagehot, they can smile patronisingly, but they also know not to mock too forcefully. The women's interest is protected from too much criticism, for the women are concerning themselves with the symbols of nationhood and family. Loyal men cannot attack the womanly interests without risking themselves being criticised as unpatriotic. Their absences on the great days are not radical statements. Instead, they affirm conventional masculinity, and, thereby, they affirm the conventions of that private realm which is being publicly celebrated on the television screen. The men's absences are only brief. Soon, they return home. The normal life, which has just been brilliantly commemorated in their absence, is resumed, not that it had been foresaken.

FAMILY MATTERS

It would be wrong to exaggerate the numbers of absent friends and present critics. Only a minority of women were critical, and many men were present at their family celebrations. There was also the occasional critical male who attended. As was shown in Chapter 2, the radical son, under questioning from his mother, admitted to watching the royal weddings on television, although he claimed to have forgotten his reactions to the scene (interview 41).

A most Durkheimian scene would have greeted the eyes of a passer-by who, on Prince Charles's wedding day, peered through the window of the family home, belonging to the credit controller and her husband, the fireman (interview 22). Red, white and blue streamers were hung on the windows of the small, modern detached house. The passer-by would have seen the mother and father watching the television in the front-room. On the father's head was a bowler-hat, painted in the national colours. The table cloth was made in the same patriotic pattern, and a bottle of wine had been opened. Throughout the day, the picture would have been the same. During the whole broadcast, the fireman and his wife had sat there watching, she bare-headed and he wearing his celebratory hat. Such was the scene they recalled for the benefit of the interviewer.

It was a scene of domestic and national unity – the sort of scene which might be used to illustrate the chapter about ritual and social order in a sociological textbook. Yet, the divisions of gender are not absent. This was the father who pointed out that *Women's Realm* was not complemented by a *Man's Realm*. Men aren't interested in weddings, he said: 'A typical answer from any of my workmates would be "Well, you've seen one wedding, you've seen them all"'. There he was talking with his wife about that happy day, when together they had watched the whole royal wedding. The next day, back among his workmates in the man's world of the fire-station, did he talk differently?

The days of royal events, especially the royal weddings, might be women's days, largely celebrated within the family home. The nation might be given a day's holiday from work on such occasion. However, women, on their national holiday, would not necessarily be freed from domestic labour in the home. While the father claimed only to remember the royal wedding, which he spent at work, his wife had a much clearer memory (interview 39). She remembered

Princess Anne's wedding and that of Princess Alexandra. She described watching them 'on the telly, you know, and then nip, nip in the kitchen and get a bit done and nip back and watch the telly again, but I can remember them really clear'.

The retired fitter and cleaner have already been quoted (interview 52). Men were so uninterested in weddings that they would prefer to get married in registry offices, said the husband. His wife agreed that men did not share the womanly interests in weddings and wedding dresses. They had been describing how they watched Prince Charles's wedding. The husband had only watched 'perhaps the odd snatches'. But for his wife it was a very different story, raising her voice to emphasise her points: 'I never missed a moment; I got the tea ready, and then I run back in again and done a bit more, you know...it's such a, I think, especially for a woman, a man's not, err, you know, *oh her dress and the bridesmaids*...oh it was fantastic'.

It was her occasion, not her husband's – a woman's day, not a man's. She never missed a moment. Well, actually she did. She had to keep running to and from the kitchen. A bit more work. Another peep. But it was fantastic. Her husband breezed in to watch a few snatches. He could take it or leave it. She could neither leave nor take it.

There was also the critical widow, talking about watching the Coronation with her husband (interview 58). The interviewer asked whether it was something that women enjoyed more than men did. She agreed and answered personally. She remembered that her husband 'watched most of it'. Her watching of the Coronation had been continually interrupted: 'I mean I had to keep leaving off to get meals ready, because it was on all day, but he didn't say anything about me watching'. It was the same for the weddings. He did not object that she paused between domestic tasks to look at the television, which he was watching. The celebration of the national family provided no escape from the ordinary practices of gender and family. So long as she produced the meals, she could catch snatches of the event, her event. And it was royalty, not family, which she criticised.

No two families are exactly similar. Each family will have its own distinctive routines, secrets and patterns of power (Silverstone *et al.*, 1989; Wallman, 1984). A different pattern of talking about the royal events emerged when the women in one working-class family spoke (interview 50). In this family, females outnumbered males; the mother and two older daughters, as against father and thirteen year old boy. During the interview, the father and son were absent at football, and the younger daughter's boyfriend was skulking upstairs. The women had been left to themselves. Undisturbed, they could mock the male lack of interest.

Together the women constructed an account of the father watching royal events on the television. 'Your dad sits and watches it, doesn't he?', said the mother to her daughters. 'Only because he has to', laughed the older daughter. Yeah, agreed her mother, he wouldn't switch it on himself, but 'if it's on and we're here, he'll sit and watch it and he'll make the odd comment every now and again and we all jump on him'. They were all laughing. The mother continued: 'He'll say', and she mimicked a deep voice, '"Oh, I'm not saying anything else", he makes an odd comment like "Yeah, cost me three months wages that one", you know and we all jump on him'.

It was a tale of victory. The male was mocked in his absence. But would they – could they – have spoken thus, had he been present? Could they have jumped upon him in just the way which they spoke about doing? Walter Benjamin (1973) wrote in his essay 'Theses on the Philosophy of History' that history is a spoil of war which goes to the victors. The women, in telling their version of the family history, were celebrating triumph: they force the male to watch the women's events and then they all jump on him if he makes so much as a comment. When the father had returned from the football match, perhaps a different family history would have been told; and a different present would have been enacted. Or, perhaps he would still have to say his points by saying that he's not saying anything. Whatever might be, the women were enjoying their moment together at home, in their realm. None of them thought to call the boyfriend down.

THE ROYAL FORCE OF EROS

The most dedicated fans of royalty might not have the most interesting stories to tell. Such women may have always taken their royal enthusiasms for granted. By contrast, those who have tried to resist the appeal might have the more interesting stories to tell. The downgrading of the women's interests ensures that some women will attempt to resist the attraction. They might wish to avoid saying the 'stupid things' which one mother ascribed to other women (interview 41). But also, like her, they might find themselves saying those very same things.

197

The three mothers talking together provide a case in point (interview 54). They were featured in Chapter 5, when they discussed their desire for the elegant meal-times of royals. These left-of-centre *Guardian* readers were not the sort of women to be attracted by the royal gossip of the women's magazines. Sue said she would never have talked to her two friends if either had decorated their houses with flags for Prince Charles's wedding. They were skirting delicately around their own interest in the royal wedding, and were wondering whether men would ever admit to watching such weddings. Then Sue took the plunge: 'Well, I have to admit that I enjoyed watching that wedding'. The phrasing was cautious: it was something to be confessed. Lynn quickly expressed agreement. 'Yes, I did', said the teacher, 'the Princess Di wedding, yeah, it's all the clothes'. It was the clothes – not royalty, her words whisper. Sue interrupted to continue her confession: 'but I didn't want to enjoy it, but I actually did; I had it on and watched it'. 'Yes, that's right', said Lynn, sharing the experience of enjoying the unwanted pleasure. 'But Andrew wouldn't have watched it', said Sue of her husband. 'No', agreed Lynn. She understood.

There was more confession and justification to be said within the protectorate of this all-woman's conversational realm. Lynn went on to specify that she was not drawn by the royal aspect: 'It's the spectacle of it, it was the bridesmaids and all of the dresses...it wasn't just a Royal Family'. Sue agreed. A few moments later they were talking about the courtship of Prince Charles and Lady Diana. Sue, leading the way, said why she found the young royals interesting:

(Interview 54)

Sue: ...they're of an age when they are actually (.) going out and going out with people, and I think that kind of youthful, sexual element is, is very attractive (.) it's something that people like reading about

Lynn: I can't imagine Charles being sexual {*laughs*}

Sue: You know what I mean

Lynn: Yeah

The resistances against admitting interest were being weakened. Sue continued her confession: 'Despite myself, I found that I was interested'. Lynn still denied that she had been interested. Sue interrupted her: 'Well, you were interested at the time, I remember you being interested'. Lynn's resistances were slipping: 'Was I?', she asked, 'Was I?'. 'Yeah', said Sue firmly. They were all laughing.

Lynn, her resistance having been contradicted in this safe atmosphere of mutual confession, talked about Princess Diana. It was at this point that she made the remark, quoted previously, about loving to see what the Princess wore. Ann said that she had enjoyed seeing Lady Diana being transformed 'from a rather chubby nineteen year old' into a glamorous figure: 'It's just interesting watching that'. Sue contradicted her: 'She wasn't chubby'. She's incredibly attractive, said Ann. Both said they were jealous of the Princess's looks. By now, they were all speaking without inhibition about matters which they were now claiming to be intrinsically interesting.

As a Freudian might have predicted, once resistances have been removed, the force of Eros is revealed. Sue claims that the magnetic power – the force which people like to read about – is a sexual one. The royal personae are sexual beings. This interest contains a salacious tendency, which newspaper-readers so readily deplore and from which they attempt to dissociate themselves. It is a gossipy interest, which is difficult to admit, especially to males. The confessions are made by women to themselves, old friends understanding each other. Even so, the creation of the confidences was not all plain sailing. At first, Lynn interprets Sue, as if her friend were talking about the male in the story. They laugh at the notion of Prince Charles as a sexual being. You know that's not what I meant, says Sue. They know that it was not what she meant. That was the joke.

It was the force of Eros within Lady Diana's life – her looks, body and clothes – which interested these women. Their remarks illustrate a more general point about the woman's interest in royalty: the women were looking at women. There might be a sexual element, as Sue said, but they were not gazing at royals as objects of their own sexual desires. That was ridiculous, as their laughter at Prince Charles confirmed. In this respect, their gaze was very different from the male gaze. In the interviews, males occasionally made sexual innuendoes, of a sort not made by women. One husband talked about seeing a bit of royal leg (interview 10). A remark was attributed to the absent boyfriend, who remained upstairs during the interview (interview 50). Although he might have claimed to know nothing about royalty and would not even recognise the Queen, his girlfriend claimed that he 'fancies Lady Diana...he likes Diana, he thinks she's a bit of alright, he does, it's the truth'.

The women did not talk in this way; none said that they tried to catch a glimpse of a prince's leg. It was the sexuality of a princess which interested the three friends. As the other interviews revealed, when women talked about their interest in clothes, it was the clothes on the bodies of the female royals, especially the young females, to which they referred. 'I can't recall anything Charles wears', said a district nurse, when they were discussing women's interest in royal clothes (interview 42). 'Yes, but he's always got to wear a suit', said her mother, a clerk. 'Yes', replied her daughter, 'but you're attracted to the clothes that the women are wearing, that's why you would look'.

In this women's realm, males appear only as peripheral figures. Males are not expected to understand, let alone appreciate, the gentle geography of this terrain. Women are celebrating the beauty and clothes of fellow women. There was no interest in what Prince Charles wore. It was forgotten. His body was a joke.

This women's world is easily mocked by the male, and indeed downgraded by the female, especially when a serious interest in the world of public affairs is being claimed. Accordingly, this world presents problems to the analyst: how can it be understood without either being downgraded or accepted uncritically on its own imaginary terms? Certainly, its pleasure principle and its aesthetics deserve to be taken seriously. An interest in the embroidery of a gown and the cut of its material is no more absurd, and certainly far less aggressive, than an interest in teams of men hitting or kicking balls. C.L.R. James (1963), in his Marxist analysis of cricket, could claim that W.G. Grace 'had enriched the depleted lives of two generations' and 'had done no harm to anyone' (p.183; see also James, 1989). Could not the same be said of the beautiful clothes produced for the royal occasions? Do not these occasions embody the forces of Eros, freed from those aggressively masculine forces of Thanatos which beset sporting events?

The point could be pushed a bit further. The critical reversal of Eros and Thanatos, envisaged by Herbert Marcuse in *Eros and Civilisation*, could be read into the scene of a royal wedding. For a brief moment of holiday, the aesthetic of playfulness triumphs over the severity of performance – the possibilities of the private predominate over the public. The dialectic of impulses seems to be reversed: Eros, the force of life and beauty, is triumphing over the deadly seriousness of Thanatos. On the royal holiday, the bride, and not the groom – the woman and not the man – captures the spectator's eye. And the spectators are presumed to be principally female on this woman's day.

The interest in glamorous fashion reverses the ordinary order of things. Objects of labour are transformed into objects of aesthetic pleasure. The women, who are claiming an interest in clothes, are women for whom ordinary clothes are articles to be washed, to be mended, to be ironed. This is the condition of life within the ordinary woman's realm. These are the same conditions which can make the women's realm of fashion appear so alien to men.

The reversals of the ordinary into the aesthetic of the royal wedding might be said to hint obliquely at the possibilities for a different ordering of the world. To use Marcuse's phrase, the reversals portray, if only for a brief moment, a female Eros triumphing over the aggression of a male Thanatos. However, this is too simple, indeed too sentimental, a depiction. It should not be forgotten that the royal events, and their celebration, are firmly encased within the institutions of the present social order. Most notably, they are encased within the institution of the family, which they so brilliantly represent; and they are encased within the institution of the nation.

Women can be heard to speak about their interests in royal weddings, as if the 'royalness' of the event could be subtracted. This means subtracting the 'national' element, and playing with the illusion that it is only the private world of an interesting family which is being celebrated. But it can never be thus. The royal event is a national enactment, and, as such, it is a celebration of the world of nation states. Subtracting the national element involves a forgetfulness, which is itself an act of ideological imagination.

This forgetfulness is revealed even as the celebrated moment is recalled. Again, the absences have particular significance. The women, talking about the royal wedding and about its feminine beauty, were recalling women's clothes. The male apparel was largely absent in this talk; or if present, it was dismissed as merely a suit, scarcely worthy of memory. In this collective act of forgetfulness, Thanatos is overlooked. Eros may have stood there, a shy figure in her carefully prepared, memorable beauty. Her white dress had magnificently unfolded. Next to her, stood the bridegroom wearing a military uniform of the nation. Hung around his clothes was a sword, a weapon of death. All about, there were armed soldiers of the state. Thanatos had been invited too. It was a fantastic day.

201

8

THE HERITAGE OF THE FUTURE

The family discussions about the Royal Family have enabled patterns of common-sense thinking to be identified across divides of class, gender and generation. Similar thoughts have been echoed by males and females, young and old, in detached private houses and in cramped council flats. Voices, heavy with regional accent or using the modulated tones of the middle-class, could be heard repeating similar themes – equating monarchy with Britain's uniqueness, voicing anger at 'hangers-on', ascribing greater interest to women, expressing sympathy for the hard life of royals and so on. Not only were the same common-places uttered in different settings, but similar patterns of discussion could be heard: demands that 'they' should set examples were being pitted against sympathetic declarations that 'they' were only human after all.

As speakers used the common-places of common-sense, so also were they expressing their own individuality. No two voices had identical tones, nor did they say the same things. The family members were doing various bits of family business, as they spoke. In consequence, the discussions gave glimpses of lives being uniquely led. As was said in Chapter 1, it was the intention that people would be present in this psychological account – it would be a 'populated psychology'.

This final chapter draws together some of the themes from the previous chapters. Having done this, it seeks to go further, by exploring one aspect of monarchy which might contribute to the fascination which the institution exerts in contemporary times. There is the possibility that the Royal Family is a post-modernist phenomenon, well fitted to post-modernist times and to post-modernist ways of thinking. To pursue this possibility, it is necessary

202

to examine whether the ways in which people talk about monarchy bear traces of what has been called post-modernism. One aspect is particularly crucial. This is the depiction of time – how the past is construed and how the future is imagined. These construals of time offer a hint about monarchy's popularity. In the changing times of post-modernist consciousness, monarchy provides reassurance, for it appears to resist obsolescence by presenting today as the heritage of the future.

PANGLOSS AS A CYNIC

If the general tone of contemporary common-sense is marked by cynicism, then the cynical tone of talk about monarchy is indicated by two absences. In the first place, the sacral spirit was lacking; virtually no-one believed that the Queen ruled by God's grace. The second absence is related to the first. There is an almost complete absence of uncritical deference. The modern common-sense is suffused with egalitarian themes: 'they're' only human like 'us', and 'they're' doing a job of being royal. Should 'they' place themselves too far above 'us', then 'we' have common strategies of mockery. Loyal royalists would happily join in the jokes and the criticisms: they mock the bald spots and complain about the royal manners. All this is part of being loyally interested in the family upon the throne.

Cynicism is often associated with rebelliousness, for it undermines the pretensions and claims of social superiors. Peter Sloterdijk (1988) refers to cynicism as 'existence in resistance, in laughter, in refusal' (p.218). However, the mockery and cynicism do not lead to a rebellious republicanism. The cynical consciousness might expose the images as images, but the exposure was part of the show, for the royal job contains its own negations. The royal conjurors are to continue performing before an audience, which claims to see through the tricks but which sympathises with the performers on that very account.

There was an undertow of anger, which was openly directed against the privileged hangers-on and which was ready to explode against royals thought to be evading their duties. Anger and envy are neither repressed, nor are they sublimated into an idealised image of royals. Instead, they are constrained rhetorically. The themes of envy are accompanied by common-places, which assert what is 'on-the-other-hand'. In so doing, speakers contain envy within safe bounds. As a result, there is an ideological settling down, accomplished by features of talking, which have been called here 'double-declaiming' and 'coupon-filling'.

In making claims about the royal way of life, people were doubly making claims about their own selves. The acceptance of the royal way entailed an ideological affirmation of ordinary life. Common-sense was providing metaphorical coupons to be filled in. The coupons, which invited envy of the royal particulars, solicited comparative celebration of 'our' whole life. By coupon-filling and double-declaiming, the jealous thought is hemmed in.

As jealousy is safely contained, then present ways of living are affirmed. Thus, there was a comforting, Panglossian tendency within the cynical consciousness. In Voltaire's satire *Candide*, Pangloss was the rationalist philosopher who, despite unimaginable disaster, kept fast to his position that the present moment represented the best possible world. Each misfortune was adduced as a further proof that all was to the good. Rationalism, rather than religion, guided Pangloss's faith in the present order. Echoing around a nation in economic and political decline, the tones of a cynical Pangloss can be heard; at least they can be so heard when the topic turns to monarchy.

As outlined in Chapter 2, it was said that no other country had the heritage and history of Britain. The rest of the world, and the Americans in particular, envied 'us' for 'our' Royal Family. The cynical heirs of Pangloss were living in the most envied of nations. So, too, within the nation there were signs enough to comfort a Pangloss. As speakers double-declaimed about the royal and ordinary way of life, so they concluded that royals led the unenviable life. 'We' are thankful that 'we' do not suffer the hardships which 'they' have to endure. In fact, 'they' might even envy 'us'. A Pangloss, living in cynical times, does not naïvely call being a subject of the Queen of England the best possible position in the best possible nation. The tone is more competitive, with a hint of sourness; the absolute of 'the best' has been replaced by the comparisons of envy. Still, a Panglossian tone is recognisable: being a subject of the Queen is the most enviable position in the most envied of nations.

ROYALTY AND POST-MODERNISM

The common-sense themes, which have been heard in the interviews, can be compared with what is often called 'post-modernism'. Some observers of contemporary culture have claimed that the late twentieth century has seen the emergence of a 'new structure of feeling', which can broadly, and imprecisely, be termed 'post-modernist' (Harvey, 1989). At first sight, the label seems to fit monarchy well. Contemporary monarchy is not a perfectly preserved survival from a past, pre-modern age; its rituals frequently are 'invented traditions', the product of modern times (Cannadine, 1983). There again, monarchy does not express the spirit of modernism: its obvious anachronisms and its cumbersome quaintness contradict the pragmatic ethos of modernism. Instead, the label 'post-modernist' seems ready to encompass monarchy in a snug, conceptual embrace.

There has been much debate about what exactly 'post-modernism' is, and how it differs from 'modernism'. As Lash (1990) points out, the term has become a vogue word and 'everybody has an opinion on the subject' (p.2). Post-modernism is most conveniently described in terms of the architectural reaction against modernism. If modern architecture, with its concrete and glass, rejected traditional styles, then post-modernist architecture rejects this rejection. The post-modernist looks back to traditional styles, but does not do so naïvely nor in a spirit of romanticism. The post-modernist's use of the past contains elements of pastiche and self-parody. The myths of the past are not to be re-created, and, in this sense, there is cynicism in the reproduction of the past. A gothic arch, a Georgian pillar and a plastic drain-pipe are intermixed in a collage of anachronisms. The daily collage of royal photographs – stepping from horse-drawn barouches to helicopters – wearing crowns and *haute couture* – would seem to represent a quintessentially post-modern mixing of epochs. The invented traditions are not re-creating past myths of royal divinity. The very appearance of being an anachronism – an up-to-date anachronism – might be said to mark monarchy as a phenomenon attuned to a post-modernist structure of feeling.

It is not difficult to see post-modernist features in the current displays of monarchy. For instance, royalty itself has entered the argument against modernism, which post-modernism has been conducting. The most notable example is that of Prince Charles and his views on architecture. In 1984, the heir to the throne shook the Royal Institute of Architects when he condemned the proposed plans for an extension to the National Gallery as 'a monstrous carbuncle'. He complained that St Paul's was being 'dwarfed by yet another glass stump, better suited to downtown Chicago' (*The Times*,

31 May 1984). His choice of phrase, as well as his architectural taste, echoed the past.

More important than the Prince's own dislike of modernist buildings is the general belief that his architectural mission is appropriate to his royal position. A Gallup survey, conducted in December 1988, asked respondents whether the Royal Family should speak out on various issues. Fourteen different topics were presented and architecture attracted the second highest degree of assent (after the 'environment and pollution'), attracting even higher figures than did the issues of 'family life' and 'crime and punishment'. It is doubtful whether such high agreement would have been recorded had the royals' most famous architectural spokesperson been defending the modernist carbuncles. In the family discussions, there was scarcely a word against Prince Charles for his architectural mission. Yes, said a middle-aged mother, it was good that Prince Charles has spoken out on architecture: 'That's done a lot of good, I haven't met one person that didn't agree with him, from all walks of life' (interview 21).

The myths of nationalism may, in the main, be modern creations, nevertheless they have fitted uneasily with the philosophy of modernism and, especially with its internationalism. Prince Charles's critique of modernism is suffused with nationalist themes, which express an earnestly romantic conservatism. His talk of an organic unity between houses and earth does not quite match the ironic tones of much post-modernism. However, nationalist themes *per se* might not be out of place within the themes of post-modern sensibility. Waldemar Januszczak, a modernist critic of the Prince of Wales, sees post-modernism as inherently nationalist, for 'modernism was a deliberately international movement', whose styles aimed to transcend national differences. Januszczak suggests that the Prince's views, and their popular reception, match the 'dangerously patriotic' times of today, in which 'all beliefs in the similarities between nations are being erased by the new tides of nationalism and fundamentalism' (1990, pp.6–7). Thus, the critic of post-modernism sees shadows of nationalism behind the post-modernist pastiche and the royal parade.

A further aspect of the post-modernist style is its cynical knowingness. The post-modernist consciousness is said to recognise images as mere images, whilst accepting the image as the reality, or as the hyper-reality (Kroker and Cook, 1988). This style is marked by self-reference, for it demystifies the image by revealing how it is produced; and this revelation is itself part of the image.

Urry (1988) claims that in the post-modernist age 'the media have also undermined what is to be thought of as properly backstage, what could be made public and what can be kept private' (p.40). As Jean Baudrillard writes, the distinction between public and private space is lost: 'The one is no longer a spectacle, the other no longer a secret' (1985, p.130).

It is not hard to insert the case of monarchy into these general descriptions of post-modernism. Dayan and Katz (1985), in their analysis of Prince Charles's wedding, make the point that the audience is part of the televised spectacle; in this way, the distinction between stage and audience is blurred. The private life of the public family can no longer be a secret, for the royals' job entails the public presentation of the private realm. In fact, the regular publication of trivial details about royal lives is only comprehensible in a society which already understands that the private and public spheres can be collapsed into each other. 'We' expect to see the pictures of royal toddlers playing with their toys, the princesses wearing casual clothes, and princes sharing a joke. The sight of such photographs is not puzzling to the modern eye.

It is said that the splendid procession of the 1953 Coronation was augmented by seven coaches borrowed from Sir Alexander Korda's film studio (Brown and Cunliffe, 1983). What could be more post-modern than an audience watching the appearance of real film-props in the film of the historic event? Nor does the revelation do anything to detract from the splendour of the occasion. No disillusion sets in, but the filmed parade is possibly made all the more real, because some of its elements are recognisable from real films.

The question of post-modernism can be taken further. It is not enough to draw parallels between royal parades and those cultural products which have been called post-modernist. If post-modernism denotes a new structure of feeling, then it should be manifested more widely than in architecture, coronations and the public performance of princes. The thinking of ordinary people would be suffused with post-modernist themes. Moreover, if monarchy, in its public presentation, is quintessentially post-modern, then the existence of post-modernist tendencies in ordinary thinking would ensure that the anachronistic institution is not popularly thought to be absurd.

To examine this, it is necessary to take seriously the possibility that post-modernism is more than a cultural style, but is a feature of ideology. It is a characteristic of ideology that it settles people down into social positions of inequality. Therefore, to propose that post-modernism is a feature of ideology is to claim more than that post-modernist tendencies are to be found in ordinary ways of talking. There is the additional claim that these tendencies of talk can settle down speakers, soothing discontented itches and dispelling tremors of fear.

The family discussions revealed that some themes of post-modernist consciousness are to be heard in words spoken in ordinary living-rooms. There was a knowing demystification and an even more knowing call for further mystification. The reality of images was taken seriously. It was common-sense that the royal job was to present public images. Defenders of the Crown felt no incongruity in talking of the royal job as a form of public relations. Hypocrisy could even be countenanced, for the public image of the private was, in one sense, to be more real than private truth. Yet, the cynical consciousness claims to be too knowing to be fooled by such images; it claims to distrust the public images. Again, distinctions are blurred, this time the distinctions between the real and the image, as well as the distinction between private and public. And, meanwhile, the Panglossian theme is expressed: how hard it is for 'them' to produce the right public images; how fortunate 'we' are, not to have such a job. In this way, the merits of ordinary life are affirmed in the face of extreme wealth.

Despite all this, care should be taken when applying the label of 'post-modernist', lest the novelty of today's monarchical phenomena be exaggerated. As has been shown earlier, parallels can be drawn between what is said now and what was written by that most Victorian of figures, Walter Bagehot. There are similar claims to see behind the image, whilst advocating the public transmission of the image; similar compounding of the private and public realms of royalty; similar cheeky familiarity while discussing majesty. And, of course, there is the continuity of nationalism. If Bagehot was aiding the establishment of the modern state, then one might say that modernity in its earliest stages already contained the seeds of its own cynicism.

HERITAGE AND CHANGING TIMES

Clearly, things have not remained constant since the days of Bagehot. Times – and particularly royal times – have changed, and these changes, whether or not they include totally new structures of feeling, must be taken into account. So too must the depiction of the changing times themselves, for the construal of time is crucial to ideology. It makes all the difference, for example, whether people believe that their world is advancing towards a bright, new future, whose attainment is threatened by old institutions and privileges; or whether, fearing the future, they cling to symbols of the past, easing the terror of a disappearing present. The absence of an image of a better future can itself be a means of reconciliation with the discontents of the present.

Bagehot could not have foreseen the mass commercialisation of royalty's private life. As Cannadine (1983) has shown, the last hundred years have seen an exponential growth in mass-marketed royal souvenirs. Published revelations about royal private lives are now common in a way not seen even two generations ago (Nairn, 1988). Today, it is hard to appreciate the shock in 1950, when Marion Crawford, the former governess to the present Queen, published *The Little Princesses*, her gushing account of life behind the palace walls. *Woman's Own*, in eighteen successive issues, serialised extracts, and its editor claimed with slight exaggeration that 'before "Crawfie's" memoire we had no royal stories' (see Pearson, 1986, p.46).

Perhaps the growth of books claiming to reveal the hidden life of the palace represents an increase in the desire for secret information about royalty. On the other hand, the desire itself might not be novel. In the early nineteenth century, the public followed with interest the disclosures about George IV's wife. Modern reporters would be hard put to compete with the salacious details broadcast about Princess Caroline. During the debate of the 1820 Bill of Pains, servants were called before parliament to give evidence whether the Princess's bed-linen bore the tell-tale stains of adultery (see *New Annual Register, 1820*, pp.199–202). What was said in parliament was repeated in the broad-sheets of the street. The scandal carried political themes, and the more that the Princess was exposed to public inspection, the more the public sympathised with her, condemning the King as her persecutor (Clark, 1990).

Possibly the prurient interest in Princess Caroline's bed-linen might seem familiar in the twentieth century. It is conceivable there has always been a desire – and thus a potential market – for revelations about the royal bedchamber. In a previous chapter, a father was heard to be embarrassed by his interest in the bedroom of his neighbours. A hundred, or two hundred, years ago there would have been similar men with similar interests. That is not the point. Even if some desires have remained unchanged, there may be differences in the promise of their satisfaction. Nowadays, the daily press, and the publishers of popular books, regularly tantalise by promising to reveal all about royal lives.

When people today claim that newspapers did not previously pander to the shameful desires of others, they are doing more than expressing criticisms and denials. They are also construing time, for they are comparing the present world with an imagined past world of respectful newspapers. This sort of common-sense construal of time limits the Panglossian optimism: the best possible place might not be experiencing the best possible of times. Moreover, this depiction of time's passage indicates a difference between the confidence of Bagehot and the uncertainties of post-modernism.

Walter Benjamin, in his 'Theses on the Philosophy of History', wrote that the modern world experiences time in a particular way – as a 'progression through a homogeneous, empty time' (1973, p.263). History is felt to be progressing onwards, filling empty calendars at an even pace. This construal of time expresses a low-key optimism. There is a sense of progression. There is also a crucial absence. As Benjamin wrote, this depiction of time contains no image of a radically different future which will rupture the homogeneous progress in order to redeem the past.

The conditions for this view of time as continual progression are conditions of social change. Eric Hobsbawm (1983) has argued that the rapid transformations of society, during the past two hundred years, have produced the supply of, and demand for, 'invented traditions'. Change itself does not necessarily produce ideologies of optimism or pessimism. It is possible to view change with a sense of optimism: history is leading progressively towards betterment. On the other hand, changes can produce bewilderment: the past is disappearing and the familiar social landmarks of one generation are being rejected by the next. Theorists of the post-modern have pointed to a collapse of optimism in the latter part of the twentieth century as providing the condition for the post-modern sensibility. Post-modernism's pastiche of past styles questions the assumption of uniform progress into a better future.

This loss of optimism is reflected in mass culture. Robert Hewison (1987), discussing the heritage industry in Britain, argues that rapid social change and pessimism about the future have contributed to the growing market for nostalgia. Today, Britons, cynical about the present and fearful for the future, flock by the thousand to theme parks, where they celebrate past times by riding in trams and by sucking souvenir humbugs. This is a fitting comment upon the state of the nation, suggests Hewison: 'When museums become one of Britain's new growth industries, they are not signs of vitality, but symbols of national decline' (p.84).

The age which is producing the heritage parks, is the same age which is producing the industry for mass-marketed royal books and souvenirs. Today's nostalgia is not a romantic conservatism which actually seeks to turn the clock backwards. Nostalgia has its hint of self-parody: the actors, employed to play Victorian passers-by in the heritage theme parks, fool no-one. The visitors can play at living in past times without leaving the contemporary world. They can recall times of national self-confidence, as the nation declines politically and is faced with incorporation into the supra-national institutions of Europe. So, perhaps, one can play at being a loyal subject of an ancient monarchy, simultaneously believing and disbelieving, applauding and mocking.

THE DIALECTIC OF PAST AND PRESENT

The argument outlined above needs to be supported in two ways. First, evidence is required to show that people construe present times as bewildering and that nostalgia for an imagined past offers reassurance against a threatening future. Second, even if time is construed in these ways, the connection with the appeal of monarchy must be demonstrated.

The construal of time today is not simple, but it contains contrary themes. As families talked about past and present, there was a strong sense of change, which was understood in terms of both progress and loss, optimism and bewilderment. Common-sense provides both liberal and conservative accounts of history to articulate these depictions of change (Billig, 1990a). The liberal narrative tells a tale of advance: in olden times there was poverty, disease and inequality; today, life is so much better; 'we' are freer, richer and more equal; 'we' know things today, which were unknown previously. This is not the only tale to be told by common-sense. A conservative history can be reproduced: in the past, life was simpler and more ordered; children obeyed their parents; there was respect for authority; people looked up to royalty, and so did the newspapers; everyone stood to attention when the national anthem was

211

played. Life might have been harder, but it was friendlier and more genuine. An image of an ordered, deferential society (a *Gemeinschaft*) is constructed and celebrated in this account.

The conservative history is not only told by older people who might be fondly imagining the times of their youth. The common-sense memory of past time can be evoked by those who did not personally experience it (Halbwachs, 1980; Schwartz, 1990). The young can easily recall the myths of past harmony and order. A twenty-three year old wife, a payroll officer, was talking about the days of her parents and of her 'parents' parents' (interview 32). In those times, there was more patriotism; old people weren't attacked in the street. 'In my parents' day, and certainly in my grandparents' day', she said, 'you were quite alright to leave your front door open with five pounds on the kitchen table'. She continued: 'Morals were different then, I think the morals for which the Royal Family stand for were upheld ninety-five percent over the rest of the country'.

The conservative and liberal narratives of past time were often pitted against each other in an argumentative dialectic. A seventeen year old trainee printer said he'd like to have lived in olden times, in castles and so on (interview 22). His mother argued back: 'We've got to be better off now', she said. The father, a fireman, agreed with her: 'We're materially better off, aren't we'. But then he spoke of loss. There's no neighbourliness now, he continued, 'when I was younger, people would sense that somebody hadn't got the means to pay for groceries'. And so on. A further 'on-the-other-hand' was due. He switched back to the narrative of progress: in the past 'they didn't have the material things that we've got, even things we just take totally for granted, like hot running water and a bath'. 'They were a mucky lot', said his wife.

We're losing too many traditions, said another father: 'It's, you know, forcing the country apart' (interview 1). The ordered unity of the *Gemeinschaft* was crumbling. His wife then put in a good word for the 'mod cons' of modern living. But, answered the father, 'our kids are losing out; anything, everything they want, they've only got to press a button – and there, it's there'. Three mothers were discussing the same themes (interview 54). Lynn was talking about the 'cruelty' and 'the harshness of life' in olden times. 'I couldn't bear not having a bath for weeks on end', put in Ann. But there was more to be said. Ann continued: today life is getting 'more sort of antiseptic and lacking the sort of realities'. Around and around it could go:

progress and cleanliness versus order and authenticity – gain versus loss. The present is not unarguably the best possible of times.

In this dialectic between past and present, there is an assumption of change: an imagined past has been supplanted by the present. The processes of change are not finished, but change is the unchanging condition of today. 'We live in a changing world, don't we', said a father (interview 3). It was a common-place thought. There was no-one to disagree.

The change from the past could be talked about in terms of progress or of loss, but, either way, there is an omission. As the arguments for the present confront those for the past, the future slips from the argumentative agenda. It becomes a blank category, whose nature is to be extrapolated from the gap between past and present. The fireman was thinking ahead to the time when his teenage sons will be middle-aged: 'Things will have progressed that much further' (interview 22). He drew an analogy from his own life. There were things which he never dreamt of when young, but which he now takes for granted: 'Silly things like soft margarine out of the fridge and the milk not going off'. It will be like that in the future, as time continues along its homogeneous way. He gave no specific examples of future changes. But that was the nature of his argument: all that could be predicted was the unpredictability and the inevitability of change.

Despite his talk of advances along the lines of softened margarine and unturned milk, there would also be loss. He talked of the disappearance of neighbourliness. His wife agreed: 'I mean we used to live next door to my auntie and uncle and you knew the people weren't far away'. Everyone knew everyone else in those days. That had gone. The mother spoke about 'the changing way of the world' and 'of the awful things that happen'. The secure, ordered past was being contrasted with the dangerous changes of the present. The future would bring further change and further loss.

A sixty-one year old wife was talking of her own children: 'I mean they're a different generation, I mean you can't expect them to say and do things that we were brought up to do really, I think we've got to accept change' (interview 4). Change was the reality, to be accepted. And feared: 'Oh dear, oh dear, what are we all coming to?', exclaimed a fifty-nine year old retired school cleaner (interview 47). Her question, so common-place in its utterance, was its own answer. The answer was anything but Panglossian in tone.

If change is the claimed reality, then, the self, in contemplating the future, is imagining a foreign terrain. This sense of foreignness was expressed by a husband and wife, both in their thirties (interview 34). What changes, asked the interviewer, will there be 'when William does get to the throne?'. 'I wouldn't like to think that far ahead', said the wife. There'll be changes, said her husband: 'We can hope that nothing is destroyed in the country'. 'It'll be normal to them whatever it is', she said, 'it wouldn't be normal to us'. As the empty calendars of the future are progressively filled with losses and gains, the present self will have become out of date. It will have outlived its sell-by date. That is the future to be common-sensically imagined, and feared.

THE OLD-FASHIONED BREATH OF FRESH AIR

In Chapter 2 respondents were heard to equate monarchy with the heritage of the nation. They said that the nation's future existence depended upon the continuation of monarchy, and, thus, upon the continuation of the past. The threat to the nation's continuity was seen to come from the United States: without the Royal Family 'we' will become just another state of America, having abandoned 'our' heritage. No-one mentioned monarchy protecting the nation against integration into Europe.

It would be easy to argue that royalty is seen as a symbol of past times, and that, in an age of change, it offers a fixed point for an unimaginable future. Certainly, claims along these lines were to be heard in the family discussions. A thirty-eight year old sales manager, said of monarchy: 'It represents something that's been there for a long time and, and hopefully gives some continuity to how we'll carry on' (interview 7).

Nevertheless, monarchy is more than a symbol of times past, for it reflects common-sense's dialectic between past and present. The Royal Family, as a family, represents both change and continuity across time. Its representation of continuity is obvious. Nevertheless, as a continuing family, the royals always have a younger generation who can be seen to be moving in a modern direction, leaving their elders appearing 'old-fashioned'. Common-sense can praise this progress. Princess Diana is 'great', said a sixteen year old receptionist, 'she's brought real life into it' (interview 9). The point is that there is always another generation to bring in 'real life'. Formerly, it was those royals who have now grown middle-aged or old. A retired bank manager and his wife, both in their sixties, were reminiscing about when the young Duke of Edinburgh was courting the future Queen of England (interview 12). The Duke had driven a sports car, said the husband, and that was 'unheard of' those days. Yes, the Duke had 'brought a breath of fresh air in'. Each generation of royals can bring a new breath of air, and be praised by their contemporaries for so doing.

When the father said it was 'a changing world' in which 'we' live, he was specifically talking about the Royal Family (interview 3). He said: 'They have to change, have to move with the times to a certain degree'. And then he added: 'I don't think the Queen does, do you Linda?'. His wife agreed: 'She's never changed, has she? But I think the younger ones have, haven't they'. 'All children change from what their parents are, don't they', added her husband, 'same as ours do'. 'We' and 'they' have to move with the change of time. There is no hope of arresting the movement. Not even the Queen of England can manage that. Homogeneous time has to be filled, and each generation will differ from the previous.

Moving with the times presents particular problems for royalty. 'They' can be criticised for being too old-fashioned and they can be criticised for discarding the past too hastily. There can be endless discussion whether a young prince or princess is being too formal or not formal enough. The sales manager might have said that the Royal Family represented continuity with the past (interview 7), but the royal continuity did not represent absence of change. He said that 'in a world that changes as much as it does, in some respects they're the one thing that doesn't change quite so much'. He went on: 'Although they need to modernise and have done in some ways, it's a fine line between going too far and not going far enough, so that they get too remote'.

The modern breath of fresh air was, above all, a humanising one, forcing 'them' down from 'their' remote pedestal. Each generation was becoming less formal, less remote; the deferential society was becoming more egalitarian. 'They're more human now', said a sixty-six year old woman (interview 37). And she liked that. 'I like the idea that they're not put on a pedestal any more', said a forty-seven year old housewife and domestic cleaner (interview 61; quoted in Chapter 3). But others might worry that some of the younger royals were going too far in that direction.

Double-declaiming is to be heard in this argumentative dialectic. When a young girl praises 'Di' for making royalty less stuffy, she is locating herself on the side of the moderns. The double-declaiming is not confined to a young girl making claims for her own generation, speaking in the presence of her parents. She is doing something which is much more generally done. She is making a claim for the present, and for her present self. Even her parents do the same in their way, for the common depictions of the past involve claims for present. This is just as true when the conservative accounts of a lost past are being given. The depictions of past times as ordered, safe and friendly are also depictions of past simplicities. Experiences might have been more authentic in those days – no button-pressing to produce a televised image – but the experiences are depicted as naïve – the people of the past entertained beliefs which 'we' have seen through. Their sense of order was based upon a deference towards superiors who are now exposed as being just like 'us'. Max Horkheimer's remark, quoted in Chapter 4, about the modern child seeing through the super-ego of the father is particularly pertinent. As empty time is filled, each generation claims to expose naïve illusions which were believed by its elders. In claiming this, present speakers lay claim to a superior sophistication.

The mother and daughter, who worked in the same secretarial office, were talking about the diminishing respect for royalty (interview 23). It was during this exchange that the mother made her comment, quoted in Chapter 6, that today 'we know them warts and all'. The context was a contrast between past and present. Nowadays, she said, there isn't 'a respect generally for the Royal Family that there was then'. It was because we know them warts and all: 'Whereas then, they was someone you could consider to be better than us; whether they were or not is a different matter; we considered they were better than us, they were sort of God's chosen people'. She went on: 'They're in the paper every day' and, once again, she mentioned the warts and all. It was then that she made her remark, also previously quoted, that in those days you thought that 'they didn't have natural functions, not like we did'.

As she spoke, she was locating herself in the modern world, in which the royal warts are known by sophisticated subjects. She was distancing herself from religious deference, just as in Chapter 3 she could be heard distancing herself from the old-fashioned notion of divine right. In former times, royalty was believed to be better than 'us'. She specifically casts doubt on that belief (whether or not it's true is a different matter, she says). She mocks the naïvety of earlier times, even that of her youthful self: she claims that it used to be

216

believed that royal figures had no lavatorial requirements. Nowadays, we have seen through such childish illusions. 'We' do not bow down in deference, naïvely believing in the superiority of kings and queens. 'We' *know* what was previously unknown. As she depicts the past, and as she laughs at its naïveties, the speaker asserts that she is no deferential subject. So speaks a keen royalist of today.

Each generation might claim its own sophistication, and these claims can be used to accomplish family business. In Chapter 6, the grandparents portrayed the great-grandmother as a gullible figure of the past: she believed all she read in newspapers, so they claimed (interview 38). A forty-three year old father was joking about his own parents collecting pictures of royalty: 'There's a magazine cutting of Charles and Diana by the kitchen door' (interview 14). He explained this in terms of generation. His parents were typical of their times: 'They were brought up to doff their cap to the lord'. He was claiming that he had progressed beyond such deference.

A teenage daughter and her friend were denying that they respected royalty (interview 24). The daughter's friend spoke generally: 'The further down you get in generations', she said, the less respect there was for royalty. The daughter was trying to brand her father's generation amongst the uncritically respectful. He argued back, locating the jump from naïvety to sophistication in the gap between his generation and that of his own parents: 'From my parents, and your grandma and grandad, to what we've got, I think we respect them more now because of what they tend to do in society, whereas my mother and father respected them probably because they were king or queen; they'd been brought up to respect monarchy, whereas we've not had it that way'. The 'we' included him and his modern daughter. He had unmasked his parents' superego, so he was claiming. His daughter was claiming to unmask his.

The young, the middle-aged and even the old could agree that the progress of rationality was inexorably sweeping away the imagined deference and naïvety of an always-previous generation. Royalty could not expect 'us' to be obedient subjects of old, and 'they' correspondingly had to move with the times. Moreover, the lost naïvety, ascribed to past times, cannot be naïvely recaptured by an ego which claims its own sophistication. There can be nostalgia; but nostalgia is not simply expressed, lest the speaker abandons the knowledge of the present, which makes the nostalgia possible. This complication was illustrated by the discussions between the office supervisor and his wife, a cleaner (interview 1).

In their talk, the dialectic between past and present was played out. Both, at different times, could voice a praise for past times – even a wish to return to the past. But as the wish was expressed, so it was argumentatively countered. The husband, as quoted earlier, repeated the conservative history that modern life had lost the authenticity of olden times. When he spoke thus, his wife countered with the liberal themes of material progress. The exchange had started when they were talking about castles and stately homes, which they often visited on their holidays. The husband declared that 'I think sometimes it would pay us to go back in time'. His wife cut in: 'The trouble is we wouldn't be in the castle, we'd be the serfs'. There might be nostalgia, but the contemporary ego has no wish to defer to feudal lords.

When they talked about royalty, the positions of husband and wife were reversed. The wife gave the conservative account of history, claiming that she liked 'the old days', when royalty had more privileges. Her husband disagreed, saying that it was good that 'they' were coming off the pedestal: 'It shows to the public that they are human the same as us'. But, said the wife, the more 'they' come down from the pedestal, 'then the next generation admires them less'. She worried that the royals were becoming too informal: 'I think it'll get lax, more lax, more lax, until it's nothing'. The progress of time, which her husband was supporting, would sweep 'them' away. She looked back to the reign of Queen Victoria:

> 'If you look back to the time of Victoria, I mean, I mean, say for instance, Charles and Di they kissed on the balcony, right, when they got married, that would never have been allowed in Victoria's time, would it? So, it's, again it's bringing them down a little bit. I mean to me it was alright, it didn't bother me, but the morals are going as, as, the time goes on and it's just reaching them as well.'
>
> (interview 1)

At first sight, she seems to be arguing for a return to past times. However, her nostalgic self remains rooted in the present. Her language indicated lack of deference: it was 'Charles and Di', not the Prince and Princess of Wales. She specifically distinguishes herself from the moral selves of Victorian times. As she talks about the Prince and Princess's kiss upon the balcony, she pointedly says that 'it was alright' by her: it didn't bother her. She was no Victorian prude, to be upset by a public embrace. She blocks off that line of potential criticism.

In so doing, she was heading in a familiar argumentative direction. Her denial of prudery resembles that of the estate agent, quoted in Chapter 4, who, in arguing that the future king could not marry a woman with a sexual past, specifically said that he personally wasn't bothered (interview 42). It was the public image which mattered. After the mother had complained about the kiss upon the balcony, the interviewer asked whether royalty should have different morals from other people. 'No', replied the mother, 'but they should be very strict, very strict what's allowed in public'. Again, it was the public image of morality which mattered, whether or not it was followed in private. Her nostalgia included the demand that 'they', the royals, should set examples, which 'we' need not follow. 'They' should be like old-fashioned royalty, but 'we' are not to be deferential serfs. Moreover, in private, even 'they' need not follow the examples which 'they' should set so strictly in public. This is no advocacy for a return to former naïvety. 'They', the royals of today, should act publicly as if 'they' belong to yesteryear, when 'we' know that 'they' do not.

The mother's championing of past time itself belongs resolutely to the present. She herself is not a Victorian, as she makes clear. One might call her nostalgia typically post-modern. Public and private realms seem to be being distinguished, but they are blurred in the distinction: the strict public display is to be a public image of private morality. The mother wants royalty to borrow from the images of the past, but without reproducing past superstitions and deference – just as a post-modern building might reproduce a gothic cathedral arch, whilst subtracting God's grace. As her cry for a return to the past is uttered, so there is a knowing wink towards the present. There is also a quick, frightened glance towards an unknown future.

REMEMBERING THE PRESENT

Bagehot, too, winked knowingly, as he advocated that the majestic parade be continued. His wink differs from today's, for *The English Constitution* expressed a confidence in the future. Bagehot recognised that society was changing, but he considered that a reformed monarchy would aid the successful management of those changes. The constitutional arrangement, which he was proposing, was a nineteenth-century machine built to last – a solid piece of engineering, complete with polished oak and brass fittings. Bagehot believed that the constitutional machinery would continue to operate, so long as the ill-educated masses clung to their superstitious illusions about kings and queens. That was the basis of his wink.

Today, the descendants of Bagehot's masses have seen through the illusions. In place of a confidence in the future, there is a sense of puzzlement: oh dear, oh dear, what are we all coming to? Monarchy seems to offer reassurance that not all is changing beyond recognition. It symbolises both the past's continuity into the present, and the continuity of the present into the future. The continuity of monarchy, and indeed the continuity of the nation, into the future suggests that the present, too, might not be lost in future times. Instead, 'our' times might be saved, if not redeemed, as the heritage of the future.

To understand how monarchy might represent this continuity and this mixing of times, it is necessary to stress one important aspect about royalty. Its fame is completely unlike that of any other celebrity in the modern world. This cannot be emphasised too much, lest parallels with other aspects of contemporary life mislead. For instance, the Royal Family is sometimes likened to a soap opera. Rosalind Coward (1983), in a witty analysis, sees similarities between the 'Windsors' of Buckingham Palace and the 'Ewings' of Dallas. In a number of respects, there are parallels between fictional and royal 'soaps'. In both cases, continuing sagas of private life are unfolded before the eyes of mass audiences. Both have a particular female dimension. Just as women are said to be the most interested viewers of soap operas (Hobson, 1982; Livingstone, 1990), so, as was seen in the previous chapter, the royal story is held to be a woman's realm. Nevertheless, the parallel is inherently limited. So too is the analogy that the royals are 'show business stars', and that monarchy is a branch of show business.

Royals are uniquely different from other show business celebrities and from the characters in fictional dramas. In the first place, neither the stars of the entertainment industries, nor the characters in soap operas, are held to embody a national heritage and the future continuity of a nation. There is a second crucial factor which confirms the uniquess of royal fame. In contemporary life, there are no other figures who are guaranteed a lifetime of celebrity from the moment of birth. Indeed, the interest of the media guarantees fame from the moment of possible conception. This fame is transmitted across generations. The sons and daughters of today's film stars and

220

sporting heroes will fade into anonymous obscurity, unless they manage to gain celebrity in their own right. But it is not so with the royals – they, their unborn children and grandchildren are known to be famous, whatever they do.

Wd/
yes.

In a world of obsolescence, the transmission of royal celebrity across the generations has special significance. For example, the family stories of brief encounters with royalty can themselves be transmitted from generation to generation. Chapter 3 presented the moment when the mother was re-telling to her daughter the time when the latter, as a baby, was briefly held by Princess Margaret (interview 23). The daughter well knew the significance of the lady who had held her; there was no need for the mother to explain the point of the story. If a favourite star of the mother's generation had done the holding, the significance would have a diminishing future return. The next generation will care little for a touch from a figure whose transient fame was linked to the experiences of the previous generation. Who, today, would care that Douglas Fairbanks Junior had briefly held their mother? Or, in future times, that their mother had been held by Madonna? It might matter to the mother's mother, but not to the grandchildren. By contrast, the daughter had a story which she could pass on to her children: 'The Day I Was Held By the Queen of England's Sister'. The story would be meaningful to an audience as yet unborn.

Here is an exception to the rule of obsolescence, foreseen by each generation in the changing world. The thirty year old wife might have said that she didn't wish to think into the future, when Prince William will be king (interview 34). Her husband mentioned that there will be disorientating changes, which will seem 'normal' to the people of those times, but not to 'us'. The future was to be foreign land, except for one matter. The national frame for the imagining was familiar: a known figure from a familiar family will be upon the throne.

Present royal moments, whether those of the great televised occasions or the moment when an ordinary person receives the touch of a royal hand-shake, are construed as being inherently memorable (Nairn, 1988; Ziegler, 1977). Thus, collective memory is something which is defined as being worthy of remembering and re-telling (Edwards and Middleton, 1987 and 1988; Middleton and Edwards, 1990). In Chapter 2, a mother was heard to ask her critical son whether the royal wedding wasn't something about which he, in the fullness of time, could tell his grandchildren (interview 41).

221

The young bachelor had laughed and argued back with his mother. As so often is the case, the absent words in the argument were significant. He did not reply with words to the effect that 'my grandchildren won't know what the hell I'm talking about'. Both he and his mother knew that the event was memorable, even for the unborn.

Times might be changing and the Royal Family might have to move with them. Nevertheless, the permanence of royal fame suggests that the present moment is not to be completely overtaken. In this sense, the past heritage of royalty – or, the imagining of its historical continuity – offers a promise for a future which might otherwise be a disconcerting blank. 'Our' lives will run in parallel to 'theirs' and the continuity will be reassuringly shared. Overwhelming transience and obsolescence seem to be held in check, while a touch of royalty dignifies the present as the heritage for the future.

If this is correct, then monarchy today is attuned to times whose common-sense lacks optimistic visions for the future. Moreover, monarchy contributes to the limitation of that vision for the future, which is contained within the liberal account of historic progress. The movement of time towards progressive equality is seen as threatening. Royalty could not survive such equality, so it was said; and if royalty cannot survive, then the nation will be cut dangerously from its past, from its present and from itself. The premise of 'royalness', which is a premise of inequality, limits the imagining of the future. A future without inequality – and, thus, without royalty – is to be feared, even dismissed as unimaginable.

Such limiting of the imagined future can be reproduced at a personal level, when, for instance, people, in talking of royalty, also talk of their own future. This was illustrated by the fifteen year old daughter of the couple who have been cited arguing about the merits of past and present (interview 1). If one wanted a single symbol of monarchy's ideological significance, then perhaps one should not look to the well-known photographic images: royals in their official finery, waving from the balcony; a queen, chatting to strangers, whose faces register delight at the honour; the wonderful wedding scenes. A fitting symbol is a fifteen year old girl, talking confidently of royalty in the security of her family home. Her mother and father are sitting beside her. Her older brother is there too, in the crowded living-room of the suburban home. As she talks of royalty, she talks of the future, her future.

She justifies monarchy in terms of an imagined scene in her adult life, and, in so doing, she depicts the future as a reproduction of the present. She was talking of the royal babies: 'It will be nice when they're older and you can think, "Well, I saw them when they were babies and now look at them, they're so grown up"'. The young girl imagines that, in years to come, she will be reassured by the continuity of the richest family in the land. Her imagined future is homely and familiar; its front door is closed upon disturbing dreams of different times. And the young girl is reassured now by the prospect. It is a settling thought for unsettling times.

APPENDIX

INTERVIEW DETAILS

Interview Relationship, Age, Occupation, Newspapers

1   Mother, 42, housewife/cleaner
            Father, 42, office supervisor
            Son, 18, electronics technician
            Daughter, 15, school student
            Sun, Sunday Express, local

2   Father, 42, motor mechanic
            Mother, 39, shop manager
            Son, 18, upholsterer
            Daughter, 17, school student
            News of the World, local

3   Father, 48, shopkeeper
            Mother, 45, shopkeeper
            Son, 17, student
            Daily Mirror, Sunday Telegraph

4   Husband, 64, ex-engineer
            Wife, 61, ex-office supervisor
            Daily Telegraph, Sunday Times, local evening

5   Husband, 56, engineer
            Wife, 50, housewife
            Daughter, 19, sales demonstrator
            Son, 16, YTS upholsterer
            Daily Express, Observer

6   Wife, 48, part-time bar-worker
Husband, 48, manager
Son, 21, electronics technician
Daughter, 18, computer clerk
Sunday Express, local

7   Mother, 39, housewife, ex-market gardener
Father, 38, sales manager
(two young children present but not contributing)
Daily Express or *Daily Mail*

8   Mother, 77, retired, ex-housing officer
Son, 50, helicopter pilot
Observer

9   Grandmother, 70?, retired ex-clerk
Daughter, 43, housewife/cleaner
Granddaughter, 16, clerk
Sun, Sunday Express

10   Father, 46, engineer
Mother, 43, home-help, ex-bar-worker
(daughter present but not contributing)
Daily Express, local

11   Father, 41, engineering consultant
Mother, 38, housewife
Daughter, 14, school student
Daughter, 13, school student
Observer

12   Husband, 62, retired bank manager
Wife, 60, housewife
Daily Telegraph, Sunday Express

13   Husband, 43, dentist
Wife, 42, ex-teacher
Daughter, 12, school student
Daily Express, Sunday Express, Sunday Times

14   Wife, 43, clerk
        Husband, 43, engineer
        Son, 18, trainee mineral surveyor
        Son, 16, school student
        Daily Mail, Mail on Sunday

15   Husband, 53, ex-upholsterer
        Wife, 51, ex-lacemaker
        Today, News of the World

16   Father, 64, retired manager
        Mother, 56, voluntary worker
        Daughter, 27, traffic warden
        Daily Telegraph, Sunday Express, Sunday Times

17   Father, 49, engineer
        Mother, 40+, housewife/bar-worker
        Son, 14, school student
        Son, 12, school student
        Daily Telegraph, Sunday Telegraph

18   Husband, 33, civil servant
        Wife, 30, part-time civil servant
        Daily Mail, Sunday Telegraph

19   Friend (male), 31, hairdresser
        Friend (male), 27, teacher

20   Father, 46, manager
        Mother, 44, retired, ex-teacher
        Daughter, 21, airline clerk
        Son, 19, university student
        Guardian, Observer, local

21   Wife, 48, housewife
        Daily Mail

22   Father, 44, fireman
        Wife, 41, credit controller
        Son, 17, YTS printer
        Son, 15, school student
        Sun, local

23   Mother, 48, secretarial
Daughter, 25, secretarial
Daily Mirror, People, News of the World

24   Mother, 43, secretarial
Father, 42, salesman
Daughter, 16, school student
Daughter's friend, 16, school student
Daily Mirror, Sunday Mirror. Friend's family: *Star, Sunday Mirror*

25   Mother, 44, housewife, ex-teacher
Husband, 41, architectural technician
(brief interruptions from daughter, 13, and son, 11)
Observer

26   Husband, 52, salesman
Wife, 43, secretarial
Daily Mail, Independent, Sunday Times

27   Husband, 48, engineer
Wife, 44, secretarial
Daughter, 19, hairdresser
Daughter, 16, college student
Sunday Express, local

28   Husband, 38, computing consultant
Wife, 32, nurse
Sunday Times

29   Father, 67, ex-toolmaker
Husband/son-in-law, 39, hairdresser
Daughter/wife, 36, market researcher
Daily Telegraph, unspecified Sunday papers

30   Father, 43, researcher
Mother, 41, ex-teacher
Daughter, 11, school student
Observer, local

31   Mother, 45, housewife/typist
Daughter, 19, pool attendant
Local

32   Wife, 23, payroll officer
Husband, 22, technician
Daily Mail or *Today*

33   Husband, 34, marketing
Wife, 32, housewife
Sunday Times, Mail on Sunday, local

34   Husband, 38, unemployed, enrolled on part-time
computing course
Wife, 30, childminder

35   Husband, 44, manager
Wife, 43, shop assistant
Daughter, 19, university student
Daughter's boyfriend, 19, university student
Son, 17, trainee technician
Daily Express, Mail on Sunday. Daughter: *Guardian*

36   Wife, 36, school meals supervisor
Husband, 45, electrical engineer
Son, 17, electrical apprentice
Daughter, 14, school student
Fostered girl, 13, school student
Daily Mirror, Sun, Sunday Express

37   Husband, 71, ex-engineer
Wife, 66, housewife
Daily Express, Sunday Express

38   Great-grandmother, 87, ex-print worker
Grandmother (a), 66, ex-domestic cook
Grandfather (a), 64, ex-army, civil service
Grandfather (b), 60, ex-bank clerk
Grandmother (b), 59, ex-cook
(Great-grandmother is mother of grandfather (a);
grandparents (a) are parents of husband of 28;

grandparents (b) are parents of wife of 28)
G-grandmother: *Sun, Daily Mirror.* (a): *Sun, Daily
Mirror,* local. (b): Occasional *Sunday Times*

39   Father, 41, security officer
Wife, 39, cleaner
Son, 23, plumber
Son's wife, 21, ex-factory worker
Father and wife: *Star, Sunday Mirror, News of the
World.* Daughter and husband: *Sun*

40   Wife, 87, ex-farm worker
Husband, 80+, ex-farm worker
Daily Telegraph, Sunday Telegraph

41   Wife, 53, health products business
Husband, 53, engineer
Son, 30, photographer
Son, 27, finance assistant
Local. Older son: *Observer*

42   Grandfather, 59, school laboratory technician,
ex-electrician
Grandmother, 55, clerk
Father, 42, estate agent
Mother and daughter of grandparents, 34, nurse
Sunday Express, Mail on Sunday, local

43   Wife, 31, charity worker
Husband, 29, local government

44   Husband, 29, factory technician
Wife, 29, clerk
Local

45   Single woman, 49, teacher
Daily Mail

46   Mother, 46, housewife, ex-factory worker
Daughter, 15, school student
Sun, People, local

47   Mother, 59, ex-cleaner
Daily Mirror, People, News of the World

48   Wife, 55, cleaner, childminder
Husband, 50, gas servicer
Daughter, 15, school student
Daily Mirror, People

49   Wife, 47, cleaner
Sun, People

50   Wife, 44, cleaner
Daughter, 22, shop worker
Daughter, 19, catering assistant
Daily Mirror, People

51   Wife, 63, ex-factory worker

52   Husband, 67, ex-fitter
Wife, 57, ex-cleaner
Sun, Daily Mirror, Sunday Mirror

53   Mother, 62, widowed housewife
Daughter, 24, secretarial
Daughter's husband, 22, nurse
Mother: *Daily Mirror.* Daughter and husband:
Guardian, Observer

54   Mother, 39, single parent, teacher
Mother, 39, clothes pattern-cutter
Mother, 38, teacher
Guardian. Guardian. Local

55   Wife, 44, supermarket cashier
Husband, 42, fitter
Daughter, 11, school student
Daily Mirror, Sunday Mirror, local

56   Mother, 47, cleaner
Daughter, 16, factory worker
Star, News of the World

57 Father, 50, lorry driver
    Mother, 40, domestic cleaner
    Daughter, 18, catering worker
    Daughter, 16, school student
    Second daughter's boyfriend, 18, labourer
    Star, News of the World

58 Mother, 59, ex-shop worker, factory worker
    Son, 18, motor mechanic and part-time bouncer
    Daily Mirror

59 Husband, 62, quality assurance manager
    Wife, 61, housewife, ex-cleaner
    Son, 24, technician
    Local

60 Mother, 68, ex-cleaner
    Son, 43, care-taker
    Son's wife, 30, secretarial
    Star, Sun, Sunday Mirror

61 Wife, 47, domestic cleaner
    Husband, 47, telephone engineer
    Son, 21, plumber's assistant
    People, local

62 Husband, 26, clerk
    Wife, 25, dental nurse
    Mail on Sunday, local

63 Husband, 53, waste disposal operator
    Wife, 45, hospital orderly

REFERENCES

Aboud, F. (1988) *Children and Prejudice*, Oxford: Blackwell.

Adorno, T.W., Frenkel-Brunswik, E., Levinson, D.J. and Sanford, R.N. (1950) *The Authoritarian Personality*, New York: Harper and Row.

Aebischer, V. (1985) *Les Femmes et le Langage*, Paris: Presses Universitaires de France.

Alexandra, Queen (1908) *Queen Alexandra's Christmas Gift Book: Photographs from My Camera*, London: Daily Telegraph.

Anderson, B. (1983) *Imagined Communities*, London: Verso.

Andrews, A. (1975) *The Follies of Edward VII*, London: Lexington Press.

Atkinson, J.M. and Heritage, J. (eds) (1984) *Structures of Social Action*, Cambridge: Cambrige University Press.

Bacon, F. (1906) *Essays*, London: J.M. Dent.

Bagehot, W. (1867/1965) *The English Constitution*, Glasgow: Fontana.

—— (1965) *Historical Essays*, ed. N. St. John-Stevas, Garden City, New York: Anchor Books.

—— (1968) *The Collected Works* (ed. N. St. John Stevas), Cambridge, Mass.: Harvard University Press.

Baistow, T. (1985) *Fourth-Rate Estate: an Anatomy of Fleet Street*, London: Comedia.

Barker, M. (1981) *The New Racism*, London: Junction Books.

—— (1989) *Comics: Ideology, Power and the Critics*, Manchester: Manchester University Press.

Barthes, R. (1972) *Mythologies*, London: Jonathan Cape.

—— (1983) *Selected Writings*, London: Fontana.

Bartlett, F. (1932) *Remembering*, Cambridge: Cambridge University Press.

Baudrillard, J. (1985). The ecstasy of communication. In *Postmodern Culture*, ed. H. Foster, London: Pluto Press.

Benjamin, W. (1973) *Illuminations*, London: Fontana.

Benn, T. (1988) *Out of the Wilderness: Diaries 1963–67*, London: Arrow.

Billig, M. (1987) *Arguing and Thinking: a Rhetorical Approach to Social Psychology*, Cambridge: Cambridge University Press.

—— (1988a) 'Rhetorical and historical aspects of attitudes: the case of the British monarchy', *Philosophical Psychology*, 1, 83–104.

—— (1988b) 'Common-places of the British Royal Family: a rhetorical analysis of plain and argumentative sense', *Text*, 8, 191–218.

—— (1988c) 'The notion of "prejudice": some rhetorical and ideological aspects', *Text*, 8, 91–110.

—— (1989a) 'The argumentative nature of holding strong views: a case study', *European Journal of Social Psychology*, 19, 203–22.

—— (1989b) 'Conservatism and the rhetoric of rhetoric', *Economy and Society*, 18, 132–47.

—— (1990a) Collective memory, ideology and the British Royal Family. In *Collective Remembering*, eds D. Middleton and D. Edwards, London: Sage.

—— (1990b) 'Stacking the cards of ideology: the history of the *Sun Royal Souvenir Album*', *Discourse and Society*, 1, 17–37.

—— (1991) *Ideology and Opinions: Studies in Rhetorical Psychology*, London: Sage.

Billig, M., Condor, S., Edwards, D., Gane, M., Middleton, D. and Radley, A.R. (1988) *Ideological Dilemmas: a Social Psychology of Everyday Thinking*, London: Sage.

Birnbaum, N. (1955) 'Monarchs and sociologists', *Sociological Review*, 3, 5–23.

Bloch, Marc (1973) *The Royal Touch: Sacred Monarchy and Scrofula in England and France*, London: Routledge and Kegan Paul.

Bloch, Maurice (1987) The ritual of the royal bath in Madagascar: the dissolution of death, birth and fertility into authority. In *Rituals of Royalty*, eds D. Cannadine and S. Price, Cambridge: Cambridge University Press.

Blumler, J.G., Brown, J.R., Ewbank, A.J. and Nossiter, T.J. (1971) 'Attitudes to the monarchy: their structure and development during a ceremonial occasion', *Political Studies*, 19, 149–71.

Bocock, R. (1974) *Ritual in Industrial Society*, London: George Allen and Unwin.

Brown, C. and Cunliffe, L. (1983) *The Book of Royal Lists*, London: Sphere Books.

Brunt, R. (1988) 'Right royal opposition', *Marxism Today*, September, 20–5.

Cannadine, D. (1983) The context, performance and meaning of ritual: the British monarchy and the 'invention of tradition'. In *The Invention of Tradition*, eds E. Hobsbawm and T. Ranger, Cambridge: Cambridge University Press.

Chaney, D. (1983) 'A symbolic mirror of ourselves: civic ritual in mass society', *Media, Culture and Society*, 5, 119–35.

Clark, A. (1990) 'Queen Caroline and the sexual politics of popular culture in London, 1820', *Representations*, 31, 47–68.

Colley, L. (1984) 'The apotheosis of George III: loyalty, royalty and the British nation', *Past and Present*, 102, 94–109.

—— (1986) 'Whose nation? Class and national consciousness in Britain, 1750–1830', *Past and Present*, 113, 97–117.

Coward, R. (1983) *Female Desire*, London: Paladin.

Crawford, M. (1950) *The Little Princesses*, New York: Harcourt Brace.

Crossman, R.H.S. (1979) *The Crossman Diaries: Condensed Version*, London: Methuen.

Dayan, D. and Katz, E. (1985) Electronic ceremonies: television performs a royal wedding. In *On Signs*, ed. M. Blonsky, Oxford: Blackwell.

Dupuis, J. (1990) 'Louis XX ou Jean IV? Profession prétendant', *Le Nouvel Observateur*, August 16–22, p.8.

Durkheim, E. (1968) *The Elementary Forms of Religious Life*, London: George Allen and Unwin.

Edelman, M. (1977) *Political Language*, New York: Academic Press.

Edley, N. (1991) 'Monarchy in the mirror: a social psychological analysis of representations', unpublished Ph.D. thesis, University of Loughborough.

Edwards, D. and Middleton, D. (1987) 'Conversation and remembering: Bartlett revisited', *Applied Cognitive Psychology*, 1, 77–92.

—— and —— (1988) 'Conversational remembering and family relationships: how children learn to remember', *Journal of Social and Personal Relationships*, 5, 3–25.

Edwards, D. and Potter, J. (in press) 'Nigel Lawson's memory: Neisser, truth and discourse analysis', *Applied Cognitive Psychology*.

Elster, J. (1983) *Sour Grapes*, Cambridge: Cambridge University Press.

Fiske, J. (1987) *Television Culture*, New York: Methuen.

Folger, R. (1986) Rethinking equity theory: a referent cognitions model. In *Justice in Social Relations*, eds H.W. Bierhoff, R.L. Cohen and J. Greenberg, New York: Erlbaum.

Forbes, H.D. (1986) *Nationalism, Ethnocentrism and Personality*, Chicago: Chicago University Press.

Fraser, N. (1989) *Unruly Practices: Power, Discourse and Gender in Contemporary Social Theory*, Cambrige: Polity Press.

Fraser, C. and Foster, D. (1984) Social groups, nonsense groups and group polarization. In *The Social Dimension*, ed. H. Tajfel, Cambridge: Cambridge University Press.

Freud, S. (1964a) Group psychology and the analysis of the ego. In *Standard Edition of the Complete Psychological Works*, Volume 18, London: Hogarth Press.

—— (1964b) Totem and taboo. In Standard Edition of the Complete Psychological Works, Volume 13, London: Hogarth Press.

Furnham, A. and Bochner, S. (1986) *Culture Shock*, London: Methuen.

Gellner, E. (1983) *Nations and Nationalism*, Oxford: Blackwell.

—— (1987) *Culture, Identity and Politics*, Cambridge: Cambridge University Press.

Gilbert, G.N. and Mulkay, M. (1984) *Opening Pandora's Box*, Cambridge: Cambridge University Press.

Golding, P. and Middleton, S. (1982) *Images of Welfare*, Oxford: Martin Robertson.

Gramsci, A. (1971) *Prison Notebooks*, London: Lawrence and Wishart.

Guillaumin, C. (1972) *L'Idéologie Raciste, Genèse et Langage Actuel*, Paris: Mouton.

—— (1986) Sexism, a right-wing constant of any discourse: a theoretical note. In *The Nature of the Right*, ed. G. Seidel, Amsterdam: John Benjamins.

Gurr, T.R. (1970) *Why Men Rebel*, Princeton: Princeton University Press.

Habermas, J. (1987) *Theory of Communicative Action*, Cambridge: Polity Press.

Halbwachs, M. (1980) *The Collective Memory*, New York: Harper Row.

Hall, S. (1986) Varieties of liberalism. In *Politics and Ideology*, eds J. Donald and S. Hall, Milton Keynes: Open University Press.

Hamilton, W. (1975) *My Queen and I*, London: Quartet.

Harris, L.M. (1966) *Long to Reign Over Us?*, London: William Kimber.

Harvey, D. (1989) *The Condition of Postmodernity*, Oxford: Blackwell.

Heald, G. and Wybrow, R.J. (1986) *The Gallup Survey of Britain*, Aldershot: Croom Helm.

Helkama, K. (1987) 'A world at peace as a personal value in Finland: its relationship to demographic characteristics, political identification and type of moral reasoning', *Current Research on Peace and Violence*, 10, 113–23.

—— (1988) 'Two studies of Piaget's theory of moral development', *European Journal of Social Psychology*, 18, 17–37.

Henriques, J., Hollway, W., Urwin, C., Venn, C. and Walkerdine, V. (1984) *Changing the Subject*, London: Methuen.

Heritage, J. (1988) Explanations as accounts: a conversation analytic perspective. In *Analysing Everyday Explanation*, ed. C. Antaki, London: Sage.

Hewison, R. (1987) *The Heritage Industry*, London: Methuen.

Hewitt, J.P. and Stokes, R. (1975) 'Disclaimers', *American Sociological Review*, 40, 1–11.

Hobsbawm, E. (1983) The invention of tradition. In *the Invention of Tradition*, eds E. Hobsbawm and T. Ranger, Cambridge: Cambridge University Press.

Hobson, D. (1982) *Crossroads: the Drama of a Soap Opera*, London: Methuen.

Hoey, B. (1987) *Monarchy: Behind the Scenes with the Royal Family*, London: BBC Books.

Hogg, M.A. and Abrams, D. (1988) *Social Identifications: a Social Psychology of Intergroup Relations and Group Processes*, London: Routledge.

Hoggart, R. (1958) *The Uses of Literacy*, Harmondsworth: Pelican.

Horkheimer, M. (1941) 'The end of reason', *Zeitschrift für Sozialforschung*, 9, 366–88.

Howitt, D. (1982) *Mass Media and Social Problems*, Oxford: Pergamon.

James, C.L.R. (1963) *Beyond a Boundary*, London: Hutchinson.

—— (1989) *Cricket*, London: Allison and Busby.

Jameson, F. (1988) Cognitive mapping. In *Marxism and the Interpretation of Culture*, eds C. Nelson and L. Grossberg, London: Macmillan.

Januszczak, W. (1990) 'The last crusade', *Weekend Guardian*, February 3–4, pp.4–7.

Jennings, H. and Madge, C. (1987) *May 12 1937: Mass Observation Day Survey*, London: Faber.

Jensen, K.B. (1990) 'Politics of polysemy: television news, everyday consciousness and political action', *Media, Culture and Society*, 12, 57–77.

Jones, E. (1951) The psychology of constitutional monarchy. In *Essays in Applied Psycho-Analysis*, Volume 1, London: Hogarth Press.

Kroker, A. and Cook, D. (1988) *The Post-Modern Scene: Excremental Culture and Hyper-Aesthetics*, London: Macmillan.

Lacan, J. (1977) *The Four Fundamental Concepts of Psycho-Analysis*, London: Hogarth Press.

Lacey, R. (1977) *Majesty*, London: Hutchinson.

Lant, J.L. (1979) *Insubstantial Pageant: Ceremony and Confusion at Queen Victoria's Court*, London: Hamish Hamilton.

Lash, S. (1990) *The Sociology of Postmodernism*, London: Routledge.

Lauerbach, G.E. (1989) 'We don't want war, but...: speech act schemata and inter-schema-inference transfer', *Journal of Pragmatics*, 13, 25–51.

Leith, D. and Myerson, G. (1989) *The Power of Address*, London: Routledge.

Lerner, M. (1975) 'The justice motive in social behaviour', *Journal of Social Issues*, 31, 1–19.

—— (1980) *The Belief in a Just World*, New York: Plenum.

Lévi-Strauss, C. (1985) *The View From Afar*, Harmondsworth: Penguin.

Livingstone, S.M. (1990) *Making Sense of Television*, Oxford: Pergamon Press.

Lukes, S. (1977) *Essays in Sociological Theory*, Oxford: Oxford University Press.

McGuire, W.J. (1964) Inducing resistance to persuasion: some contemporary approaches. In *Advances in Experimental Social Psychology*, Volume 1, ed. L. Berkowitz, New York: Academic Press.

McLellan, D. (1986) *Ideology*, Milton Keynes: Open University Press.

Macpherson, C.B. (1962) *The Political Theory of Possessive Individualism*, Oxford: Clarendon Press.

McRobbie, A. (1981) Just like a 'Jackie' story'. In *Feminism for Girls*, eds A. McRobbie and T. McCabe, London: Routledge and Kegan Paul.

Maitland, K. and Wilson, J. (1987) 'Pronominal selection and ideological conflict', *Journal of Pragmatics*, 11, 495–512.

Marcuse, H. (1969) *Eros and Civilisation*, London: Sphere.

Martin, J. (1986) When expectations and justice do not coincide: blue collar visions of a just world. In *Justice in Social Relations*, eds H.W. Bierhoff, R.L. Cohen and J. Greenberg, New Jersey: Erlbaum.

Marx, K. (1915) *Capital*, Volume 1, Chicago: Charles H. Kerr.

Marx, K. and Engels, F. (1970) *The German Ideology*, London: Lawrence and Wishart.

Masters, B. (1973) *Dreams about H.M. the Queen*, St Albans: Mayflower.

Merton, R.K. (1976) *Sociological Ambivalence and Other Essays*, New York: Free Press.

Middleton, D. and Edwards, D. (eds) (1990) *Collective Remembering*, London: Sage.

Montgomery-Massingberd, H. (1986) *Her Majesty the Queen*, London: Willow Books.

Morley, D. (1986) *Family Television: Cultural Power and Domestic Leisure*, London: Comedia.

Morley, D. and Silverstone, R. (1990) 'Domestic communication – technologies and meanings', *Media, Culture and Society*, 12, 31–55.

Morton, A. (1989) *Theirs is the Kingdom*, London: Michael O'Mara.

Nairn, T. (1988) *The Enchanted Glass: Britain and its Monarchy*, London: Radius.

—— (1989) Britain's royal romance. In *Patriotism: the Making and Unmaking of British National Identity*, Volume III, ed. R. Samuel, London: Routledge.

Nelson, J.L. (1987) The Lord's anointed and the people's choice: Carolingian royal ritual. In *Rituals of Royalty*, eds D. Cannadine and S. Price, Cambridge: Cambridge University Press.

New Annual Register, 1820 (1821) London: Thomas McLean.

Nicolson, H. (1952) *King George V: His Life and Times*, London: Constable.

Pearson, J. (1986) *The Ultimate Family: the Making of the Royal House of Windsor*, London: Michael Joseph.

Perelman, C. and Olbrechts-Tyteca, L. (1971) *The New Rhetoric*, Notre Dame, Ind.: University of Notre Dame Press.

Plato (1971) *Gorgias*, Harmondsworth: Penguin.

Potter, J. and Edwards, D. (1990) 'Nigel Lawson's tent: attribution theory, discourse analysis and the social psychology of factual discourse', *European Journal of Social Psychology*, 20, 405–24.

Potter, J. and Wetherell, M. (1987) *Discourse and Social Psychology*, London: Sage.

—— and —— (1988) 'Accomplishing attitudes', *Text*, 8, 51–68.

Price, S. (1987) From noble funerals to divine cult: the consecration of Roman Emperors. In *Rituals of Royalty*, eds D. Cannadine and S. Price, Cambridge: Cambridge University Press.

Ricoeur, P. (1986) *Lectures on Ideology and Utopia*, New York: Columbia University Press.

Robinson, J.B. (1988) Time diary evidence about the social psychology of everyday life. In *The Social Psychology of Time: New Perspectives*, ed. J.E. McGrath, Newbury Park: Sage.

Roby, K. (1975) *The King, the Press and the People: a Study of Edward VII*, London: Barrie and Jenkins.

Rose, R. (1965) *Politics in England*, Boston: Little, Brown.

Rose, R. and Kavanagh, D. (1976) 'The monarchy in contemporary culture', *Comparative Politics*, 8, 548–76.

Sampson, E.E. (1977) 'Psychology and the American ideal', *Journal of Personality and Social Psychology*, 36, 1332–43.

—— (1988) 'The debate on individualism: indigenous psychologies of the individual and their role in personal and societal functioning', *American Psychologist*, 43, 15–22.

—— (1990) Social psychology and social control. In *Deconstructing Social Psychology*, eds I. Parker and J. Shotter, London: Routledge.

Schwartz, B. (1986) Conservatism, nationalism and imperialism. In *Politics and Ideology*, eds J. Donald and S. Hall, Milton Keynes: Open University Press.

—— (1990) The reconstruction of Abraham Lincoln In *Collective Remembering*, eds D. Middleton and D. Edwards, London: Sage.

Schwartz, B., Zerubavel, Y. and Barnett, B.M. (1986) 'The recovery of Masada: a study in collective memory', *Sociological Quarterly*, 27, 147–64.

Seidel, G. (1975) Ambiguity in political discourse. In *Political Language and Oratory in Traditional Society*, ed. M. Bloch, London: Academic Press.

Sennett, R. and Cobb, J. (1976) *The Hidden Injuries of Class*, Cambridge: Cambridge University Press.

Shils, E. and Young, M. (1953) 'The meaning of the Coronation', *Sociological Review*, 1, 68–81.

Shorter, E. (1975) *The Making of the Modern Family*, Glasgow: Fontana.

Shotter, J. (1990) *Knowing of the Third Kind*, Utrecht: ISOR.

Sibony, D. (1990) 'Le fantasme du prince', *Nouvel Observateur*, August 16–22, p.13.

Sigal, C. (1986) America's favourite soap. In *The Queen Observed*, ed. T. Grove, London: Pavilion.

Silverstone, R., Morley, D., Dahlberg, A. and Livingstone, S.M. (1989) Condemned to the family: the household context of information and communication technologies. Working paper, Centre for Research into Innovation, Culture and Technology, Brunel University.

Simmonds, D. (1984) *Princess Di, the National Dish*, London: Pluto Press.

Sloterdijk, P. (1988) *Critique of Cynical Reason*, London: Verso.

Smith, A.D.S. (1979) *Nationalism in the Twentieth Century*, New York: New York University Press.

—— (1986) *The Ethnic Origins of Nations*, Oxford: Blackwell.

Smith, P. and Gaskell, G. (1990) The social dimension in relative deprivation. In *The Social Psychological Study of Widespread Beliefs*, eds C. Fraser and G. Gaskell, Oxford: Oxford University Press.

Sun Book of Royalty, The (1984) London: Invincible Press.

Tajfel, H. (1981) *Human Groups and Social Categories*, Cambridge: Cambridge University Press.

Tajfel, H. and Turner, J.C. (1985) The social identity theory of intergroup behaviour. In *Psychology of Intergroup Relations*, eds W.G. Austin and S. Worchel, California: Brooks-Cole.

Taylor, D.M. and Moghaddam, F.M. (1987) *Theories of Intergroup Relations*, New York: Praeger.

Taylor-Gooby, P. (1983) 'Moralism, self-interest and attitudes to welfare', *Policy and Politics*, 11, 145–60.

Thompson, J.B. (1987) 'Language and ideology: a framework for analysis', *Sociology*, 35, 516–36.

Thornton, M. (1986) *Royal Feud: the Queen Mother and the Duchess of Windsor*, London: Pan.

Urry, J. (1988) 'Cultural change and contemporary holiday making', *Theory, Culture and Society*, 5, 35–56.

van Dijk, T.A. (1987) *Communicating Racism*, Newbury Park: Sage.

Vickers, B. (1988) *In Defence of Rhetoric*, Oxford: Clarendon Press.

Victoria, Queen (1868) *Leaves from the Journal of Our Life in the Highlands from 1848 to 1861*, London: Smith, Elder and Co.

—— (1908) *The Letters of Queen Victoria*, Volume 1, London: John Murray.

REFERENCES

Voltaire (n.d.) *Philosophical Dictionary*, Volume 2, London: E. Truelove.

Wallman, S. (1984) *Eight London Households*, London: Tavistock.

Walster, E., Berscheid, E. and Walster, G.W. (1976) New directions in equity research In *Advances in Experimental Social Psychology*, eds L. Berkowitz and E. Walters, New York: Academic Press.

Wetherell, M. and Potter, J. (1988) Discourse analysis and the identification of interpretative repertoires. In *Analysing Everday Explanation*, ed. C. Antaki, London: Sage.

Whitehorn, K. (1986) Queen of hearts. In *The Queen Observed*, ed. T. Grove, London: Pavilion.

Williamson, J. (1987) *Consuming Passions*, London: Boyer.

Wilson, E. (1989) *The Myth of British Monarchy*, London: Journeyman.

Wilterdink, N. (1990) 'The monarchy contested: anti-monarchism in the Netherlands', *The Netherlands' Journal of Social Sciences*, 26, 3–16.

Young, K. (1984) Political attitudes. In *British Social Attitudes: the 1984 Report*, eds R. Jowell and C. Airey, Aldershot: Gower.

Ziegler, P. (1977) *Crown and People*, London: Collins.

Zizek, S. (1989) *The Sublime Object of Ideology*, London: Verso.

NAME INDEX

SUBJECT INDEX